Web of Life and Cosmos

Human and Bigfoot Star Ancestors

Krsanna Duran

Atlantis Phoenix
Missoula, Montana

Atlantis Phoenix
Missoula, Montana
AtlantisPhoenix.com

Copyright © 2013, 2015 by Krsanna Duran

All rights reserved. No part of this publication may be reproduced, distributed or transmitted in any form or by any means, including photocopying, recording, or other electronic or mechanical methods, without the prior written permission of the publisher, except in the case of brief quotations embodied in critical reviews and certain other noncommercial uses permitted by copyright law. For permission requests, write to the publisher at the above address.

Order online at www.atlantisphoenix.com.

Email: phoenix@atlantisphoenix.com.

Quantity sales available

Fourth Edition 2015

Previously published as

Bigfoot and Human Ancestors: UFOs, Planetary Changes and Species

ISBN 978-0615942988 paperback

Cover design by Radiant Arts
Photos by Philip Baird and 10000 BC Gobekli Tepe
Art by Hartmut Jager
Images from Wikimedia Commons

Contents

Introduction 1
    The Mayan Story 5
    Himalayan Adepts and Atlantean Records 7
    Birthing the Earth 9
    Extraterrestrial, Shamanic, and
    Near Death Initiations 14

Timeline 23

One   Crisis, Die-Offs, Mutants, and Savants 31
    Lemuria, Atlantis, and Sumer 35
    Gods in the Garden 39
    Towering Figures, a Great City 48
    A New World Order After the Great Floods 53

Two   Ages of Humankind 61
    Cosmic Radiation, Magnetism, and Sun Stone 63
    Ancestors' Gateways 69

Three   America's Mother Culture 71
    Mother Earth, Father Sky, and Cosmos 74
    Sun, Moon, and Venus 78
    Sun Stone Signature 82
    Microcosmic Portrait of the Macrocosm 86
    Toltecs, Aztecs, and Rome 88

Four   Cosmos 95
    Human 95
    Earth 98
    Sun 105
    Milky Way 109

Five	Mystery Ancestors	113
	Arcturian Genesis	115
Six	Web of Life	128
	Properties of the Quantum Web	135
	Cosmic Fire	137

Appendices

    Earth-Human Calendar 147

        Planet-Changing Fracture Region Pinpointed
        with TimeStar Earth Map 152

        TimeStar Earth Map 155

        Mapping with Crop Circles 156

        Islands Rising, Sinking 159

    Origins of Crop Circles 165

        Megalithic Britain's Crop Circle Context 174

    Symbols and Communication. 177

    UFO Communications.. 185

References

Index

Biography

Introduction

Strange lights in the skies, coming and going with stunning speed, heralded changes few imagined in 1942. Nikola Tesla wrote about wireless communication with other planets in 1901, and was certain Earthlings could communicate with Mars and Venus. Before Tesla could invent interplanetary technology, spacecraft from other worlds came to Earth.

Britain's Prime Minister Winston Churchill classified a 1942 report of unidentified flying craft top secret, and spoke about fear of undermining religious faith. Supreme Commander of Allied Forces in Europe, Dwight Eisenhower followed suit with Churchill's knee-jerk policy for craft that Air Forces first called foo fighters and then unidentified flying objects, the UFO.

In the decade following World War II, human-appearing extraterrestrials contacted citizens from all lifestyles, and explained to some that sons of God in Genesis 6 were extraterrestrials who had parented children on Earth. Our ancestors were extraterrestrials from the stars. Governments and militaries blocked the ancestors' return and clamped down news outlets.

A news release issued by the U.S. Army about a flying saucer crash at Roswell, New Mexico on July 8, 1947 was retracted the next day.[1] Three months later in October the National Security Act of 1947 authorized the National Security Agency (NSA) to deal with flying saucers at the highest levels of secrecy. Extraterrestrial crews from ancestral civilizations responded by contacting lone individuals to explain their presence by 1949. This grassroots strategy of directly contacting individuals who, in turn, inform neighbors and friends of the Ancestors' presence has been the primary means of informing the public of UFO activity since 1947.

Governments continue to deny the UFO presence when craft appear, hover, zoom and disappear while thousands of people watch. Hundreds of thousands of people witnessed the mile-wide array of Phoenix Lights in 1997 and masters of the stars over Mexico City in 1991.[2] These two highly documented mass sightings of UFO are especially important, because they directly and indirectly pointed to areas where modern UFO activity proliferated in 1947 and America's first civilization in Mexico.

In the Phoenix Lights sightings, UFOs, some as large as football fields, traveled in a V-shaped formation across the state of Arizona and into Sonora, Mexico on March 13, 1997. Observed by thousands of witnesses, the silent formation was visible for 106 minutes. Witnesses reported stars behind the UFOs disappeared from view when they were overhead and then reappeared when the formation had passed, indicating the craft were solidly structured. A second series of stationary lights, which some witnesses described as a huge carpenter's square-shaped UFO containing lights, was visible over Phoenix. Fife Symington, then governor of Arizona, initially ridiculed reports of UFOs, but several years later, he admitted seeing a UFO he called "otherworldly."

The single most highly documented and longest spree of UFO displays in the twentieth century began in Mexico City. Crowds jammed the streets of the most densely populated metropolis in the western hemisphere awaiting an historic solar eclipse July 11, 1991 when it started. One of the longest eclipses in the twentieth century, Maya timekeepers had predicted its date one thousand years earlier.[3,4] At the moment of totality when the sky slipped into darkness, a brilliant light shone where the last rays of the sun had flickered moments earlier. Motionless while it gathered attention, some thought the light was Venus. Then the structured craft burst into a whirling dance of light, flashing high and low, but staying in view of cameras waiting for the sun's return. Without slowing, the light disappeared as suddenly as it had arrived and instantaneously appeared eighty miles south in Puebla, where cameras scanned the sky waiting for the first rays of the sun to shine. In the massive wave of UFO displays throughout Mexico after the star masters' spectacular return, television anchor Jaime Maussan collected more than 5,000 videos of unexplained lights and craft in the following decade.

Ancestors from the stars are characterized in mythologies and traditions from the earliest times of human history. Our archetypes are the ancestors' legacy forwarded to the future species. They folly, compete, dominate, and love in eerily familiar ways.

Modern introduction of the Ancestors began with Tibetan adepts who mentored Helena Blavatsky in the nineteenth century, preceding by a hair's breadth relativistic and quantum sciences. The adept Koot Hoomi wrote about the extraterrestrial scope of humanity in an 1882 letter:

> "Therefore, whenever I speak of humanity without specifying it you must understand that I mean not humanity of our fourth round as we see it on this speck of mud in space but the whole host already evolved."[5]

A Russian by birth and seeker of ancient wisdom by choice, Helena Blavatsky blazed a trail to the Ancestors' tree of life with her landmark treatise on cosmogenesis in 1890:

> "My chief and only object was to bring into prominence that the basic and fundamental principles of every exoteric religion and philosophy, old or new, were from first to last but the echoes of the primeval "Wisdom Religion." I sought to show that the TREE OF KNOWLEDGE, like Truth itself, was ONE; and that, however differing in form and color, the foliage of the twigs, the trunk and its main branches were still those of the same old Tree, in the shadow of which had developed and grown the (now) esoteric religious philosophy of the races that preceded our present mankind on earth."[6]

The extreme antiquity of civilizations that Blavatsky reported had no parallels in the nineteenth century, when many believed the Lord had created the world in exactly seven days some 6,000 to 10,000 years beforehand. Critics loudly proclaimed that lost continents did not exist, had never existed, and could not exist when Blavatsky informed them Atlantis had existed on a now-lost continent in the Atlantic. Geologists believed the oceanic crust was too "firm" for the continents to "simply plough through," in Blavatsky's day, when scientists ridiculed Albert Wegener's theory of continental drift as late as 1915. Wegener's theory was widely adopted fifty years later, in the 1960s, when surveys detected magnetic anomalies in ocean floors that could only be explained by the movement of landmasses. Today, continental drift is the basis of tectonic science.

In the late twentieth century, the sunken microcontinents of Avalonia and Baltica in the Atlantic Ocean were discovered. Positive proofs for Blavatsky's account of continents rising and sinking over eons in cyclic processes were discovered more than 100 years after her death.[7]

A steady stream of new sciences in the twentieth century laid new foundations for recognizing and aligning ancient sciences and civilizations that Blavatsky wrote about in her landmark book, *The Secret Doctrine: The Synthesis of Science, Religion, and Philosophy*, published in 1888. With the advent of relativistic and quantum sciences soon after Blavatsky's death in 1891, landmark discoveries continue to exponentially accelerate.[8]

1. A "cosmic impact" that scattered molten debris over four continents, causing fires so hot that glass and nano diamonds formed in the eastern USA, in its path across North and Central America, the Atlantic Ocean and North Africa was dated at 12,800 years before present (BP).[9]
2. Vestiges of a mother language shared throughout Europe and Asia 15,000 BP are deeply embedded in modern languages.[10,11]
3. A continent sunken in an area that some histories identify with Atlantis near the coast of Brazil in the Atlantic Ocean was discovered in 2013.[12]
4. A landmass in the Indian Ocean that sank in a continental breakup 85 million years ago (MYA) was discovered in 2013.[13]
5. A web connecting distant galaxies, which scientists likened to the web that Spider Woman cast in American Indian lore, was photographed using light from a quasar in 2014.[14]
6. Harvard scientists challenged long-held views about the Earth's formation with evidence of an Ancient Earth encased deeply in the mantle of modern Earth in 2014[15]

Scientists continue to debate the origin and nature of the object that scattered debris across half a hemisphere 12,800 BP. The Madrid Codex from the Yucatan portrayed fire descending from the sky, causing the Earth to shift on its axis and resulting in massive flooding 12,500 BP, which Mayanist Brasseur de Bourbourg deciphered in the nineteenth century.

Mayan codices, murals, and oral traditions render ancient events similar to Plato's account of Atlantis and Blavatsky's history of Mu. Sanskrit literature that began trickling into Europe and America in late nineteenth century also gave comparable histories. Among early Mayanists whose work merits more consideration in the light of new scientific discoveries are Abbe Charles Etienne Brasseur de Bourbourg and Augustus Le Plongeon.

The Mayan Story

Charles Etienne Brasseur de Bourbourg

Speaking twelve languages and fortified with the ecclesiastical credential of Abbe, Brasseur sailed to Mexico in 1845 in pursuit of his childhood dream to discover Mayan mysteries, inspired by reading about them. In the next twenty years, he found in private archives a number of rare manuscripts that had been all but forgotten. These included *Annals of the Cakchiquel,* the *Popul Vuh,* Bishop of the Yucatan Diego de Landa's *Relation des choses de Yucatán,* and the *Troano Codex* that Hernan Cortes had taken to Spain after his 1519 conquest of Mexico, all of which Brasseur translated and published.

De Landa's theocratic presence in the Yucatan proved to be more problematic than helpful. Brasseur had learned several dialects of Mayan language and was able to study numerous artifacts on site with native people. He deduced a scenario that reflected an actual event, which the cosmic impact discovered in the twentieth century would certainly have caused. Although Brasseur believed the catastrophe the Maya recorded was the same as Plato's account of Atlantis, he deciphered a date 1,000 years earlier than Plato's 11,500 BP, or 12,500 BP, when North America continued to reel from damage the exploding object caused. This independently discovered date is an important feature of his direct observations of the Maya, but his European education offered only Plato's account of Atlantis for context of the catastrophic events the Maya recorded. The series of catastrophes recorded in the Mayan codex have no parallel in Plato's rendition of Atlantis, but are evidenced in consequences of volcanic eruptions.

Augustus Le Plongeon

Le Plongeon sailed with his wife Alice to Mexico in 1873. After learning to speak Maya at Merida, they traveled to sites in the Yucatan, surveyed buildings in the ancient ruins, took hundreds of photographs, and carefully drew murals, over the course of twelve years.

In the Mayan ruins, Le Plongeon encountered a world defined by cosmic order and natural forces. "The Maya deified all phenomena of nature and their causes, and then represented them in the shape of human beings or animals," Le Plongeon wrote. "Their object was to keep for their initiates the secrets of their science."

At Kabah, a Yucatan site, Le Plongeon identified a mural that depicted the submersion of ten countries and an inscription for Mu, and believed it was in the Indian Ocean:

"...there occurred terrible earthquakes which continued without intermission until the thirteenth Chuen [Mayan date]. The country of hills and mud, the "Land of Mu" was sacrificed. Being twice upheaved, it suddenly disappeared during the night, the basin being continually shaken by volcanic forces. Being confined, these caused the land to sink and rise several times and in various places. At last the surface gave way and the ten countries were torn asunder and scattered in fragments: Unable to withstand the force of the seismic convulsions, they sank with their sixty-four millions of inhabitants, eight thousand and sixty years before the writing of this book."[16]

Le Plongeon discovered the Chac-Mool sculpture at Chichen Itza after observing spots on a shield in a mural that were identical to spots on a sculpture of a human-headed jaguar reclining on its side. *Chac-Mool* means *Big Red Jaguar*, and the jaguar typically represents transformation and sorcerers.[17] (*The Jaguar Within: Shamanic Trance in Ancient Central and South American Art* by Rebecca R. Stone beautifully describes and illustrates the jaguar in transformative symbolism.[18]) The Olmec, who laid the foundations for Mexico's civilization by 3000 BCE, revered transforming human-jaguar babies, or were-jaguars, and introduced the earliest imagery of the Feathered Serpent (Quetzalcoatl) at La Venta circa 900-1000 BCE.

Morphing serpents, jaguars and birds in transforming guises merged in the Feathered Serpent to become the primary religious and political figure of Mexico by 600 CE. Accepting only butterflies and flowers on altars, the peaceful Feathered Serpent denounced sacrifices. The Feathered Serpent first appeared with a full collar of feathers in central Mexico at Teotihuacan. A winged jaguar rested at the base of Teotihuacan's Pyramid of the Sun when it was excavated in the early twentieth century.

> "Jaguars appear to be more clever at Teotihuacan than jaguars anywhere else in the Mesoamerican world. They seem on first acquaintance to perform a whole variety show of trained animal acts, such as straddling corn-grinding tables, wearing flowers and feathered ruffs, blowing on shell trumpets, swimming among waves, and shaking rattles. They appear both as cubs and as gravid cats. Men dress up as jaguars, and jaguars wear netted garments."[19]

Realizing the human-jaguar body marked the burial site of a person deemed important, Le Plongeon dug twenty-four feet below the surface and found the nine-foot Chac-Mool sculpture. In the *Troano Codex*,

Le Plongeon interpreted images of Chac-Mool's wife, Queen Moo (Macaw), sailing east. He repeatedly translated the name Mu from inscriptions and located it in the Indian Ocean. He believed the Maya had traveled to the Indian Ocean and reached Africa, India, and the Indus Valley.[20] Although he correctly translated the name "Moo," as Brasseur had done before him, Le Plongeon attempted to relate it to the familiar Western knowledge base. Helena Blavatsky introduced Mu in her 1888 book *The Secret Doctrine*, a decade after Le Plongeon translated the name from the Maya's codex.

Himalayan Adepts and Atlantean Records

As a witness of ancient archives, Helena Blavatsky's access to records in Tibet, India, and South America in the nineteenth century was unparalleled for Americans and Europeans. The Editorial "Foreword" to the 1927 edition of her book *The Voice of the Silence*, originally published in 1889, states the book was printed at the Panchen Lama's request, and that his staff and Chinese scholars had verified Blavatsky's translation of Tibetan words. It also mentions that Blavatsky had studied for several years at Tashilunpo and knew the Panchen Lama very well. The Fourteenth Dalai Lama wrote the foreword for the 1989 centenary edition of Blavatsky's book.

Helena P. Blavatsky, 1877

Blavatsky provides rare references that elucidate clues about Atlantis and Mu, which Brasseur and Le Plongeon independently found in Mexico. Her nineteenth century accounts of a very ancient human presence on the Earth are matched by accounts of modern UFO contacts and Vedic history. Vedic scholar Michael Cremo presents evidence of human life on Earth hundreds of millions of years in the past.[21] Linda Moulton Howe reports interviews with a now-retired military intelligence officer who spent thirty years tracking extraterrestrial activities dating to more than 100 MYA.[22]

Madame Blavatsky introduced Mu to the Western world in 1888. She reported learning about Mu in *The Book of Dzyan*, written in Atlantis, and preserved in Tibet where she studied. She wrote about Atlantis and Mu with great care to emphasize the two civilizations were separate but successive in both time and space.

After studying with a Vedantan master in Tibet for three years in the 1860s, Helena Blavatsky wrote about Mu and Atlantis in *The Secret Doctrine*. Her aim in writing the book was to show that the roots of all religions on Earth stemmed from a single source. Regardless of how tangled and disparate in exoteric expression religions have gotten, their shared origin is still discerned in their oldest roots.

As a young man Mahatma Gandhi, India's great liberator, studied with Blavatsky and other Theosophists before returning to India with Theosophical books. Mahatma Gandhi explained to his biographer Louis Fischer:

> "Theosophy is the teaching of Madame Blavatsky. It is Hinduism at its best. Theosophy is the Brotherhood of Man...Jinnah and other Moslem leaders were once members of the Congress. They left it because they felt the pinch of Hinduism patronizing...They did not find the Brotherhood of Man among the Hindus. They say Islam is the Brotherhood of Man. As a matter of fact, it is the Brotherhood of Moslems. Theosophy is the Brotherhood of Man."[23]

The Mahatmas who mentored Blavatsky carefully considered English terms to introduce their doctrine in the West. Sanskrit and English are vastly different languages with many words that do not transliterate. The Mahatmas propounded their measures of time in English as planetary rounds and rings, with human evolutions described as races and subraces, over cycles measured in hundreds of thousands and millions of years. Blavatsky's renditions of Tibetan and Sanskrit literature have proven to be remarkably faithful in detail to the original texts translated by native scholars in the twentieth century.

Few Westerners had opportunity to imagine materials conveyed in Vedic texts, much less see them, when Blavatsky arrived in New York in 1873 to announce that the Brothers of her Lodge had sent her to share their knowledge with the world. Blavatsky met with a volley of mixed reactions, from curiosity to bitter criticism, on a par with reactions to UFO reports in the twentieth century.

The Mahatmas monitored Blavatsky's progress and provided guidance in letters written in distinct red and blue ink that literally materialized in thin air. Many of the Mahatmas' letters are presently in the

British Museum, where their handwritings have been analyzed repeatedly, with the conclusion that Blavatsky did not write them. Reports of witnesses who saw the letters materialize are well documented in *The Esoteric World of Madame Blavatsky: Insights into the Life of a Modern Sphinx* by Daniel Caldwell. Historical accounts and occult science that Blavatsky learned with the Mahatmas uncannily presaged discoveries made in the twentieth century.

Birthing the Earth

New micro and supercontinents continue to be discovered well into the twenty-first century. *National Geographic* announced a newly found supercontinent in August 2011.

"There are people who have put forth models of earlier supercontinents. One, called Columbia, [may have] existed from 1.8 to 1.5 billion years [ago]," Loewy said.

And at 2.4 to 2.6 billion years ago (BYA), there seems to have been another major event," she said. "There appear to have been multiple cycles throughout time."[24]

A virtual plethora of sunken continents has been discovered since Blavatsky wrote about Atlantis and Mu in 1888. Modern continents originated from a handful of supercontinents that formed successively starting 2.1 billion years ago after a global scale collision. Dates for Columbia and Rodinia vary depending on the model for them. More is known about Pangaea, which rifted to form North America, South America, Africa, and the Atlantic Ocean.

1. Columbia — 2.1 BYA
2. Rodinia — 1.1 BYA and 750 MYA
3. Gondwana, Laurasia (later called Laurentia), Baltica, and Siberia — 514 MYA
4. Pangaea — 237 MYA

The very ancient Avalonia and Baltica microcontinents that survived transitions of two supercontinents (first Gondwana and then Pangaea) are feasible candidates for locations of Atlantis. After separating from Pangaea, Avalonia and Baltic collided in what is now the North Atlantic, and Avalonia is embedded in the crust of Great Britain, Wales, Newfoundland, Canada, New England, and the Atlantic floor.

The Baltic Shield from the ancient Baltica continent comprises much of Norway, Sweden, Iceland, and other parts of Scandinavia.

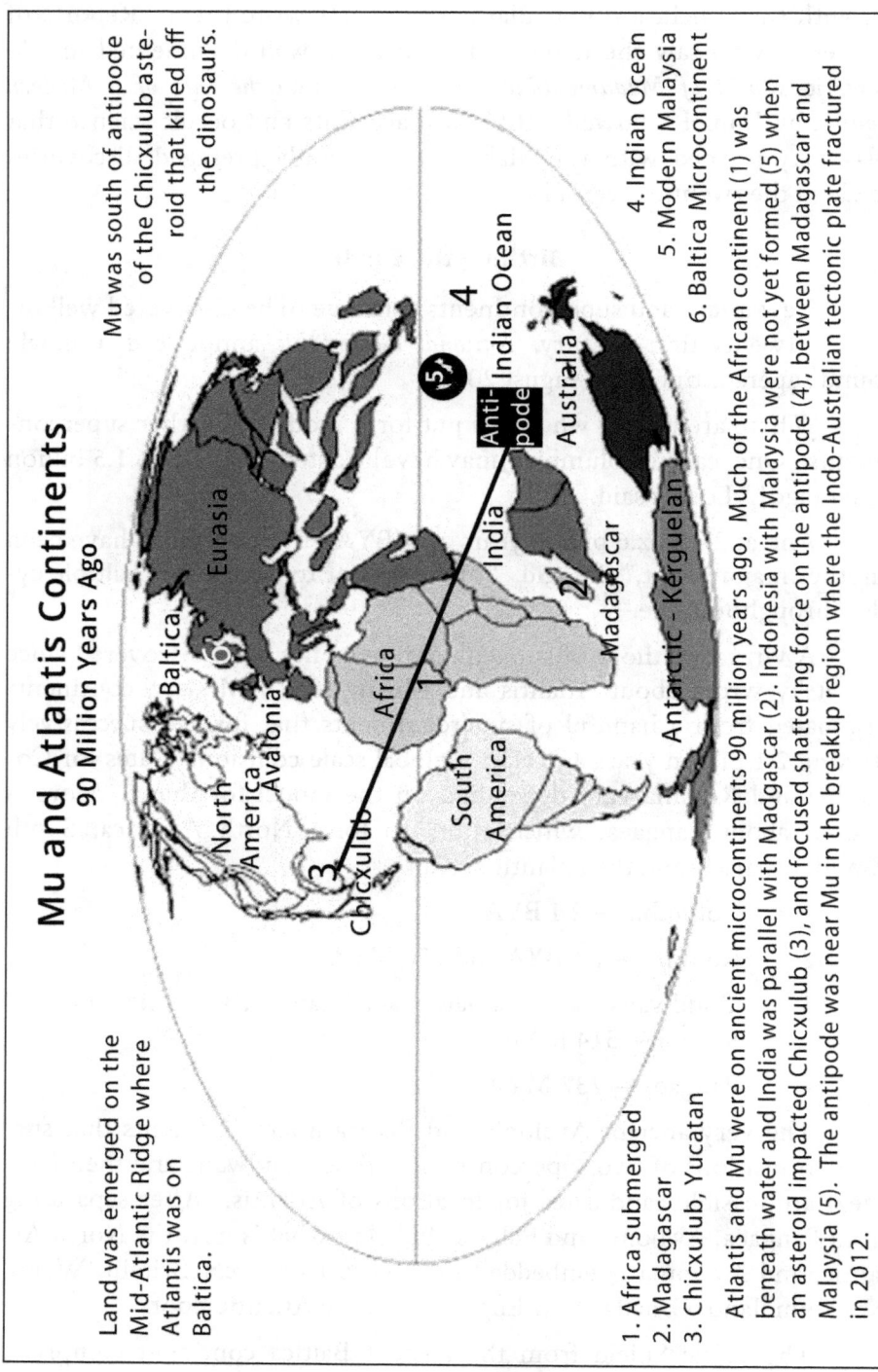

Mu and Atlantis Continents
90 Million Years Ago

Land was emerged on the Mid-Atlantic Ridge where Atlantis was on Baltica.

Mu was south of antipode of the Chicxulub asteroid that killed off the dinosaurs.

1. Africa submerged
2. Madagascar
3. Chicxulub, Yucatan
4. Indian Ocean
5. Modern Malaysia
6. Baltica Microcontinent

Atlantis and Mu were on ancient microcontinents 90 million years ago. Much of the African continent (1) was beneath water and India was parallel with Madagascar (2). Indonesia with Malaysia were not yet formed (5) when an asteroid impacted Chicxulub (3), and focused shattering force on the antipode (4), between Madagascar and Malaysia (5). The antipode was near Mu in the breakup region where the Indo-Australian tectonic plate fractured in 2012.

Shields are portions of continental crust that have not tectonically deformed, and are called cratons.

Very little land is on the modern Mid-Atlantic Ridge, but this was not always the case. The lengthy mountain range and granite continental rock inside the Ridge show landmasses have been on it. Iceland straddles the Mid-Atlantic Ridge and the Azores Islands are mountaintops that rise from it.

The Kerguelen plateau extending into the Antarctic was discovered to be a microcontinent in 1999. Kerguelen was above water three different times over a period of eighty million years "before it went underwater for a final time about 20 million years ago... Floor samples indicate that the land was covered by a coniferous forest. Unlike Hawaii, which resembles a chain of columns punctuating the ocean floor, the Kerguelen Plateau is as large igneous (volcanic) province encompassing a large amount of ocean-floor real estate. Today, most of the plateau lies one to two and one-half kilometers below the ocean surface. Two small portions, however, remain above the surface."

A time when Africa emerged from the bottom of the ocean and the Atlas Mountains were half sunk, as Blavatsky described, challenged the nineteenth century mind.[25] Africa was, in fact, connected to the Antarctic and South America 150 MYA when, according to Blavatsky, the first island of Mu rose above the water. Although the African continent was already formed, much of it remained beneath water 150 MYA, as the Kerguelen plateau is beneath frozen water yet still identifiable today.

Blavatsky's Mahatma anticipated these discoveries about continents and plate tectonics in an 1882 letter.[26]

> "In the Eocene Age — even in its 'very first part' — [50 to 33 MYA] the great cycle of the fourth Race [of] men, the Atlanteans, had already reached its highest point, and the great continent, the father of nearly all the present continents, showed the first symptoms of sinking — a process that occupied it down to 11,446 years ago [9564 BCE], when its last island, that, translating its vernacular name, we may call with propriety Poseidonis [Atlantis], went down with a crash.[27] By the bye, whoever wrote the review of Donnelly's Atlantis is right: Lemuria can no more be confounded with the Atlantic Continent than Europe with America. Both sunk and were drowned with their high civilizations and "gods," yet between the two catastrophes a short period of about 700,000 years elapsed;

"Lemuria" flourishing and ending her career just at about that trifling lapse of time before the early part of the Eocene Age, since its race was the third...why not bear in mind that, under the continents explored and fathomed by them, in the bowels of which they have found *ere* are the "Eocene Age" and forced it to deliver them its secrets, there may be, hidden deep in the fathomless, or rather unfathomed ocean beds, other, and far older continents whose stratums have never been geologically explored; and that they may someday upset entirely their present theories, thus illustrating the simplicity and sublimity of truth as connected with inductive "generalization" in opposition to their visionary conjectures. Why not admit — true, no one of them has ever thought of it — that our present continents have, like "Lemuria" and "Atlantis," been several times already submerged and had the time to reappear again, and bear their new groups of mankind and civilization; and that, at the first great geological upheaval, at the next cataclysm—in the series of periodical cataclysms that occur from the beginning to the end of every Round — our already autopsized continents will go down, and the Lemurias and Atlantises come up again. Think of the future geologists of the sixth and seventh races. Imagine them digging deep in the bowels of what was Ceylon and Simla, and finding implements of the Veddahs, or of the remote ancestor of the civilized Pahari — every object of the civilized portions of humanity that inhabited those regions having been pulverized to dust by the great masses of travelling glaciers during the next glacial period —"

The landmasses of Gondwana, Laurasia, Baltica, and Siberia had already formed and separated 514 MYA. Then they came back together with the Antarctic as Pangaea 237 MYA, before again separating to form most of the modern world. The Antarctic was free of ice with a tropical climate 150 MYA when Africa was still connected to the Antarctic and South America. Blavatsky wrote about Lemuria, or Mu:

"There is a period of a few millions of years to cover between the first "mindless" race and the highly intelligent and intellectual later "Lemurians", [sic] there is another between the earliest civilization of the Atlanteans and the historic period.

"As witnesses to the Lemurians but a few silent records in the shape of half a dozen broken colossi and old cyclopean ruins are left. These are not allowed a hearing, as they are "productions of blind natural forces," we are assured by some; "quite modern" we are told by others..."[28]

"An old continent is also suspected to have existed on the Eastern coast [of Africa]. Only Africa, as a continent, was never part and parcel of either Lemuria or Atlantis, as we have agreed to call the Third and Fourth Continents. Their archaic appellations are never mentioned in the Purânas, nor anywhere else. But with simply one of the esoteric keys in hand it becomes an easy task to identify these departed lands in the numberless "lands of the gods," Devas and Munis described in the Purânas, in their Varshas, Dwipas, and zones. Their Sweta-Dwipa, during the early day of Lemuria, stood out like a giant-peak from the bottom of the sea; the area between Atlas and Madagascar being occupied by the waters till about the early period of Atlantis (after the disappearance of Lemuria), when Africa emerged from the bottom of the ocean, and Atlas was half-sunk.

"It is of course impossible to attempt, within the compass of even several volumes, a consecutive and detailed account of the evolution and progress of the first three races — except so far as to give a general view of it, as will be done presently. Race the first had no history of its own. Of race the second the same may be said. We shall have, therefore, to pay careful attention only to the Lemurians and the Atlanteans before the history of our own race (the Fifth) can be attempted.

"What is known of other continents, besides our own, and what does history know or accept of the early races? Everything outside the repulsive speculations of materialistic science is daubed with the contemptuous term "Superstition." The wise men of to-day [nineteenth century] will believe nothing. Plato's "winged" and hermaphrodite races, and his golden age, under the reign of Saturn and the gods, are quietly brought back by Hæckel to their new place in nature: Our divine races are shown to be the descendants of Catarrhine apes, and our ancestor, a piece of sea slime."[29]

The ancient continent off the east coast of Africa that Blavatsky and her mentors suspected had existed was confirmed with the 2013 discovery of a landmass in the Indian Ocean that sank in a continental breakup 85 MYA.[30] The first mountain peak of Mu, Sweta-Dwipa in the Indian Ocean, was near the Antarctic Plate and the Kerguelen microcontinent discovered in the twentieth century. In the millions of years since the ancient land of Mu rose, the again sunken peaks have drifted to the coasts of Java and Christmas Island in the break-up region of a history-making tectonic fracture in 2012.

An adept in her own right, Blavatsky initially consulted with the growing Spiritualist movement in America with the intent of teaching the principles of phenomena they pursued. In the Spiritualist movement she met Henry Olcott, a co-founder of the Theosophical Society in 1875, and initiated him into adept phenomenon.[31] With the realization that over-indulgence of phenomena obscured the true spiritual nature of humankind, she concluded her work with the Spiritualist movement co-founded the Theosophical Society with three primary objectives:

- Form a Universal Brotherhood of Humanity,
- Promote the study of the world's religions and sciences, and
- Investigate the hidden mysteries of Nature, psychic and spiritual powers.

The objectives Blavatsky laid out with the Theosophical Society dominated the UFO movement and the Ancestors' return in the twentieth century. After UFO contact at White Sands in 1949, Daniel Fry founded the Understanding organization and devoted his life to it. George van Tassel's 1956 book, *Religion and Science Merged*, introduced the sons of God in Genesis 6 as fathers of modern humans and reiterated the necessity of synthesizing science and religion.[32] Among the many perplexing elements of UFO contacts, psychic and "paranormal" features are perhaps the most mind-bending for modern experiencers and investigators alike. Yet, these elements were most characteristic of human experience in the first light of civilization, but had been segregated into religious mythos. Groundbreaking research reopened cold cases of psychic humanity in the twentieth century and floodgates of the Ancestors' legacy opened with new understanding of UFO visits.

Extraterrestrial, Shamanic and Near Death Initiations

Science and religion splintered so forcefully during the Renaissance, after an Inquisition against Galileo for observing that the Earth orbits the Sun, that scientists escaped Rome's excesses by abandoning theology. A de facto peace with Rome separated science from religion, allowing sleeping dogs to rest quietly. Most scientific research of the soul in the twentieth century was done with near death experiences, in which the soul leaves the body at death and then returns again to live.

Emeritus professor of psychology at the University of Connecticut, past president of the International Association of Near Death Studies and author of numerous books and articles, Dr. Kenneth Ring spearheaded seminal research of near death experiences in the 1970s.

Dr. Ring concluded that the deep structure of psyche in shamanic initiations, UFO encounters, and near death experiences are identical.[33] Extraordinary knowledge and achievements follow death-like states in all cultures and times, when the mind and soul transcend the limits of the purely material. Near-death experiences exceed expectations of physical sciences to invoke shamanic states and supernormal life.[34]

The vision of Nick Black Elk, a spiritual leader and healer among the Lakota (Sioux), inspires and heals generations that follow him. Born in Wyoming in 1863, at the age of nine he suddenly fell prone and unresponsive in a death-like state for days. Later in life as an elder Black Elk related his vision to biographer John Neihardt:

> "And while I stood there I saw more than I can tell and understood more than I saw; for I was seeing in a sacred manner the shapes of all things in the spirit, and the shape of all shapes as they must live together like one being. And I saw that the sacred hoop of my people was one of many hoops that made one circle, wide as daylight and as starlight, and in the center grew one mighty flowering tree to shelter all the children of one mother and one father. And I saw that it was holy."[35]

In his vision, Black Elk was taken to what mythologist Joseph Campbell explained as "the *axis mundi*, the central point, the pole around which all revolves...the point where stillness and movement are together..." Black Elk was residing at the axis of the six sacred directions. Campbell viewed Black Elk's statement as key to understanding myth and symbols.[1]

Black Elk was from a long line of medicine men and healers; his father was a medicine man as were his paternal uncles. Black Elk had many visions throughout his life that reinforced what he had experienced as a boy. He worked among his people as a healer and holy man the rest of his life.

Wallace Black Elk, Lakota spiritual leader and healer who called Nick "grandfather," served as a Native American representative to the United Nations and an international lecturer. Born on the Rose Bud Reservation in South Dakota in 1921, Wallace carried his elder's vision and the stone sent to him in a UFO encounter throughout his life. He parachuted into Africa and later served as a code talker during World War II, before breaking ground in the modern era of UFOs.

When Wallace was twelve, as memory served him, he did a sweat lodge while visiting his cousin Benjamin, while some of the family sat on the front porch of their home. *Inipi*, the Lakota word for sweat lodge, literally means *Stone People's Lodge*. Coverings of hides and blankets seal sweat lodges from all light and tightly secure the door. While in the lodge, Wallace heard the family screaming, but could not leave until he completed all the songs for the ritual.

A rock flew through the sealed door and came to rest between Wallace's feet. He picked up the rock and held it. When the sweat lodge ended, Wallace ran out to the family to find out what had happened. They said a glowing disc had hovered over the sweat lodge during the rounds of songs, and then flew away as suddenly as it had come.

Wallace Black Elk and I discussed our UFO experiences at length. He blessed my pipe (*chanunpa*) and passed forward his vision and knowledge of the Ancestors. He worked with and spoke about the Star Ancestors, whom he identified with the flying craft America's Air Force called UFO.[36]

Contact with the extraterrestrial "Alan" and Daniel Fry in 1949 transpired with the national security state's domination of human-extraterrestrial relations. Alan reported his ancestors included humans from Lemuria, who had departed the Earth more than 1,000 generations earlier, or before 20,000 BP. This period marked the beginning of glacial melt that culminated in ravaging floods soon after the still-unidentified "cosmic impact" 12,800 BP. His ancestors possessed flying craft but had never attempted interstellar flight, until the complete collapse of civilization spurred them to risk escape to Mars.[37]

A group from Mu took refuge in the Himalayas while considering a course of action. A portion of the survivors elected to remain on Earth, where they believed they would be safe from contamination. Seven craft attempted flight to Mars and four succeeded, while three were lost. Those who reached Mars eventually developed technology to simulate a planet and are no longer dependent on a physical planet for survival.[38]

National Security Act initiatives in the Cold War, following World War II, directed the agenda of silent deception that guided information given to Americans about extraterrestrials. Claiming that witnesses hallucinated UFOs and extraterrestrials commenced with recommendations of the Robertson Panel in 1953, convened at the CIA's request. Dr. Leo Sprinkle, Professor of Psychology at The University of Wyoming, conducted the first formal study of UFO experiencers using a battery of standardized psychological, personality, and IQ tests in the late 1960s. The study found that as a group UFO witnesses have normal psychological functions, and individuals who report direct communication with extraterrestrials tend to have higher-than-average IQs and psychic functions.[39,40]

Dr. Sprinkle's findings have been replicated in subsequent studies, including one done by Dr. John Mack, Harvard Professor of Psychiatry and Pulitzer Prize winning biographer. After conducting a decade-long study of 200 individuals who experienced UFO contact in the 1990s, Dr. Mack spoke about attitudes towards UFOs.[41]

> "You have to start with a certain mentality which pervades the Western way of thinking, but it is coming throughout the world, which is that the planet is a kind of piece of real estate that belongs to us, and that we can divide it up into countries and there's a marketplace for goods and for all kinds of resources...and we have no responsibility beyond what we take from the Earth. In other words, we act like the Earth essentially belongs to this one [human] species...We have reached the place where basic resources are running out and the planet is becoming more and more polluted...the yield of fish from the seas is going down...
>
> "In effect we are in an extraordinary planetary crisis, because of our inability to understand what native peoples all over the world understand, which is that there is a very delicate web of life and that web of life is being destroyed by this species. So that's the background, but then what happens in these experiences is that the message comes through to people who have had no particular environmental sensitivity or awareness, and the message is "your planet is dying; this is not your planet; it does not belong to this one [human] species." And they are shown images of vast exquisite beauty of the planet all over the earth, and then those images are shown alongside of pictures of the sea polluted, trees dying, species disappearing. And they often react with shock when they see this. And it creates a very deep sadness but, at the same time, a strong motivation on the part of many experiencers if they can get past the trauma, the initial trauma of the experiences, they become very mo-

tivated to do something about this situation. They want to talk publicly about it, but again... in the beginning you [Whitley Strieber] spoke about derision and ridicule, and that's a big problem because this phenomenon is so frightening to many of us in the West. Not so much because of what the aliens do or don't do to people. That's a part of it.

"But the deeper fear is that it tells us something about ourselves and the universe that is completely shattering to our worldview. Because it says that there are beings, creatures —whatever you want to call them — intelligences who have powers, who have vision, who have intelligence and technological capabilities that we simply don't have. And that they can reach us and do with us what they will. What they do is not that destructive. But the fact that we are not in control, that there are other beings that come through to us in this way, it kind of topples the arrogance that is pervasive, in the sense that we are alone somehow in the universe...we are the smartest beings in the cosmos. And this is a shock to discover that what native peoples all over the world — of course, have known and still know, and we used to know this too — that the universe is filled with beings with intelligence which don't necessarily manifest in the material form, although they may. This is opening people to this kind of awareness...but the point is that people are afraid to speak up about this, because the tendency is to be laughed at or in some way embarrassed for speaking about what is a deep truth for these individuals."

Notes

[1] Corso, Philip, Col. (Ret.). 1998. *The Day After Roswell.* Pocketbooks: New York, NY. pp 22-23

[2] Kitei, Lynne D., M.D. 2004. *The Phoenix Lights.* Hampton Roads Publishing Company: Charlottesville, VA. pp 1-11

[3] Bricker, Harvey M. and Victoria R. 2011. *Astronomy in the Maya Codices.* American Philosophical Society: Philadelphia, PA. pp 4-10, 53-59, 249-261

[4] Kramer, Miriam. "Ancient Maya Predicted 1991 Solar Eclipse." Live Science. January 8, 2013. . http://www.livescience.com/26070-maya-predicted-1991-solar-eclipse.html

[5] Sinnett, A.P., compiled by Alfred Trevor Barker. 1923. *The Mahatma Letters to A.P. Sinnett from the Mahatmas M. and K.H.* T. Fisher Unwin Ltd: London. Letter XV from Koot Hoomi to A. O. Hume, received July 10, 1882. pp 88-99

[6] Blavatsky, H. P. "Mistaken Notions on 'The Secret Doctrine'" *Lucifer* magazine, June 15, 1890, pages 333-35 (*H.P. Blavatsky: Collected Writings*, Volume XII, compiled by Boris de Zirkoff. 1980. Theosophical Publishing House: Wheaton, IL. pp 234-237)

[7] Blavatsky's foreknowledge (prescience) of sunken continents before the discovery of microcontinents and supercontinents 100 years after her death confirms the accuracy of her source of information. Astrophysicist Robert Nemiroff and his students at Michigan Technological University in Houghton did a search of social media with the internet to find evidence of prescience that could indicate time travelers among us in 2013. Blavatsky's 1888 account of sunken continents meets the scientific criteria of prescience Dr. Neimiroff's study used.

[8] Since 2012 when the first edition of "Web of Life and Cosmos" was prepared, three subsequent editions have been issued to keep pace with the rapid release of new scientific findings central to this book's subject.

[9] Wittke, James H., etal. "Evidence for deposition of 10 million tonnes of impact spherules across four continents 12,800 years ago." *Proceedings of the National Academy of Sciences for the United States.* Published online before print May 20, 2013,

[10] Ghose, Tia. "Before Babel: Ancient Mother Tongue Reconstructed." *LifeScience.* May 6, 2013. www.livescience.com/29342-ancient-mother-tongue-reconstructed.html

[11] Pagel, Mark, etal. "Ultraconserved words point to deep language ancestry across Eurasia." *Proceedings of the National Academy of Sciences of the United States of America.* May 6, 2013. Downloaded 5-6-13. www.pnas.org/content/early/2013/05/01/1218726110.full.pdf+html

[12] Than, Ker. "Lost Lands Found by Scientists." National Geographic News. May 11, 2013.
http://news.nationalgeographic.com/news/2013/13/130509-brazilian-atlantis-lost-continents-geography-world/

[13] ____"Ancient Lost Continent Discovered in Indian Ocean." National Geographic News. February 27, 2013. .
http://news.nationalgeographic.com/news/2013/02/130225-microcontinent-earth-mauritius-geology-science/

[14] "Cantalupo, Sebastiano, etal. "A cosmic web filament revealed a Lyman-a emission around a luminous high-redshift quasar." *Nature international weekly journal of science.* doi: 10. 1038/nature 12898. Published online January 19, 2014.

Simulations of structure formation in the Universe predict that galaxies are embedded in a 'cosmic web', where most baryons reside as rarefied and highly ionized gas. This material has been studied for decades in absorption against background sources."

[15] "Scientists May Have Identified Echoes of Ancient Earth." June 9, 2014. Phys.org. .
http://phys.org/news/2014-06-scientists-echoes-ancient-earth.html

[16] Tompkins, Peter. 1976. *Mysteries of the Mexican Pyramids.* Harper & Row Publishers: New York. pp 171-172

[17] Le Plongeon, Augustus. 1877. *The Mayas, The Sources of Their History. Proceedings of the American Antiquarian Society of April 26, 2876 and April 25, 1877.* Press of Charles Hamilton: Worcester. pp 56-58

[18] Stone, Rebecca R. 2011. *The Jaguar Within: Shamanic Trance in Ancient Central and South American Art.* The University of Texas Press: Austin. p 4

[19] Kubler, George. 1972. "Jaguars in the Valley of Mexico." Reprinted from *The Cult of the Feline.* Dumbarton Oaks, Trustees for Harvard University: Washington D.C. p 1

[20] Le Plongeon, Augustus. 1881. *Vestiges of the Maya or, Facts Tending to Prove that Communications and Intimate Relations Must have Existed, in very Remote Times.* Hamburg, Germany: Tradition Classics. pp 32-33

[21] Cremo, Michael. 2005. *Forbidden Archaeology: The Hidden History of the Human Race.* Los Angeles, CA: Bhaktivedanta Book Publishing, Inc. pp 796-814

[22]. Linda Moulton Howe discussed in radio interviews that she had interviewed a former intelligence specialist who reported he had spent 30 years during his career tracking activities of three extraterrestrial groups believed to have been involved with earth for hundreds of millions of years. She emphasized the immense number of hundreds of millions of years. Her report of the intelligence specialist's comments was especially interesting, because it corroborates the immense spans of time Helena Blavatsky's Mahatmas reported as well as time measures postulated in the Vedic calendar and literature. On July 11, 2012 I requested in an email a reference for the interview: "I would like to get the name and date for a report that Linda mentioned in a [radio interview] report. She said a former (military) intelligence specialist had spent most of his career tracking three different ET groups who appear to have been involved with earth for millions of years. If I can get an identifying reference I'll look up the info in the archives. Best regards, Krsanna Duran"

Linda Moulton Howe's response: "I have never publicly reported any of the material - so nothing beyond my mention on COAST radio. Thanks for your interest in my work, Linda Moulton Howe, Science/Environment Reporter and Editor"

[23] Cranston, Sylvia. 1993. *HPB: The Extraordinary Life and Influence of Helena Blavatsky Founder of the Modern Theosophical Movement.* New York, NY: G. P. Putnam's Sons. p 194

[24]. Lovett, Richard A. "Texas and Antarctica Were Attached, Rocks Hint." National Geographic. August 2011.

[25]. Lewis, Martin W.; Kären E. Wigen. 1997. *The Myth of Continents: a Critique of Metageography.* University of California Press: Berkeley, Los Angeles and London. pp 31-35

[26]. Sinnett, A.P., compiled by Alfred Trevor Baker. 1923. *The Mahatma Letters to A.P. Sinnett from the Mahatmas M. and K.H.* Letter XXIIB, II, 1882: Koot Hoomi replies to queries. pp 149-178

[27] Ibid. Dating the peak of the father of modern continents, the Pangaea supercontinent that had not yet been discovered in 1882 comma? is remarkable. The Arcturians, who seed modern humans (the Fifth race) with their DNA, according to the Arcturian Maez ("Mystery Ancestors," Chapter Two), had been on Earth and departed long before they introduced Bigfoot and Neanderthal. Spelling Neanderthal ? They introduced Bigfoot to determine whether environmental conditions were suited for their return. This implies the environment had not been suitable for

them in the past, either at the time they left and/or later. Species that mixed with Arcturian species to constitute modern humans had been in evolution long before the civilization of Atlantis took root.

[28] Blavatsky, H. P., edited by Boris de Zirkoff. 1888. *The Secret Doctrine*. Wheaton, IL: The Theosophical Publishing House. pp Vol 2, 263-276

[29] . Ibid.

[30] Than, Ker. "Ancient Lost Continent Discovered in Indian Ocean." National Geographic News. February 27, 2013. . http://news.nationalgeographic.com/news/2013/02/130225-microcontinent-earth-mauritius-geology-science/

[31] Caldwell, Daniel. 2000 *The Esoteric World of Madame Blavatsky*. Quest Books, Theosophical Publishing House: Wheaton, IL. pp 54-55, 57-77

[32] Van Tassel, George. 1958. *Religion and Science Merged*. Ministry of Universal Wisdom, Inc. Yucca Valley, CA pp 15-19

[33] Ring, Kenneth Ph.D. 1989. "Near Death and UFO Encounters as Shamanic Initiations." *ReVision*, Vol. 11, No. 3, Winter 1989 http://www.near-death.com/experiences/articles011.html

[34] Many who experience death and then return, such as neurosurgeon Eben Alexander, carry forward the thrust of near death and supernormal research.

Alexander, Eben. 2012. *Proof of Heaven: A Neurosurgeon's Journey into the Afterlife*. Simon & Schuster Paperbacks: New York, NY. pp 7-10

[35] Neihardt, John. 2008. *Black Elk Speaks: Being the Life Story of a Holy Man of the Oglala Sioux*. University of Nebraska Press: Lincoln, NB. p 33

[36] Black Elk, Wallace and William F. Lyons. 1990. *Black Elk: Sacred Ways of a Lakota*. New York, NY: HarperCollins Paperbacks. p 32, 91, 92

[37] . Fry, Daniel. 1973. *To Men of Earth*. Merlin, OR: Merlin Publishing Co: Merlin, OR. pp 82-83, 110-111

[38] . Ibid.

[39] Sprinkle, R. Leo. 1999. *Soul Samples*. Granite Publishing , LLC: Columbus, NC. pp 143-154, 237-238

[40] Mack, John E. 1999. *Passport to the Cosmos: Human Transformation and Alien Encounters*. Crown Publishers: New York, NY. pp 22-49

[41] Dreamland Radio, November 14, 1999. http://www.unknowncountry.com

Timeline

Years Before Present @ 2000 CE	Event
66 MYA	Explosion of Planet K in orbit between present-day Mars and Jupiter showered the surface of the Earth with debris, leaving only Antarctica untouched. (Van Flandern, *Dark Matter, Missing Planets and New Comets: Paradoxes Resolved, Origins Illuminated*.) Of the eight major craters the debris made, the one at Chixculub in southern Mexico continues to affect the Earth's balance profoundly. The equatorial axis modernly aligns between longitudes of the Chicxulub crater and its antipode in the Indian Ocean, shown on the TimeStar World Map, page 121. In 2012 the first-ever observed tectonic fracture began breaking up the Indo-Australian Plate in the region of the Chicxulub impact's antipode, which has drifted to the modern coasts of Java and Christmas Island. The Indo-Australian Plate fractured in volcano cones that became extinct 45 MYA, following massive volcanic eruptions after the debris impact.
275,601 BP	Resonant cycle culminating in modern human species in 2012 begins with Neanderthal, who created art, made tools, and buried its dead. Its final surge in 2012 corresponded with the ascending bronze age of Sri Yukteswar's yuga cycle. Earth was a nature preserve shared by a variety of ET civilizations, after it had been virtually destroyed in a cosmic explosion billions of years earlier and thrown into the present third orbit.
	Three primary extraterrestrial civilizations maintained genesis-creation gardens on Earth when the modern human timewave dawned: Arcturus-Lemuria, Aldebaran-Atlantis, and Mars-Sumer.
212,000 BP (210,000 BCE)	Atlantis as a colony with Germanic human workers Aldebaran had earlier introduced. The Mars-Sumer colony had steadily grown to become a political force with workers hybridized in the fabled Garden of Eden. Arcturus established Lemuria in the Pacific Ocean where Bigfoot, Neanderthal, and Cro-Magnon lived side-by-side with Homo erectus when territorial conflicts had started circa 250,000 BP.

52,772 BP (50,772 BCE)	The first of three breakups Atlantis experienced was 52,772 BP when rays produced with crystal technology were focused on the planet's surface to destroy large animals overrunning some regions. This resulted in a series of catastrophes with only five major islands remaining in the Atlantic. (Drs. Gregory and Lora Little and John Van Auken, *Edgar Cayce's Atlantis*)
30,000 BP (28,000 BCE) to 24,000 BP (22,000 BCE)	A violent destruction of Atlantis between 30,000 and 24,000 BP occurred when Atlantean crystal power stations were set too high. In both destructions, people moved to other places on the Earth. The third and final destruction of Atlantis was brought about by war circa 12,000 BP. (Ibid.)
22,000 BP (20,000 BCE)	An enclave of Lemurians retreated to peaks of the Himalaya Mountains above high levels of surface radiation during war with Atlantis. Some of the Lemurians elected to remain in the Himalayas and another group attempted flight to Mars during a close conjunction with Earth. Those who traveled to Mars created a self-sustaining planetoid, enabling them to travel among the stars independently of any planet.
	A Lemurian descendant from the planetoid, "Alan," initiated UFO contact with Daniel Fry in 1949 at White Sands, New Mexico. He introduced returning Lemurians who shared genetic roots with modern humans, before venturing into the stars more than 1,000 generations, or 20,000 years, earlier. Alan offered observations about Earth's plight as it emerged from World War II and entered the Cold War. (Fry, *To Men of Earth*)
	Many Lemurian "nationals" relocated to Arcturus when sinking of their Pacific home accelerated. (Kannenberg, *Time Travelers from Atlantis*) Arcturians established a center for teaching and guardianship beneath the Arctic in Hyperborea. Herodotus in his fifth century BCE Histories identified Hyperborea at the Arctic. Diodorus Siculus wrote that the sun rose and set once a year in Hyperborea, placing it in the Arctic polar region in the first century BCE.
	The planetary temperature began warming in this period and culminated in glacial flooding and beginning of the Holocene Age 11,700 BP.

15,000 BP (13,000 BCE)	A mother language shared throughout Europe and Asia suggests widespread civilization existed that was destroyed in glacial flooding. Mutation in Bigfoot's human maternal (mitochondrial) DNA that Dr. Melba Ketchum identified coincides with date for constraining change in Earth's magnetics, according to the Arcturians. Sumer's Adam and Eve are viable workers for Sumerian governor Enlil, and he decrees their descendants will inherit the Earth. Sumerian governor Enlil seizes opportunity to weaponize floods and turn them against humans of Lemuria and Atlantis, who compete with Sumer's Adam and Eve line. Contingent of 200 Sumerian scientists rebel when Sumer's Enlil wages environmental war and join with Lemurians remaining in Hyperborea under the Arctic.
13,501 BP (11,501 BCE)	Zenith of golden age is reached with closest approach to the Great Center (Vishnu Nabhi), according to Sri Yukteswar's calculation of the Hindu yugas. Descent from golden age begins. ("Ages of Humankind")
12,800 BP (10,800 BCE)	"Cosmic object(s)" scatters molten debris across four continents, and causes fire that burns North America's Older Dryas strata.
12,500 BP (10,500 BCE)	Turkey is the crossroad of mother language spoken in Asia and Europe identified by anthropologists. Astronomical alignment of the Sphinx at Giza describes the sky between the Orion and Leo Constellations 12,500BP.
12,490 BP (10,490 BCE) to 12,390BP (10,390 BCE)	Great Pyramid construction started 12,490 BP and completed 12,390 BP. (Edgar Cayce reading 5748-6.)
12,400 BP (10,400 BCE) to 12,350 BP (10,350 BCE)	The fastest and shortest reversal of the magnetic poles occurs with the Gothenburg Magnetic Excursion. After the magnetic poles flip (reverse) for fifty years starting 12,400 BP during the Great Pyramid's construction, they again reverse 12,350 BP after construction is complete, according to Edgar Cayce's dates.
12,000 BP (10,000 BCE)	Gobekli Tepe's construction in Turkey begins with exemplary crafting. The North Sea begins forming. Fresh water islands are above water in the North Atlantic.

11,700 BP (9700 BCE)	New geological period, the Holocene Age, begins with die-offs of numerous species and environmental changes.
11,564 BP (9564 BCE)	Atlantis, located on the Avalonia microcontinent in the Atlantic Ocean, sinks after in third destruction during war with Sumerian gods. It continues to sink more deeply into the planet's mantle. Provided by the Himalayan Mahatma Koot Hoomi in an 1882 letter, this is the most exact date for Atlantis sinking after third destruction by war.

Indonesians are displaced by volcanic eruptions and move toward India, where they settle on the banks of Brahmaputra River. All other tribes, including Sri Lankans and Orissans, converge on the banks of the seven rivers in the Saptha Sindhu region of India and mingle with the gods, the devi and deva. |
11,000 BP (9000 BCE)	Dravidian indigenous people of India colonized vast regions of South America, according to nuclear physicist Nunes dos Santos of the Federal University of Minas Gerais. Vestiges of the Dravidian presence in America, he says, include the phonetics of Gourani, Paraguay's national language. (Varakas, *The Scientific Dating of the Mahabharat War*.)
10,000 BP (8000 BCE)	Gobekli Tepe in Turkey is filled in with dirt with structures protected, as if preserved for posterity. Oldest astronomical calendar using a series of holes with posts for sightlines used in Scotland at Warren Field 10,000 BP.
9,500 BP (7500 BCE)	Indus Valley's early settlement begins parallel with the Neolithic culture in the Eastern Hemisphere after glacial floods.
8,000 BP (6000 BCE)	Settlements in alluvium deposited by flowing water begin in Mesopotamia with Nineveh. Settlements with public temples begin to appear in this phase. Cities of Eridu (Enki), Uruk (Inanna), and Babylon (Marduk) follow.

Postholes dug and wooden posts used at Stonehenge site 8,000 BP, discovered beneath modern parking area. Stonehenge was a funerary site that contained remains throughout Europe and the Mediterranean in its earliest uses. |
| 7561 BP (5561 BCE) | Based on astronomy with observation of Haley's comet, the war for Great Mother India (Mahabharat) commences after Krishna's birth in this era of the Hindu yugas. (Vartak, *The Scientific Dating of the Mahabharat War*) |

6700 BP (4700 BCE)	Abrupt climate change and beginning of desertification in Africa and Arabia started. Desertification was initiated by subtle changes in the Earth's orbit.
6,000 BP (4000 BCE)	Uruk, Sumerian Inanna's city, built after great floods. Mycenae established in Greece. Wayland's Smithy burial barrow (chamber) near Stonehenge built and bodies interred there 5,950 BP.
5,761 BP (3761 BCE)	Hebraic calendar begins.
5,114 BP (3114 BCE)	Long count of the Mexico's Feathered Serpent (Quetzalcoatl) begins 113 years before commencement of India's Kali Yuga era, as Sri Yukteswar calculated it. This encompasses a one-hundred-year transitional period plus thirteen years, the Feathered Serpent's signature number, for a period of 113 years.
5,101 BP (3101 BCE)	India's dark age of the Kali Yuga era begins, as Sri Yukteswar calculated it at Babaji's request. Upper and Lower Egypt unified and hieroglyphic writing introduced as flurry of human civilization building begins thousands of years after exquisite crafting at Gobekli Tepe was covered with dirt.
5,000 BP (3000 BCE)	First phase of the Stonehenge megaliths built, at site that had already been used for at least 3,000 years.
5,000 BP (3000 BCE)	Troy's first phase built in Turkey.
5,000 BP (3000 BCE)	Athens' first settlement built with descendants from Arcadia.
5,000 BP (3000 BCE)	Olmec settlement with advanced knowledge of celestial navigation in southern Mexico. (Gordon Cooper, *Leap of Faith: An Astronaut's Journey Into The Unknown*)
4,800 BP (2800 BCE)	Fu Xi invents Chinese writing; introduced with *I Ching*.
4,600 BP (2600 BCE)	Mohenjo-daro in the Indus Valley Civilization, the area of modern-day Pakistan, built circa 4600 BP. Volcanic ash covers round step pyramid at Cuicuilco in Mexico Valley; construction date for the pyramid is not known. (Hapgood, *Maps Of The Ancient Sea Kings*)
4,500 BP (2500 BCE)	Great Pyramid in Egypt renovated in 2560 BCE by Pharaoh Kufu.

4,300 BP (2300 BCE)	Babylon, Marduk's city, emerges as a small village in the south of modern-day Iraq.
4,200 BP (2200 BCE)	The most advanced civilization of the third millennium BCE, decline of Mohenjo-daro in modern Pakistan began circa 4200 BP. A catastrophic event that destroyed much of the city with bodies left lying in the streets and high radiation levels suggests that nuclear-like weapons were used at the city. Outlying cities in the area had wasted by 4000 BP.
3,996 BP (1996 BCE)	Abraham's birth in Ur of Chaldea based on Bishop Usser's timeline with the King James Bible.
3,229 BP (1229 BCE)	War of Troy under royal family of Dardanus directed by Zeus of Greece, also known as Marduk of Babylon. Aphrodite's son Aeneas sent to find location to build New Troy where Rome would be built.
2,484 BP (484 BCE)	Marduk of Babylon dies strange death and his son Nabu disappears after Babylonians reject king that Enlil's son, Sin, appointed. Control of Rome passes to Enlil's followers.
2,200 BP (200 BCE)	Teotihuacan's Pyramid of the Sun construction starts over older pyramid at site.
1,800 BP (200 CE)	Larger population moves to Teotihuacan as volcanic eruptions abate in Mexico Valley.
1,500 BP (499 CE)	Ascending Kali Yuga begins when solar system and Earth reach farthest descent from Great Center. Inertia grips the world. Barbarians gather at Rome's borders and Nahuatl tribes migrate to Mexico Valley.
1,300 BP (700 CE)	Pyramid of the Feathered Serpent constructed in ceremonial square at Teotihuacan, and emerges with a full collar of feathers. Rome collapses and Vatican assumes military role.
508 BP (1492 CE)	Columbus "discovers" America and claims possession with doctrine of discovery, on pretext that no civilization exists.
301 BP (1699 CE)	Transition into ascending Hindu Dwapara Yuga begins with end of Kali Yuga iron age. Magnetic fields begin to shift.
Dates CE	**Twentieth Century**
1899	Transitional period ends and solar system and Earth fully enter the ascending Hindu Dwapara Yuga. Planetary magnetic field weakens and temperatures rise.
1942	UFO over Los Angeles repeatedly attacked by Army but sustained no damage, sustained nuclear fission developed.

1945	Atomic bombs dropped on Japan.
1947	The Navy's Operation High Jump to the Antarctic abruptly terminated after two weeks in February. UFO crashed at Roswell, New Mexico in July. National Security Act was signed in October, provided authorization to found the Central Intelligence Agency (CIA) under the NSA. Arrangements for Operation Paperclip begin.
1948	Operation Paperclip brings presumably former Nazis to the USA to work in science projects.
1949	UFO contact with Daniel Fry at White Sands Proving Ground.
1952	Flying Saucer Air Wars when American President Truman orders Air Force to shoot down UFOs.
1954	UFO contact with George van Tassel at Giant Rock, California began followed by public displays of UFOs.
1963	American President John Kennedy assassinated in Dallas, Texas heralds shift of power in American democracy. Although the assassins have never been conclusively identified, the Central Intelligence Agency (CIA) altered evidence of bullet wounds in Kennedy's head, leaving only copies of x-rays after the originals were destroyed.
1967	UFOs hovered above nuclear missiles when the silos were shut down at Maelstrom Air Force Base in Montana (USA).
1991	Extensive UFO activity in Mexico started July 11, 1991, with eclipse predicted in Mayan calendar from Chichen Itza.
1997	Phoenix lights displayed over three states in USA and northern Mexico on March 13.

Twenty-First Century

2012	Mexico's long count ended December 21, 2012, 113 years after the Kali Yuga ended and transition into the new Dwapara Yuga in 1899 was complete. (See 3114 BCE.) History-making fracture on Indo-Australian plate April 11, 2012 in focal area of the Maya's Earth glyph from Chichen Itza.

2014	Earth's planetary magnetic field continually weakened and cosmic ray levels escalated between January and June 2014, according to the European Space Agency. After NASA announced that the solar maximum had arrived on June 10, 2014 sunspots inexplicably plummeted to zero on July 17. Sun's magnetic field failed to reverse in Cycle 24.

CHAPTER ONE

Crisis, Die-Offs, Mutants and Savants

Scientists have long believed a planet the size of Mars collided with Earth during its early formation billions of years ago. Among the evidence that mighty forces clashed with deadly might is the moon formed with debris shattered from the Earth and the continuously volcanic Ring of Fire encircling the Pacific Ocean. Friction from the collision caused the whole planet to homogeneously heat and melt, according to this theory. However, the Ancient Earth found in the belly of the planet is writing a new story that brings sharper focus to Mars.

Harvard scientists announced in 2014 that an unexplained difference in isotope ratios in one hemisphere suggests it is more ancient than the other is, indicating the entire planet did not heat evenly in an impact. Scientists named the remains embedded deep within one hemisphere of the earth's mantle the Ancient Earth.[1]

Discovering the Ancient Earth encased within modern Earth agrees surprisingly well with the Babylonian "Epic of Creation."[2] In the epic, also known as *Enuma Elish*, Marduk was a wandering planet that entered the solar system and engaged in a deadly struggle with the planet Tiamat. Eventually taming the planet, Marduk formed the asteroid belt with half of Tiamat's body and made the Earth with the other half. In Zecharia Sitchin's interpretation of Marduk's cosmic battle, after colliding with Tiamat and then creating the asteroid belt and Earth, the wandering planet was captured in the Sun's gravity and entered a long elliptical orbit around the Sun. When Marduk returned to the inner solar system 3,600 years later, according to Sitchin, it was named Nibiru.

Nibiru literally means "position of the morning star" or "planet of crossing," in Babylonian astronomy. Anciently, Jupiter and Venus were the most common morning stars, with Babylon's god Marduk ruling Jupiter. Marduk's allegorical struggle with Tiamat suggests Jupiter's involvement in the ancient cosmic battle. Among the suspects are the many moons orbiting Jupiter, neighboring the asteroid belt's orbit. In the life of solar systems, moons wander from orbits and planets explode in astronomer Tom Van Flandern's exploding planet hypothesis (eph).[3] Strong evidence indicates, for instance, that Mercury is an escaped moon from Venus and several planets exploded in the early formation of the solar system.

Encapsulating physical existences with mythological facets give context to complex situations for primitive human cultures: "Planets explode; a planet exploded and formed the asteroid belt; Tiamat was a planet that exploded and Earth formed with her body." These astronomical complexities are contextualized with Babylon's Tiamat myth in which she was a creator goddess who gave birth to the first generation of deities. When they murdered her consort and father of the gods, Apsu, Tiamat took on the form of a sea dragon and brought forth Mesopotamia's first monsters before Marduk murdered her.

Van Flandern's eph identified two planets that anciently exploded near the asteroid belt, Planet K and Planet V, accounting for at least two different sources of debris in the asteroid belt. Of the two planets, Van Flandern suggests K most likely exploded 4+ billion years ago (BYA) and V exploded 66 million years ago (MYA). Van Flandern's evidence that Mars is a former moon of another planet is compelling. NASA's MAVEN mission launched in 2013 to study Mars' atmosphere found that the red planet lost its magnetic field between 4.2 and 3.7 billion years ago, in the period when van Flandern posited K exploded.

In myth, Tiamat compares with Planet K but few clues are given about Apsu in the solar system's early formation. In one possible scenario, Tiamat's child moon, Kingu (Planet V), remained in the fifth orbit with asteroid debris while a second moon entered the fourth orbit as Mars. When Kingu subsequently exploded in Tiamat's fifth orbit, the debris repeated his mother's path and collided with Earth in the third orbit 66 MYA. Kingu's blood mixed with the Earth and his ancient mother embedded within it. Mars is the sole survivor of Tiamat and Apsu's tragic union that Marduk ended in an epic war of the gods.

With eight impact craters created by debris found around the globe in an extinction event 66 MYA, Van Flandern concluded it had the earmarks of a major planet explosion. Although a core has never been recovered from Chixculub, it was hit with so much force that the present-day equatorial axis aligns exactly between the impact crater and its antipode in the Indian Ocean. This is shown in the Earth glyph from Chichen Itza, which I used in 1998 to predict the major axis of changes

Rings of Jupiter

The largest planet in the solar system, Jupiter is a gas giant with a halo and three rings. A rocky ring along Amalthea's orbit may consist of collisional debris from that moon. NASA/JPL/Cornell University

where the Indo-Australian Plate fractured in 2012. (The tectonic plate fractured in volcano cones that became extinct 45 MYA, north of the antipode for the Chixculub crater. (See Appendix, "Earth Calendar.")

In his book *Other Tongues, Other Flesh*, UFO contactee George Hunt Williamson called the missing planet between Mars and Jupiter Maldek and its moon Malona.[4] He gleaned from UFO sources that a hydrogen weapon explosion destroyed Maldek and commented that Earth had entered its present orbit as a comet. The Earth's hypothesized entry into the third orbit after Tiamat exploded 4+ BYA was an earlier and different event from the exploding planet 66 MYA, corresponding with Kingu in the Babylonian creation epic and Maldek in Williamson's explosion account. The Billy Meier UFO contact in Switzerland gave a similar description for the planet Malona. Kingu, Maldek and Malona are different names for a planet that three extraterrestrial sources described virtually identically as early as 1953.

The astronomy and science accessible to humans in Babylon's ancient astronaut culture were among the finest in the ancient world. Jewish scribes saw the *Enuma Elish* while captive in Babylon, more than 900 years after Moses wandered the Wilderness. Sixth century Jewish scribes copied the Babylonian creation story for Genesis 1 and substituted the Judaic God for the Babylonian gods after leaving Babylon in 539 BCE. Jewish scholars posited the world was created in 3760 BCE, and compressed the chronology of stunning Babylonian texts into the framework of the Jewish calendar. Despite the implausible dates for Jewish history, the sequences of creation in the Babylonian originals give a sweeping view that compare well with geological and historical records.

During periods of geophysical quiet, a number of civilizations have occupied the Earth with a multitude of experimental species that may thrive and move into galactic life. In periods of upheaval, space faring races move to other worlds or voyage into space. Earth was entering a period of relative calm 300,000 BP when several species made quantum evolutionary leaps.

Bigfoot and tool-making Neanderthals emerged in rapid succession a little less than 300,000 years ago, according to Ida Kannenberg in *My Brother Is A Hairy Man*.[5] The period when Neanderthal began making tools is very close to the 275,601 BP beginning of Timewave Zero that Terence McKenna found by extrapolating the Chinese *Book of Changes*, the *I Ching*, as a fractal. He found in the timewave fractal segments of boundary constraints juxtaposed with self-similar segments that "surge" towards zero state. Transitions from one modality to another are called "changes in epoch." "The appearance of life in an inorganic world, of consciousness in an unconscious world, or of language in a world without language are all examples of such epochal transitions."[6]

To explain what Timewave Zero measures, McKenna used Alfred North Whitehead's extrapolation of matter as process through time. Whitehead was the first philosopher and mathematician at the dawn of the quantum revolution to elucidate quantum mechanical principles of matter as a wave with the intrinsic characteristic of time. In its process through time, matter has both 1) beginning and end and 2) physical and mental qualities.

McKenna established dates to begin and end Timewave Zero by using the explosion of the atomic bomb in 1945 as a benchmark for the last major cyclic curve in the fractal, and then using that date to find the beginning of the entire cycle. With these dates, the 275,601-year cycle ended in November 2012, a month before the Mayan Long Count's end. McKenna deferred to the long count's end on December 21, 2012 and incorporated the date into Timewave Zero.

Rupert Sheldrake's theory of morphogenetic resonance argues that resonant memory in morphogenetic fields facilitates ease in future efforts of a similar kind. Depth of the morphogenetic reservoir of the human genome had steadily increased with the success of early humans. Neanderthal was a quantum evolutionary leap into the modern human. His species was a sentient problem solver whose first and foremost survival tool in the wild was human intelligence. Neanderthal inherited the physical power of his Homo erectus ancestor along with well-developed brain capacity for processing the expanding mindscapes of genus Homo. Strong, smart, handsome, and versatile, Neanderthals made tools, created art, and buried their dead.

After early development on Arcturus, Neanderthal was introduced into the Arcturian creation garden in the North Atlantic, anciently connected to the steppes now at the bottom of the North Sea. Early humans roamed between the Americas, Mediterranean, and Africa using now-sunken land bridges. Soviet core samples taken in the '60s confirmed fresh water islands were above water in the North Atlantic as late as 12,000 years ago. (*Atlantis: Atlantology Basic Problems*)

Extraterrestrial matings with "mixtures of various evolutionary advances toward Homo erectus" preceded and overlapped the beginning of the 275,601 BP timewave. In her study, Dr. Ketchum identified a mutation in Bigfoot's human DNA between 15,000 and 12,000 BP, amid critical planetary changes.[7] Assuming a date of 275,601 BP for Sumerian genetic experiments that produced a progression of workers before Adam and Eve's creation in Eden circa 13,400 BP gives a period in line with changing planetary conditions amenable for DNA mutations.

Lemuria, Atlantis, and Sumer

Arcturus: Lemuria, Hyperborea, and Mu

Mu was the mother culture that laid foundations for the modern Earth, established by Ancestors from Arcturus who first came to Earth 225 MYA. The human species of Arcturus that lived on Earth 225 MYA has a distinctive mutation caused by the super nova of the Horsehead Nebula in the Orion Constellation. This true human mutation is entangled with extreme photon (light) radiations in Orion.

After a series of wars in Orion, the Arcturians were a vanquished species and rejoiced to have a home free from war. They devoted themselves to healing the Earth, and in that dedicated effort the Earth healed them. When they left before the meteor impact at Chicxulub, 66 MYA they returned to the Milky Way and parented numerous human species.

Lemuria in the Pacific Ocean was a younger-sister civilization to ancient Mu in the Indian Ocean. A Lemurian center north of present-day Hawaii monitored and educated the Arcturian Bigfoot and human species in Pacific areas circa 250,000 BP. The main city in the North Pacific, Posyna, began sinking after the first destruction of Atlantis 52,772 BP, and Lemurians resettled around the Pacific Rim. The Death glyph with an archaic human skull west of Chile on the TimeStar memorializes early human ancestors who died-off at the end of a long-term cycle between 100,000 and 50,000 BP. In this period, Neanderthal interbred with several novel human species and Homo s. s. emerged in the North Pacific, shown with a modern human skull on the Human glyph in the North Pacific, extending to Siberia, Alaska, and Canada on the TimeStar.

Most Lemurians relocated to Arcturus 22,000 BP, after the second destruction of Atlantis strongly affected Earth 30,000 and 24,000 BP. Lemurians who remained on the Earth moved under the Arctic to Hyperborea, where scientists who later rebelled against Sumer's Enlil and their children joined them.

Aldebaran: Atlantis and Pleiades

Colonies displaying icons of the Taurus Constellation, symbolized with the bull, have interacted with the Earth at least 780,000 years, according to UFO contact reports with Aldebarans.[8] In the UFO contact with Billy Meier in Switzerland in 1975, a Pleiadian woman using the name Semjase reported that Pleiadians first contacted the Earth 22 MYA, later founded Atlantis, and were ancestors of the Germanic people. Edgar Cayce reported that Atlantis in the Atlantic Ocean was founded approximately 212,000 years BP.[9]

Atlantis was a cosmopolitan civilization comprising numerous extraterrestrial strains that underwent three major destructions. The first of the three breakups was 52,772 BP, when rays produced with crystal technology were focused on the planet's surface to destroy large animals overrunning some regions. This resulted in a series of catastrophes worldwide, broke up the continent where Atlantis was located, and left only five major islands of Atlantis above water. A violent destruction between 30,000 and 24,000 BP occurred when crystal power stations were set too high. In both destructions, people relocated to other places on the Earth. The third and final destruction of Atlantis was caused by war, according to Edgar Cayce. When the Sumerian Enlil attempted to destroy humans and civilization during glacial flooding 13,000 BP extraterrestrial scientists, the Biblical sons of God in Genesis 6 with human children, rebelled.

Extraterrestrials of many origins mingled (or liaised) for various reasons at different times. Identifying markers for each faction are blurry, because their internal politics were less visible than the virtually monolithic extraterrestrial identity visible to primitive humans with few resources for distinguishing unique features among ubiquitously powerful forces.

Mars: Sumer

The Progenitors of Sumer are a reptilian species who hybridized with hominines to produce the Sumerian alien gods, the Anunnaki. In *UFO Highway*, Anthony Sanchez identified the Sumerian progenitor species with Mars.[10] They had anciently migrated from Zeta Reticuli 1 and subsequently to Sirius B before going to Mars 1 MYA.[11] The Sumerian aliens came to Earth about 350,000 years ago after a nuclear accident made Mars untenable for their species. Although Earth's environment was not well suited to their species, they were forced to migrate and colonized ancient Sumer, now modern Iraq. In order to preserve their species, the Progenitors hybridized with Earth's hominines.

These first offspring were the *Austra Albus* species of blondes known today as Mesopotamia's Anunnaki, according to Sanchez. In this scenario, the Progenitors died out, while their altered Anunnaki descendants survived by eventually incorporating Homo sapiens DNA into their genome. With the advanced biotechnology the Progenitors possessed, it is likely that they engineered their disappearance instead of dying out.

The name for the Anunnaki species, Austra Albus, suggests they may have hybridized with relatives of the *Australopithecus* species, which was also used for Bigfoot and Homo sapiens. In this scenario Sumer's most elite gods who had little human contact maintained higher ratios of reptilian traits than lower-ranking gods more directly associated with humankind. Enki's lower ranking directly resulted from his mother's status, which may have had fewer reptilian traits. This is suggested by Enki's relationship with and advocacy for humans in contrast to Enlil's murderous weaponizing of glacial flooding.

Marduk of Babylon
Iraq's Heritage, Musée du Louvre

In Mesopotamia, an oligarchy of elite Sumerian Anunnaki ruled with a Gray species bioengineered to serve the Anunnaki and the human species serving both the Anunnaki and the Grays. Ancient Mesopotamia's civilization was located in the Persian Gulf when it was a dry basin before flooding between 13,000 and 10,000 BP. The basin filled during the great floods and ancient Mesopotamia submerged beneath Persian Gulf waters. Limited archaeological exploration found the Mesopotamian culture was distinctly different from the one in Africa.

Gods in the Garden

Vestiges of a mother language spoken throughout Europe and Asia 15,000 BP are still found in modern languages.[12,13,14] A consistently organized language spanning a vast area with still recognizable elements thousands of years later was certainly a legacy of the Solex-Mal, the solar tongue, that UFO contactee George Hunt Williamson reported.[15] Stone Age people could walk from the crossroads of the mother language in Turkey to Atlantis on contiguous land before the great floods. Extraterrestrial parent races in colonies around the globe were racially different from native humans, albeit, select humans directly descended from extraterrestrials were similar to their parents in appearances.

Extraterrestrials were collectively titled gods and lords, acknowledging their social and scientific achievements. "When human beings began to increase in number on the earth and daughters were born to them, the sons of God saw that the daughters of humans were beautiful, and they married any of them they chose." (Genesis 6:1-2) In the epic *"Catalogue of Women"* Hesiod listed genealogies of human and godly parents of Greece's ruling aristocracy, which functionally devolved to Rome's aristocracy.

Aristocratic status and land rights passed from parent to child with patrimonial entitlement. When England's Duke of Cambridge, Prince William's son was born in 2013, his child inherited William's titled status with right of succession to the English throne. The 8 pound, 6 ounce boy was titled Prince George, Duke of Cambridge. Prince George's claim to kingship is sanctioned by the religious and political doctrine of divine right of kings, which asserts that only God can judge a king and attempts to depose kings are sacreligious violations of God's will.

The "Table of Nations" in Genesis 10 named Adam and Eve's descendants rulers of the world after the floods. Jewish scribes took Genesis from Babylon's records while the Jews were captive there in the sixth century BCE. Distinctions between the Divine source of life in the cosmos and genetic engineering by local gods ruling political kingdoms were lost in translation of Babylon's texts into institutionalized Judeo-Christian religion.

Honoring the Divine source that animates humans and aliens equally, empowering the unique evolution of each, is a critically missing link of context in Earth's history. The series of planetary catastrophes that interrupted continuously stable growth of species invited extraordinary extraterrestrial caretaking and, eventually, competition.

In Plato's Atlantis, the god Poseidon mated with the human Cleito and fathered ten sons, destined to rule the island kingdom. Plato often employed allegory for important topics, and social justice was among his frequent topics. In an allegory that places Socrates in Athens, for instance, Plato asks Socrates to defend justice (*On Justice*, 380 BCE). Both Socrates and Athens were historically factual, but Plato brought forward issues in allegorical dialogue. In Plato's Atlantis, Cleito's father was first-earth born, or the first of his lineage born on Earth, thus Cleito had one human and one godly parent. She was an aristocratic human who directly interacted with the gods on the island kingdom, which Poseidon deemed safe because Man had not yet learned to sail. Atlantis was secluded from early humans living in the wild, but easily accessible to ancient aliens with craft that could fly or submerge in water.

Ancient Sumer was strictly governed by status of genetics, birth order and gender, under the aegis of the patriarch Anu. Although Sumer's chief scientist Enki was Anu's first-born son, his mother's status was less than his younger brother, Enlil's mother. Anu ranked sixty, Enlil fifty and Enki forty. The Sumerian title "En" literally meant "lord" and conjoined with descriptors for the gods' domains of authority. Anu was Lord of Heaven and Constellations. Enlil was Lord of the Wind or sky, with "lil" meaning "wind" and Enki was Lord of the Earth, with "ki" meaning Earth. Their statuses and rankings reflected the priorities of Sumerian society, which siphoned down to human culture.

Enlil's high ranking granted him ultimate power as governor, and, when Enki created primitive workers, Enlil demanded control of them. In one incident, Enki secluded workers in a walled compound and Enlil broke down the walls.[16] When humans attained the evolutionary status to consort with gods, Enlil's rage exponentially escalated.

Poseidon's mating with the human woman Cleito in Atlantis was an archetypal human-god relationship recorded in Greece, Sumer, and Rome. In the epic *"Catalogue of Women"* Hesiod listed genealogies of human and godly parents of Greece's ruling aristocracy, which functionally devolved to Rome's aristocracy. The Greek Goddess Aphrodite's human son, Aeneas, identified the village in Italy to build the New Troy after the Trojan War. Hundreds of years later, Aeneas' descendants founded

Rome at the village and named Aphrodite Rome's founding mother. Enlil fought an uphill battle to confine humans to his desired limits.

The Lord Enlil took Enoch, Adam and Eve's fifth-generation descendant, and Enoch was no longer on the Earth, according to Genesis 5. Enoch next appeared with *The Book of Enoch* containing an eyewitness account of a war with 200 rebel scientists. A fast-paced inventory of humans to be exterminated in Genesis 6 begins with affirming Enlil's intent to eliminate man with a lifespan of 120 years. It assessed the Nephilim parented by sons of God (extraterrestrial) and human women as men of renown who were present in the past as well as in the future in verse 4. Enlil decided to destroy life on Earth in verse 7. Then he excluded Enoch's great grandson, Noah, from destruction in verse 8.

> "3) And the Lord said, "My Spirit shall not strive with man forever, for he is indeed flesh; yet his days shall be one hundred and twenty years."
>
> "4) The Nephilim [Giants] were on the earth in those days—and also afterward—when the sons of God went to the daughters of humans and had children by them. They were the heroes of old, men of renown...
>
> "7) So the Lord said, "I will wipe from the face of the earth the human race I have created—and with them the animals, the birds and the creatures that move along the ground—for I regret that I have made them."
>
> "8) But Noah found favor in the eyes of the Lord."

The Lord took Enoch when he was 365 years old and Methuselah lived for 969 years, far older than the 120 years of humans Enlil slated for extermination. Genesis is silent about which humans were limited to 120 years of life, but the Babylonian tale of "Atrahasis" specifies that the workers created to labor for the gods were designated to live 120 years. This lifespan repeated in the Judaic Genesis 2 may be a legacy inherited from the Babylonian text.

"Atrahasis" is a contender, among several, for Noah's prototype and the great floods. Atrahasis includes both a creation myth and an account of the Great Deluge, which parallels the second creation when man was created from dust in Genesis 2 and Noah's flood. Leading up to creating workers with clay, Atrahasis explains that lower-ranking gods, the Igigi, rebelled when the labor to build irrigation

Ishtar with Winged Sages

Fleur de lis and stars are at crowns of the head and serpents rise from the brows of Ishtar and sages.

Sages hold baskets symbolizing the knowledge of civilization. A supplicant levitates.

Winged sages that Ea-Enki appointed to build civilization hold satchels suggesting they carry the gifts of arts and sciences. After the great floods, Ea sent human Adapas, whom he had educated and mentored, to work with kings and build cities. The sages were emblemized with wings and fish, both symbols of the Underworld. The person receiving benediction (above) is levitating while Ishtar and the sages hold their hands in gestures of esoteric rites. The crowns and brows of Ishtar and the sages' heads are marked with metaphysical symbols. Sumerian Inanna was known as Ishtar in Assyria. An eight-pointed star symbolizing Venus was Ishtar and the Feathered Serpent's symbol. An eight-pointed rosette is embedded in the Sun Stone in Teotihuacan's region of Mexico, where Venus was the Feathered Serpent's celestial herald. The Feathered Serpent acquired a full collar of feathers at Teotihuacan. The above Assyrian cylinder seal is from Mesopotamia, circa the 7th-8th century BCE. It is housed in the Metropolitan Museum of Art in New York City, NY. © 2013 KDuran

canals was too arduous. The aristocratic Anunnaki council issued a decree to create workers and Enki prepared clay to shape them.[17]

Scholars agree that Genesis 2 constitutes a second creation, but why man was created twice with different instructions in Genesis 1 and 2 floats in murky theological water with no clear answer. The Himalayan Adept who mentored Helena Blavatsky's studies in Tibet, Mahatma Morya wrote about Genesis 1 and 2 in correspondence with A. P. Sinnett in 1882. Morya correlated principles of the esoteric inner man, the soul-mind, with the outward man in the exoteric world of causes, with Genesis 1 and 2.[18]

"He [man] starts downward as a simply spiritual entity—an unconscious seventh principle . . .—with the germs of the other six principles lying latent and dormant in him. Gathering solidity at every sphere—his six principles when passing through the worlds of effects, and his outward form in the worlds of causes . . . when he touches our planet he is but a glorious bunch of light upon a sphere itself yet pure and undefiled (for mankind and every living thing on it increase in their materiality with the planet). At that stage [in Genesis 1] our globe is like the head of a newly born babe—soft and with undefined features, and man—an Adam **before** the breath of life was breathed into his nostrils (to quote your own bungled up Scriptures for your better comprehension). For man and (our planet's) nature—it is day —the first (see distorted tradition in your Bible). Man No. I makes his appearance . . . **after** the completion of the seven rounds [equivalent to days in Genesis 1] . . . and thus he is said to be created on the eighth day (see Bible Chapter II; note verses 5 and 6 and think what is meant there by "mist" and verse 7 wherein Law the Universal great fashioner is termed "God" by Christians and Jews, and understood as Evolution by Cabalists). During this first round "animal man" runs, as you say, his cycle in a spiral.' On the descending arc . . . he has to enter every sphere not as a lower animal as you understand it but as a lower man. Since during the cycle which preceded his round as a man he performed it as the highest type of animal [in Genesis 1]. Your Lord God," says Bible, chapter I, verse 25 and 26—after having made all said : "Let us make man in our image," etc., and creates man an androgyne ape! (extinct on our planet) the highest intelligence in the animal kingdom and whose descendants you find in the anthropoids of today."

Verses in Genesis 2 that Morya recommends for comparison speak of an uncultivated world in the absence of intelligent man.

Verse 5: "Now no shrub of the field was yet in the earth, and no plant of the field had yet sprouted, for the LORD God had not sent rain upon the earth, and there was no man to cultivate the ground."

Verse 6: "But a mist used to rise from the earth and water the whole surface of the ground."

Verse 7: "Then the LORD God formed man of dust from the ground, and breathed into his nostrils the breath of life; and man became a living being."

With no rain, mist rising from the earth with the surface watered suggests irrigation canals the Igigi had built. In "Atrahasis," lower-ranking gods who cleared rivers and made channels for water for irrigation rebelled when the work became too arduous. The Anunnaki council decreed the creation of humans to do the work of clearing and irrigating the land. The kindly Enki prepared clay to fashion humankind.

Morya's 1882 letter describing the processes of soul-mind and physical evolution in the human species is consistent with the symbol set displayed by sages Enki-Ea mentored, the Adapas. Representations of the sages are archetypes for the mission to engender civilization carried out by numerous sages initiated in esoteric traditions through the ages. Shared with Lemuria-Hyperborea, these symbols point to functions of brain, chakras, and subtle energies embedded in the oldest esoteric practices in the world.

The six days of Genesis 1 comprise six of seven phases (subcycles) of spiritual entities developing human souls when they incarnated with Earth in its modern creation in the third orbit from the Sun. As species grew more complex with the planet's greater capacity to sustain life, the advancing soul-minds incarnated with the most developed animal of the epoch, the ape, before entering the human kingdom. *The Secret Doctrine* posits that every cosmic body, be it sun or planet, nebula or comet, atom or electron, is a composite of energetic and physical spheres, or globes. All have a sevenfold constitution with seven principles of energetic and physical globes of varying densities. Life streams move through the physical and non-physical globes of any celestial body in spirals. Ascent from the physical to an energetic globe is an ascending arc. Descent from an energetic globe into the physical is a descending arc.

The descending arc into the physical human species surged with the epochal end, the seventh day of the first round in Genesis 1. Life was breathed into humanity with the beginning of the second round, Genesis 2, on the eighth day. Each of the seven days in a round encompasses eons of time that vary in length. When we speak of a new day in evolutionary context, we mean a new epoch within a grander round comprising numerous cycles and subcycles.

Changing conditions of the Earth are the staging ground for the species' evolution. Using the 275,601-year benchmark for intelligent Neanderthal's emergence, the timewave for this increment ended in 2012, launching a new phase of human development. In evolutionary terms, the 2012 end of the long count rapidly followed on the heels of the Holocene Age by a mere 11,700 years BP in the geological record. Widespread devastation with glacial flooding evident in the geological record is comparable to the Hopi's third world destroyed by water and beginning of the fourth world. Surviving the floods in reeds, sometimes reed boats, and lengthy migrations to the four corners of the Earth, the Hopi were finally able to enter the fourth world in the Grand Canyon. Many Hopi report they climbed up a hollow reed and emerged from the hole where it had grown toward the sky, the *sipapu*, at the bottom of the canyon.

After the great floods Enoch wrote the first Hebraic astronomical treatise with a solar model, which he said the sons of God had explained to him. Changing materiality in humans is affirmed by Noah's exceptional "angelic" appearance, described in a fragment from *The Book of Noah*:[19] ". . . his body was white as snow and red as the blooming of a rose, and the hair of his head and his long locks were white as wool," Chapter CVI:

> "4) And his father Lamech was afraid of him [Noah] and fled, and came to his father Methuselah. 5) And he said unto him: 'I have begotten a strange son, diverse from and unlike man, and resembling the sons of the God of heaven; and his nature is different and he is not like us, and his eyes are as the rays of the sun, and his countenance is glorious. 6) And it seems to me that he is not sprung from me but from the angels, and I fear that in his days a wonder may be wrought on the earth."

The *Book of Enoch* picked up the trail with Enoch traveling with the Lord and visiting scientists who rebelled when Enlil vowed to destroy life on Earth.[20] Enoch lists the names and disciplines of leaders of 200 scientists who took an oath at Mt. Harmon to carry out a great sin, another rebellion. *"Semjâzâ taught enchantments, and root-cuttings, Armârôs the resolving of enchantments, Barâqîjâl, taught astrology [the heavens translated into modern astronomy], Kôkabêl the constellations, Ezêqêêl the knowledge of the clouds [the atmosphere], Araqiêl the signs of the earth, Shamsiêl the signs of the sun, and Sariêl the course of the moon."*

The constellations, the clouds, signs of the earth, the sun, course of the moon, and astrology translated into astronomy continue to be respected scientific disciplines. Root-cuttings that Semjâzâ taught are botanical science used by herbalists and healers throughout history and are still taught with ancient and modern medicine. The knowledge of "enchantments" identifies Semjâzâ and Armârôs as physicians with knowledge of sacred sciences passed down through Crete and Greece to the modern world.

According to Enoch, the Lord, Enlil, swore to annihilate the scientists, all their children, and all their generations. What happened after the encounter at Mt. Harmon can only be pieced together from Enoch's fragmentary account and evidence on the ground. The sons of God who rebelled controlled science and technology for Sumer's aristocracy and, other than Enki, were most capable of countering Enlil.

Glacial melt had been increasing for several thousand years, since about 15,000 BP. The water Enlil needed to produce rain for days on end was in the high atmosphere and needed only to be heated for a truly Great Deluge. Huge floods gouged holes into bedrock and tore the crust away in some places, from the Pacific Northwest and across the Atlantic, Scandinavia, and Europe as glaciers melted. Along with flooding, a "cosmic impact" scattered molten debris across four continents, from the Pacific Ocean, North America, Central America, the Atlantic Ocean, and North Africa 12,800 BP.[21] Modern scientists continue to debate what "cosmic object(s)" was capable of creating the enormous debris field. A detailed accounting of the war between the scientists and Enlil has not been unearthed, and only an analyst familiar with the capabilities of technology Enlil and the ancient astronauts possessed could give an accurate assessment. Sumerian texts repeatedly referred to "weapons of brilliance," and portions of the Sahara and Asia Minor still have unusually high radiation levels today.

Temperatures that had started to warm at the end of the glacial age cooled again after the 12,800 BP impact for 1,300 years, or until 11,500 BP. Ash and gasses from large volcanic eruptions block the sun, cause global temperatures to drop, and reduce growing seasons with resulting famines. In this period Bigfoot's DNA mutated and early signs of civilizing construction began at Gobekli Tepe in Turkey. Sequential catastrophes during the 1,300 years following the exploding object would have been devastating to Stone Age humans, Bigfoot and the habitat they relied on for sustenance.[22,23]

1. Large earthquakes on the Atlantic Seaboard, Gulf of Mexico, Caribbean Sea and Africa.

2. Fires in North America, which formed nano diamonds and burned off vegetation and watersheds.

3. Volcanic eruptions blocked the sun, reducing the growing season.

4. Flooding from increased rainfall generated by volcanic eruptions with topsoil growth and watersheds destroyed.

5. Famine for humans and animals with vegetation destroyed and short growing season.

6. Multiple-generation epigenetic effects of volcanic aerosols, low oxygen, and famine.[24]

7. Agriculture began between 11,000 and 9,000 years ago in the Gobekli Tepe region of Turkey. Cultivated grains that are cooked provide higher carbohydrates and lower nutrition than raw foods that Stone Age humans consumed. Zecharia Sitchin reported in *The End of Days* that the Sumerians Enki and Enlil negotiated providing seeds to humans to start agriculture.

The most rapid magnetic pole reversal in history took place between 12,400 and 12,350 BP. Steppes that connected Great Britain and Europe with Scandinavia subsided and the North Sea began forming 12,000 BP. So many species died in catastrophic glacial flooding that scientists declared a new geological age beginning 11,700 BP. Atlantis and Mesopotamia were both inundated during the great floods. Poseidon's Atlantis on the coast of Portugal and Spain sank 11,500 BP in its third and final destruction.

Ancient Mesopotamia had occupied the dry basin that filled with glacial floods 12,000 BP. Archaeologists have identified a civilization dating to at least 100,000 BP at the bottom of the Persian Gulf, with entirely different tool making than in Africa. After filling during the great floods, the Persian Gulf joined with the Indian Ocean 8000 BP. Comparatively little investigation has been done of the Persian Gulf civilization.

Enlil recanted his determination to destroy the Earth and offered the Covenant of the Rainbow, reported in Genesis 9:12: *"And God said: 'This [rainbow] is the sign of the covenant which I make between Me and you, and every living creature that is with you, for perpetual generations."* This was the first-ever reference to a rainbow formed by light reflecting water in the atmosphere. Clouds in high atmospheric ice, noctilucent clouds that form in the icy firmament, were observed for the first time in 1885.

Glacial flooding in the geological record that compares with the Great Deluge in Babylonian history gives feasible historical dates. With the worst of the flooding pinpointed between 13,000 and 10,000 BP, historical correlates can be compared to date the sequence of events recorded in Babylon, independently of flawed dates in the Jewish calendar.

Towering Figures, a Great City

Gobekli Tepe's elevation on a mountain ridge in Turkey was an ideal refuge above glacial floods built 12,000 BP and then inexplicably abandoned 10,000 BP when waters receded.[25] Geologist Robert Schoch, who studied erosion patterns on the Egyptian Sphinx and Gobekli Tepe, wrote about the Stone Age builders at Gobekli Tepe:

> This was supposedly the time of the brutish, nomadic, hunters and gatherers who, according to many academics, did not have the technology, governing institutions, or will to build structures such as those found at Göbekli Tepe. Clearly there is a disconnect between what conventional historians and archaeologists have been teaching all these years and the clear evidence on the ground.[26]

If anything could be more astounding than the intelligence and skill of Gobekli Tepe's builders, it is that they protected their intricate carvings before filling in the entire site, as if to preserve them for posterity, 10,000 BP. More than the first temple in the world, as some archeologists describe Gobekli Tepe, its message was literally a museum in stone and ritual center. Dr. Schoch explains:

> "Various pillars at Göbekli Tepe are decorated with bas-reliefs of animals, including foxes, boars, snakes, aurochs (wild cattle), Asiatic wild asses, wild sheep, birds (cranes, a vulture), a gazelle, and anthropods (scorpion, ants). The carvings are refined, sophisticated, and beautifully executed.
>
> "Not only are there bas-reliefs, but also carvings in the round, including a carnivorous beast, possibly a lion or other feline, working its way down a column, apparently in pursuit of a boar carved in relief. In the round, carvings of lions and boars have been uncovered, now housed in the Museum of Sanlıurfa, as is a life-sized statue of a man, which, though from Urfa, apparently dates to the Göbekli Tepe era.
>
> "Also from Göbekli Tepe are perfectly drilled stone beads. And, according to Prof. Schmidt, while some of the stone pillars were set in the local bedrock, others were set into a concrete- or terrazzo-like floor. Looking only at style and quality of workmanship, one might easily suggest that Göbekli Tepe dates between 3000 and 1000 BCE. How wrong one would be. Based on radiocarbon analyses, the site goes back to the period of 9000 to 10,000 BCE, and was intentional-

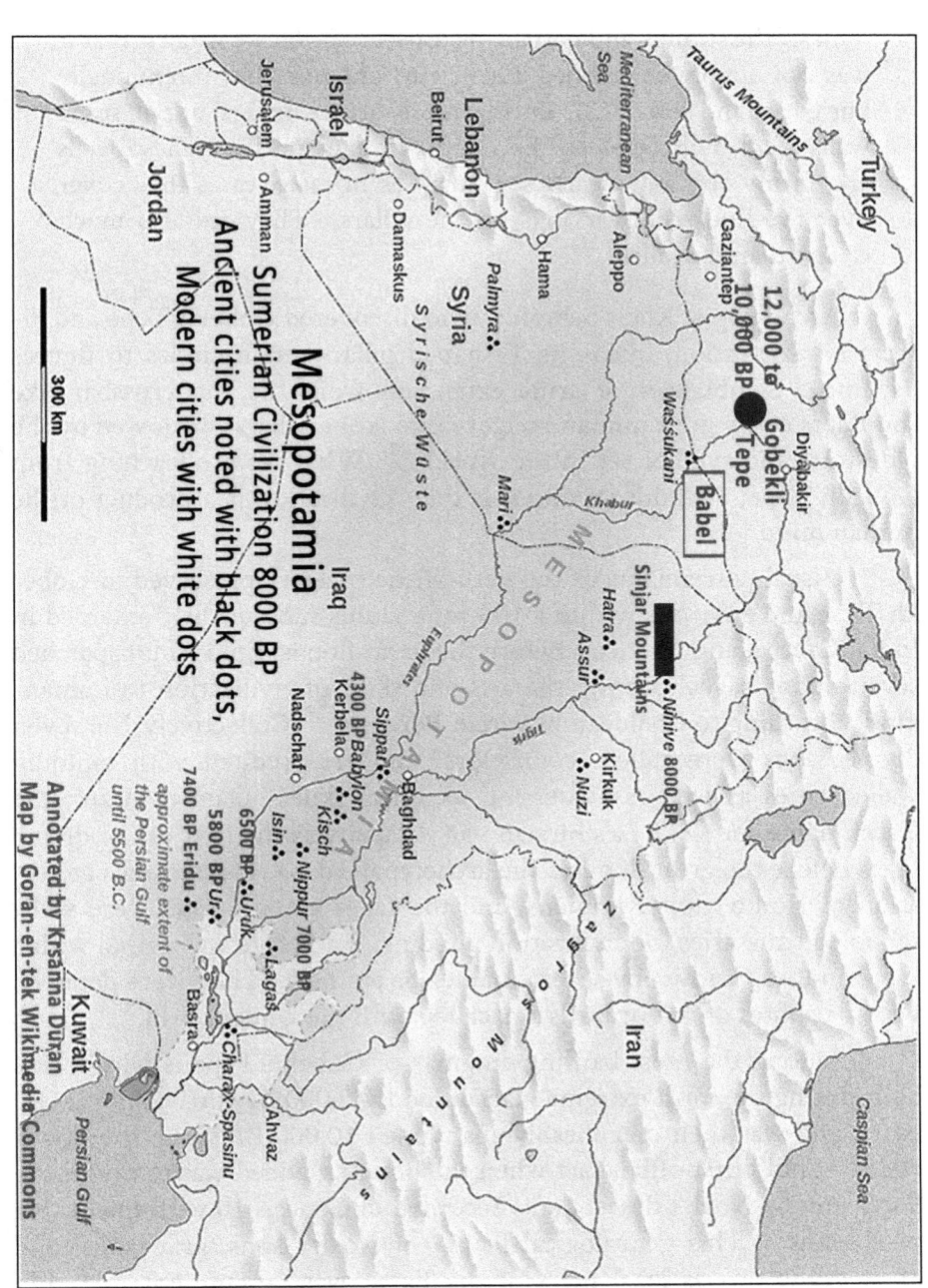

ly buried circa 8000 BCE. That is, the site dates back an astounding 10,000 to 12,000 years ago!

"One of the strange and perplexing aspects of Göbekli Tepe is that it was not simply abandoned and left to oblivion, but intentionally buried around 8000 BCE. Furthermore, before its final burial, stone walls were built between the finely wrought pillars. These walls are, in my opinion, clearly secondary as in many cases they cover over the fine relief carvings on the pillars. They are also much cruder than the pillars.[27]"

Archeologist Klaus Schmidt, who discovered Gobekli Tepe and directs its excavation, likens its T-shaped pillars set in circles to figures dancing. Semblances of arms extending from the top crossbar like shoulders eerily graft human imagery into stone pillars, shadowed by the oldest art and symbol set in the world.[28] What we are learning from Gobekli Tepe, Schmidt surmises, is that "civilization is a product of the human mind."

Visual descendants of the naturalistic imagery preserved in Gobekli Tepe and environs within a 100-mile radius subsequently emerged in India, Greece, and Mexico. Before the great floods, Enki had dispatched seven divine sages to bring the arts and skills of civilization to humankind, according to Chaldean historian Berossos.[29] Collectively, the seven divine sages were called "counselors" and are credited with building walled cities as well as possessing technical skills. Oannes (Uan), the Greek name for Enki-Ea's human son Adapa, was the first of the divine sages before the great floods. The archetypal Adapa represented a generation of Homo sapiens sapiens, and the sages among them were well-schooled emissaries for civilization building. Each sage was paired with a king, and was known by several names or epithets. They were depicted with attributes of fish or birds associated with the Underworld.

Among the most baffling enigmas of Gobekli Tepe is why it was built during the most extreme glacial floods 12,000 BP, thrived for 2,000 years, and was then inexplicably abandoned 10,000 BP when the floods ended. Enlil's first official act when the flooding ended was to divide the Earth among Noah's descendants recorded in Genesis 10 with the "Table of Nations." This genealogical listing of Noah's sons, grandsons, and great grandsons as legal heirs of the Earth was tantamount to Enlil's birthright blessing, naming Noah's descendants as his legal heirs. Enlil's stated intent in creating the flood was to destroy those who did not please him and save only those he selected, because, Genesis asserts, he had created all and was entitled to destroy all. The Table of Nations, which established a hierarchical caste system based on descent from and similarity to Sumerian gods, was well known among Sumerians, Akkadians, and Assyrians.

Sumerian civilization dominated the Mesopotamian region, stretching north into southeast Turkey, from 7000 to 4300 BP. Images of Sumerian people show them taller and slenderer than the Arabs and Hebrews in southern Mesopotamia. Sumerian men were commonly clean-shaven in images, in contrast to the Semitic people in the south. Sumerian was a non-Semitic language with Turkish and Chinese affinities. Noah's descendants were neither Jewish nor Hebrews, who emerged as a unique people 6,000 years later after Abraham's birth. Getting on Enlil's list of Noah's heirs was a matter of life and death, and the floods had shown he was deadly serious about enfranchising only Noah's descendants.

With towering T-shaped pillars symbolizing Lemuria's sunken homeland and stylized icons the sages used, survivors at Gobekli Tepe were not Noah's heirs listed in Enlil's Table of Nations. The Indus Valley east of Mesopotamia was settled 9500 BP, compared to Nineveh's 8000 BP in northern Sumer. City building in Sumer started in the north and migrated to the south, perhaps because of continued flooding in the newly formed Persian Gulf. Enki's Eridu was the first city built in southern Mesopotamia circa 7400 BP.

A plain between the Turkish and Sinjar Mountains in the north and south and the Euphrates and Tigris Rivers in the west and east meets the description for the city and tower of Babel's location circa 8000 BP. The builders journeyed from the east, where settlements were built in the Indus Valley 9500 BP soon after Gobekli Tepe was abandoned.

Sculptures depicting Vedic traditions and the classical pose of the Buddha are among cultural elements that link Gobekli Tepe environs with the Indus Valley.

Genesis describes the builders as nomads who retained the ancient mother language, but made the mistake of building in sight of Enlil and his Watchers, noted in Genesis 11:1-4:

"1. And the whole earth was of one language, and of one speech.

"2. And it came to pass, as they journeyed from the east, that they found a plain in the land of Shinar [Sumer]; and they dwelt there.

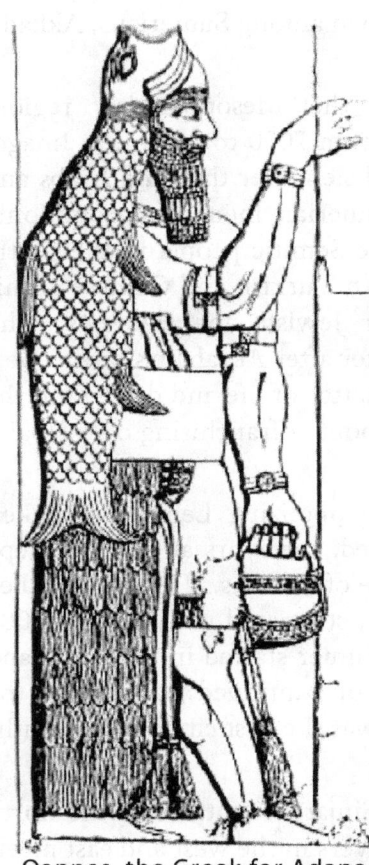

The Feathered Serpent first appeared with a satchel and the Phoenician "X" for Tau, which is also the Sumerian icon for place of the gods, in an Olmec sculpture at La Venta, Mexico (above).

Oannes, the Greek for Adapa according to Babylonian historian Berossus, carries a satchel (above).

Satchels carved in a pillar at Gobekli Tepe circa 12,000 BP (above) are identical to baskets the Adapa Oannes and the Olmec carried. A basket is carved over the in the center on the brow of the head that forms the central axis of the Sun Stone (left), of unknown origin. The pineal gland is located in the center of the brain behind the basket.

"3. And they said one to another, Go to, let us make brick, and burn them thoroughly. And they had brick for stone, and slime had they for mortar.

"4. And they said, Go to, let us build us a city and a tower, whose top may reach unto heaven; and let us make us a name, lest we be scattered abroad upon the face of the whole earth. [Nomadic survivors of the floods banded together for self-organized construction.]

Intelligent humans who could do what they imagined and built a tower to heaven is the reason Genesis 11:5-9 gives for confusing and scattering humans and their language. With one language nothing could restrain the children of men and unauthorized nations.

"5. And the Lord came down to see the city and the tower, which the children of men builded.

"6. And the Lord said, Behold, the people is one, and they have all one language; and this they begin to do: and now nothing will be restrained from them, which they have imagined to do.

"7. Go to, let us go down, and there confound their language, that they may not understand one another's speech.

"8. So the Lord scattered them abroad from thence upon the face of all the earth: and they left off to build the city.

"9. Therefore is the name of it called Babel; because the Lord did there confound the language of all the earth: and from thence did the Lord scatter them abroad upon the face of all the earth."

A New World Order After the Great Floods

The Yazidi of the Sinjar Mountain region, who incorporate indigenous beliefs with Islam, speak of experiencing two separate floods. Noah's ark passed over the mountains before landing on dry land in one flood, according to the Yazidi. Glacial melt north of the Sinjar Mountains in Turkey filled in the Persian Gulf 12,000 BP and deluged ancient Mesopotamia, which awaits greater examination with sufficient funding. The most extensive research of glacial flooding has been done in the Pacific Northwest, spearheaded by geologists under the umbrella of HugeFloods.com.[30] A temporary glacial lake 2,000 feet deep repeatedly formed in the Missoula, Montana valley.

The preemptive strike against humanity's civilization represented with the tower of Babel was so successful that cultural memory of devastating destruction had been lost by 5760 BP (3760 BCE), the date Jewish scholars concluded the world had been created. Global floods during the dates Jewish scholars calculated for the Great Deluge (2500 to 2300 BCE) are non-existent. The floods were thousands of years before Jewish and Biblical scholars believe the world was created. Rationalists disregard the powerful culture stories recorded in Babylon because dates Jewish timekeeping assigns them are impossible, i.e., savage floods 13,000 years ago are not possible within the framework of the Jewish calendar. The calendar posits the world was created thousands of years after the floods, or only 5,760 years ago.

Inanna of Sumer, Sin of Ur, and Marduk of Babylon took lead roles building neo-Mesopotamia after the floods, and recorded the ancient history of Mesopotamia to accord with the objectives of the new cities' founders. The *Enuma Elish* first emerged in Babylon, whose national god, Marduk, sponsored outstanding astronomy. Although Enlil's city Nippur exerted very little direct leadership, it was the seat of power where Enlil conferred kingship. Enlil and Sin directed the new order through appointments of human kings.

After the great floods Enki-Ea sent human sages to build civilization, according to Berossos' Babylonian history. An iconic satchel the sages carried, representing the gifts of civilization, seen at Gobekli Tepe appeared again in Mexico's earliest sculpture of the Feathered Serpent. "Feathered Serpent" translated as *Quetzalcoat*l in the Nahuatl language of central Mexico and as Kukulkan in the Mayan language in southern Mexico. In Egypt the deity *Wadjet* was a feathered serpent. In Cambodia at Angkor Wat, the great Garuda bird flying with the serpent on its back elevated the serpent.

Traces of the pre-flood mother language survived in symbolism and texts secured in ancient libraries, such as those from Atlantis Blavatsky reported seeing in Tibet. James Churchward reported studying an archaic manuscript in the private library of a rishi in India.

Civilization building, which had been slow-tracked since the Babel incident, grew with stunning speed starting 5100 BP, shown on the "Timeline." The sudden growth spurt coincided with the beginning of the Feather Serpent's long count in 5114 BP (3114 BCE). Although flying craft and UFO were memorialized in literature and art, the gods slowly receded from active involvement while continuing to covertly influence and control human affairs, often camouflaged by flagrantly self-serving human rulers epitomized in Homer's poetry.

Staging for the landmark war that continues to flow through civilization, the first defensive wall around the citadel at Troy dates to 5000 BP. Homer's *Iliad* gave intricate details about ancient Greeks and Trojans who fought at Troy, which are so accurate that Heinrich Schliemann discovered Troy's location using his directions. The *Iliad* highlights the gods' elaborate machinations to control warriors and battles for outcomes they desired from human conflict. Homer's exquisite physical and metaphysical descriptions revealed the gods in characterizing details that followed their trail to Rome, the new Troy. The gods and craft that Homer described at Troy are identical in many respects to modern UFO reports, indicating the ancient presence of advanced technology.

In the aftermath of wars between Hyperborean scientists and Sumerian gods for control of territory in Africa and Asia, areas from the Sahara Desert to Afghanistan still have unusually high radiation levels and green glass particles formed in nuclear explosions. Most Sumerian gods began leaving the surface of the planet between 2023 and 560 BCE.[31] Some gods went to the inner earth they had periodically inhabited and others to Mars where they had started 350,000 years earlier. Consummate rivals Sin and Marduk both remained on Earth to manage their claimed inheritances. In equivalency with Zeus as Jupiter, Marduk founded Rome as the god Jupiter before his death in 484 BCE.[32]

Soon after the majority of Sumer's gods had disappeared, leaving Sin and Marduk the highest-ranking gods, Marduk's reign ended with a strange death. "To judge by who was mentioned in the texts and inscriptions, we can be certain only of Marduk and [his son] Nabu of the Enki'ites; and of the Enlilites, Nannar/Sin, his spouse Ningal/Nikkal and his aide Nusu, and probably also Ishtar."[33] Shortly after Marduk's Babylonian priesthood and followers rejected a king that Sin appointed for Babylonia, Nabunaid (Nabonidus), Marduk died of a skin disease and his son Nabu disappeared. Nabunaid was the last king of Babylonia. Marduk's death in 484 BCE left Enlil's loyalists to control Rome for the Anunnaki's advantage, primed ultimately to possess the world for its God. Sin and his son Utu were the most likely candidates to step into Zeus' shoes after Marduk's death.

Judging from symbolism Marduk and Ishtar used, they were among the divine sages Enki sent to establish human civilization and then directed human sages after the great floods. The high quality of astronomy, science and libraries available to humans in Babylon attest to Marduk's fundamental intention to build human civilization.

Sin's lineage managed Rome's aristocracy for maximum leverage in religion, politics and economics after Marduk's death, laying the foundation for the Holy Roman Empire, the Nazi First Reich.[34] The German Empire forged the Second Reich in the nineteenth century. Nazi Germany carried the banner for the Third Reich in the twentieth century. Transnational corporate monopolies on planetary resources, water and food constitute the Fourth Reich in the twenty-first century.

Notes

[1] "Scientists May Have Identified Echoes of Ancient Earth." June 9, 2014. Phys.org. http://phys.org/news/2014-06-scientists-echoes-ancient-earth.html

[2] Dalley, Stephanie, translator. 2008. *Myths from Mesopotamia: Creation, The Flood, Gilgamesh, and Others*. Oxford University Press, Inc.: New York. pp 228-277

[3] Van Flandern, Tom. 1993. *Dark Matter, Missing Planets and New Comets: Paradoxes Resolved, Origins Illuminated*. North Atlantic Books. Berkley, CA. pp 277-279, 332-339, 425-432

[4] Williamson, George Hunt. 1973. *Other Tongues, Other Flesh*. Neville Spearman: London, UK. Book II pp 152-191

[5] Kannenberg, Ida M. 2013. *My Brother Is A Hairy Man: The Search for Bigfoot*. Atlantis Phoenix Books: Missoula, MT.. p 26

[6] McKenna, Terence. 1995. *Timewave Zero: Terence McKenna's Software for Time Traveling*. Blue Water Publishing: Newberg, OR. pp 5-6, 50-62

[7]. Mann, Charles C. "The Birth of Religion." *National Geographic*. June 2011. ngm.nationalgeographic.com/2011/06/gobekli-tepe/mann-text

[8] Van Helsig, Jan. 2009. *Unternehmen Aldebaran: Kontakte mit Menschen aus einem anderen Sonnensystem*. Amadeus – Verlag. Fichtenau, Germany. pp 90-93, unnumbered photos between 164 and 165

[9] Little, Drs. Gregory and Lora, and Van Auken, John. *Edgar Cayce's Atlantis*. 2008. A.R.E. Press: Virginia Beach, VA. pp 48-51

[10] Sanchez, Anthony F. 2010. *UFO Highway: The Dulce Interview * Human Origins * HAARP/ Project Blue Beam*. eBook self-published. pp 51-55

[11] Sitchin, Zecharia. 2008. *The End of Days: Armageddon and Prophecies of the Return*. Harper: New York, NY. pp 245-249

[12] Ghose, Tia. "Before Babel: Ancient Mother Tongue Reconstructed." *LifeScience*. May 6, 2013.
www.livescience.com/29342-ancient-mother-tongue-reconstructed.html

[13] Pagel, Mark, etal. "Ultraconserved words point to deep language ancestry across Eurasia." *Proceedings of the National Academy of Sciences of the United States of America*. May 6, 2013.
www.pnas.org/content/early/2013/05/01/1218726110.full.pdf+html

[14] Wittke, James H., et al. "Evidence for deposition of 10 million tonnes of impact spherules across four continents 12,800 years ago." *Proceedings of the National Academy of Sciences for the United States*.

[15] Williamson, George Hunt. 1973. *Other Tongues, Other Flesh*. Book II pp 73-94

[16] Ibid

[17] The Anunnaki (also transcribed as: Anunaki, Anunna, Anunnaku, Ananaki and other variations) are a group of deities in ancient Mesopotamian cultures (i.e., Sumerian, Akkadian, Assyrian, and Babylonian). According to *The Oxford Companion to World Mythology*, the Anunnaki: ".are the Sumerian deities of the old primordial line; they are chthonic deities of fertility, associated eventually with the underworld, where they became judges. They take their name from the old sky god An (Anu)." (Wikipedia)

[18] Sinnett, A.P., compiled by Alfred Trevor Baker. 1923. *The Mahatma Letters to A.P. Sinnett from the Mahatmas M. and K.H.* Letter No. XIII from A.P. Sinnett in January 1882 with responses by Morya. pp 70-78

[19] Charles, R.H. 1912. *The Book of Enoch*. Clarendon Press: Oxford. UK. pp 16-20

[20] Ibid. pp 264-272

[21] Wittke, James H., et al. "Evidence for deposition of 10 million tonnes of impact spherules across four continents 12,800 years ago." *Proceedings of the National Academy of Sciences for the United States*.

[22] Oppenheimer, Clive. 2011. *Eruptions that Shook the World*. Cambridge University Press: New York, NY. pp 22-52

[23] Klingaman, William K. and Nicholas P. 2013. *The Year Without Summer: 1816 and the Volcano that Darkened the World and Changed History*. St. Martin's Griffin: New York, NY. pp 121-151

[24]. Massive volcanic eruptions in the Atlantic, particularly the large number on the Mid-Atlantic Ridge, would have affected Europe in much the same way as the 2010 eruption of Iceland's Eyjafjallajökull. A "silent" crisis of heritable gene expression resulting from toxic fumes, low oxygen and famine for multiple generations might explain, at least in part, the declining culture at Gobekli Tepe. Epigenetics is a new study of how environmental factors affect the way genes are expressed without permanently altering DNA. Twins who are identical at birth but change as they age in different environments is an example of epigenetic features. Epigenetic features are heritable from generation to generation. Famines can alter gene expression that is heritable across generations.

[25]. Mann, Charles C. "The Birth of Religion." *National Geographic*. June 2011. ngm.nationalgeographic.com/2011/06/gobekli-tepe/mann-text.

[26]. Schoch, Robert M. "The Mystery of Gobekli Tepe and Its Message To Us." *New Dawn Magazine*. September-October 2010.

[27] Ibid

[28] Koerner, E. F. Konrad. "The Sapir-Whorf Hypothesis: A Preliminary History and a Bibliographical Essay." *Journal of Linquistic Anthropology*. Volume 2, Issue 2. December 1992.

[29] Dalley, Stephanie, translator. 2008. *Myths from Mesopotamia: Creation, The Flood, Gilgamesh, and Others*. pp 182-188, Seven Sages pp 327-328

Beaulieu, Paul-Alain. "Berossos on Late Babylonian History." *Special Issue of Oriental Studies*. 2006.

A text discovered at Uruk in the 1970s listing the antediluvian sages and kings that closely parallels the one in Book Two of *Babyloniaca* affirms the reliability of that portion of Berossos' texts that had passed through the hands of numerous scholars.

[30] Soennichsen, John. 2008. *Bretz's Flood: The Remarkable Story of a Rebel Geologist and the World's Greatest Flood*. Sasquatch Books: Seattle, WA. pp143-168

Huge Floods. http://www.hugefloods.com

[31] Sitchin, Zecharia. 2008. *The End of Days.* p 245

[32] In Greek religion, Zeus was god of the sky and thunder and embodied Jupiter, the king of planets. Son of Greek Titans Cronos and Rhea, Zeus overthrew his father and founded the Olympian pantheon. He subsequently acquired numerous epithets in the Mediterranean, Asia Minor, and Near East. As the founding god of Rome, he was Jupiter. The earliest mention of Zeus was in Linear B script circa 1450 BCE, contemporary with Marduk of Babylon.

Under Marduk's rule, Babylon was the largest city in Mesopotamia by the second millennium BCE when Abraham's god dispatched him from his birthplace in Ur, the moon god Sin's city, to Sin's domain in the Sinai. The Hebrews were birthed under Abraham's jealous patrons Sin and his father, Enlil, who continually struggled with Enki-Ea for control of humans.

Expansion into Troy, Greece and Rome while his bitterly fought rival, Sin, patronized Abraham and the Hebrews in the Sinai was a logical career move for Marduk's climb to dominance. Eldest son of the ancient astronaut and Sumerian god Enki, Marduk was the first Earth-born generation of Mesopotamians whose culture was strictly governed by a genetic pecking order. Although his father was the chief scientist and mastermind of Sumer's mining colony, he ranked second in prestige and authority to his younger brother Enlil because of their mother's status. Enlil was the governor of Sumer's empire on Earth, and his eldest son, Sin, was Enlil's legal heir entitled to inherit his holdings that included rulership.

In Marduk's Babylonian charter myth, *Enuma Elish,* human workers were created to perform the gods' labor before Adam and Eve's descendants were given rule of the Earth in Genesis 10. Marduk shepherded all the gods like sheep, covered the sky, diminished clouds and provided sustenance. He personified Jupiter as the morning star, Nebiru, who upheld the course of the stars in heaven. In Marduk's celestial battle with Tiamat he created the asteroid belt (hammered bracelet) and threw the rebellious Tiamat into the third orbit as the Earth.

In kingship of cosmos, gods and humans that Hesiod affirmed in the sixth century BCE, Zeus compared with the Sumerian Enlil and the Greek creator of humanity Prometheus, equivalent to the Sumerian Enki. Marduk aspired to the heights of Enlil and Enki in *Enuma Elish*. Homer's account of Zeus in the war with Troy, also written in the sixth century BCE, portrayed the god's vanity countered by other gods adept at dealing with his foibles. Communal processes of myth-making homogenized varying renditions of Zeus to produce a singular god with many, sometimes disparate, traits.

All accounts portrayed the Greek Zeus as the embodiment of Jupiter paralleling Marduk's rule of the sky, the gods, and Jupiter in the position of Nebiru, the morning star, in his fifty names listed in *Enuma Elish*:

"(48) ADDU be his name, the whole sky may he cover.
"May his beneficent roar ever hover over the earth;
"May he, as Mummu, diminish the clouds;...
"Below, for the people may he furnish sustenance.

"(49) ASHARU, who, as is his name, guided the gods of destiny;
"of all the gods is verily in his charge.

"(50) NEBIRU shall hold the crossings of heaven and earth;
"Those who failed of crossing above and below,
"Ever of him shall inquire.
"Nebiru is the star... which in the skies is brilliant.
"Verily, he governs their turnings, to him indeed they look,
"Saying: He who the midst of the Sea restlessly crosses,
"Let 'Crossing' be his name, who controls... its midst.
"May they uphold the course of the stars of heaven;
"May he shepherd all the gods like sheep.
"May he vanquish Tiamat; may her life be strait and short!...
"Into the future of mankind, when days have grown old,
"May she recede... without cease and stay away forever."

(Translation by E. A. Speiser)

[33] Ibid. pp 252-255

[34] Kirkpatrick, Sidney D. 2010. *Hitler's Holy Relics*. Simon & Schuster: New York, NY. 74-91, 251-262

CHAPTER TWO

Ages of Humankind

Compared to the Ancestors' ancient systems that integrated human evolution with Earth, Sun, and Milky Way, Western sciences are still young. The Sun is the governor of life in the solar system by all accounts, but theories explaining and predicting solar activity are diverse and debated among Western sciences. Science of America's National Aeronautics and Space Agency (NASA) is still in the making, following a series of failed predictions for the solar maximum that ended in 2012-14. ("Cosmos") Discoveries by the interstellar Voyager 1 and 2 probes when they moved into the galaxy defied many of NASA's expectations.

Hindus, Greeks and Ancient Americans reckoned successive cycles of planetary and human evolutions in long periods with mathematics symbolically encoded. Ancient calendars universally used multiple astronomical cycles, often preserved with astrological systems. The twelve-house zodiac was anciently used in pyramid centers worldwide.

Hindu sage Sri Yukteswar, Yogananda's mentor who sent him to America to establish the Self Realization Fellowship, beat anthropologists to the punch. In his 1894 book *The Holy Science*, Yukteswar determined that an error had been made in earlier calculations of Hindu ages, called yugas. In Yukteswar's model of cyclic ages, levels of magnetism vary in periods when the Sun descends away from or ascends closer to a great center over 24,000 years. Greater universal magnetism influences mental functions and organic life. He found the date to begin his calculations the old-fashioned way, using astrological ages corresponding with orbital cycles of the solar system relative to a central orbit with a dual star.[1]

"...the sun revolves round a grand center called Vishnu Nabhi, which is the seat of the creative power, Brahma, the universal magnetism...[that] regulates the mental virtue of the internal world... The sun, with its planets and their moons, takes some star for its dual and revolves round it in about 24,000 years of our earth.... When the sun in its revolution round its dual comes to the place nearest to this grand center...the mental virtue becomes so much developed that man can easily comprehend all, even the mysteries of Spirit."[2],[3]

Yukteswar's calculations for the current 24,000-year period started 13,501 years before present (BP). The entire 24,000 years are segmented into eight periods, or *"yugas."* Four yugas in a descending cycle of 12,000 years comprise a night. An ascending cycle of 12,000 years rises from the lowest point of the night towards a golden age to complete the 24,000-year cycle. Descent into night reached the lowest point in 499 CE, during the Iron Yuga when the Roman Empire collapsed. An ascending Iron Yuga immediately began at the lowest point of descent, and the journey to a golden age started again.

In Mexico's Sun Stone, an outer ring of twenty glyphs encircle a human head set inside the Movement glyph in the center. Another glyph on each corner of the Movement glyph represents a Sun, or world era. Each of the twenty glyphs in the circle represents 1/20th of the circle, the same incremental measures as Yukteswar's yugas. Each of the ancient timekeeping systems models unique features of long-period solar functions. Mexico's Sun Stone represents qualitative phases of the Sun and the Hindu yugas model the solar system's orbit in the galaxy.

Although the two systems mesh for measures of the species, climate, galactic radiations and magnetism on Earth, they are different perspectives that each encompasses 24,000 years. This shared divisor enables periods of the two solar models to integrate, even though no beginning date for the Sun Stone's cycle has been discovered. Yukteswar's beginning date for the present 24,000-year cycle provides a benchmark for comparing Hindu and Mexican cycles with a timeline of planetary, solar and galactic events.

The Feathered Serpent's long count began thirteen (13) years before the descending Bronze Yuga and ended 113 years (13 + 100) after transition into the ascending Bronze Yuga. Thirteen is the Feathered Serpent's signature number, commonly used with arithmetic puzzles messaging scale, magnitude or principle in gematria-like code. These are keys to Teotihuacan's mapping and measures of rotation in the Stone Sages map below. Coding for the Feathered Serpent is examined in the "Earth-Human Calendar" appendix.

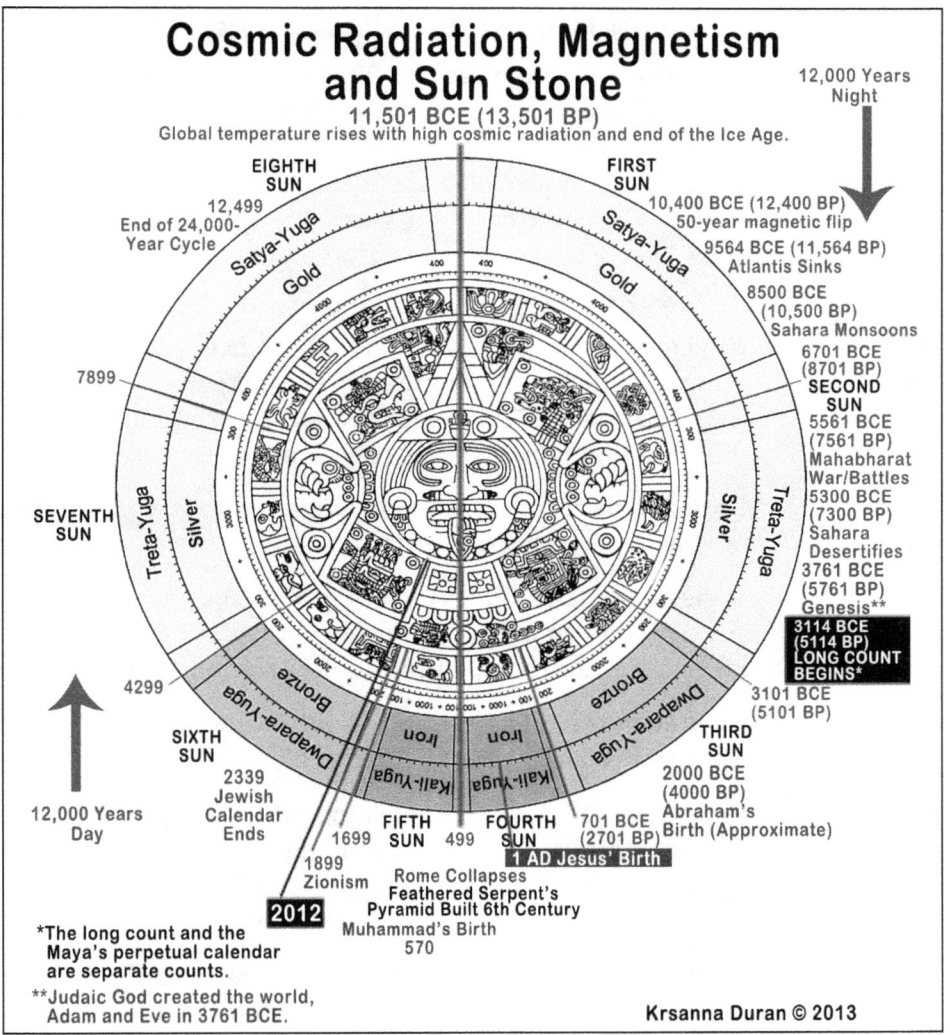

NEW CYCLE AT END OF LONG COUNT IN 2012

2014   After NASA announced on June 10, 2014 a mini solar maximum had arrived based on the number of sunspots, sunspots plummeted to zero on July 17. The Sun's magnetic field steadily weakened, and the north magnetic field did not make a full reversal. The north magnetic field briefly acted like it was going to reverse in October 2013, but soon "popped" back to its former position. The Sun's magnetic poles failed to fully reverse in 2014 during Cycle 24. The Earth's planetary magnetic fields continually weakened and cosmic ray levels escalated between January and June 2014.

2012	**FEATHERED SERPENT'S LONG COUNT AND TIMEWAVE ZERO END**
	The solar maximum at the 2012-end of the Maya's long count echoed the Maunder Minimum with very low sunspots between 1650 and 1710. The Earth's magnetic field has continually declined since 1599, the beginning of the Bronze Yuga exactly 12,001 years after the Earth's magnetic poles briefly reversed in the Gothenburg Magnetic Excursion 12,400 BP.
2010	A filament eruption engulfed an entire hemisphere of Sun, prompting NASA to announce the potential dangers of large solar flares. Despite this spectacular eruption, the mini solar maximum in 2014 was one of the lowest on record.
2009	Cosmic rays reached Space Age high with solar and planetary magnetic fields weakening.
2006	A gigantic (class-X9) solar flare mysteriously erupted amid the very low number of forty-three sunspots, indicating low magnetic activity, during a solar minimum.
2004	Solar activity began declining at fastest rate in 9,300 years. Current Bronze Yuga.
2002	Solar magnetic field is weakening and rapid pace of magnetic north toward Siberia escalating. TimeStar predicted the beginning of a solar phase shift with signs of systemic heating in solar system.
1950	Grand maximum between 1950 and 2001 was the highest fifty-year period of solar activity in 3,000 years. Grand solar maxima occur when several solar cycles are higher than average activity for decades or centuries. (Variations in peaks and lows during solar cycles continue, but the overall intensity is greater. Grand solar maxima have shown some correlation with global and regional climate changes.) Current Bronze Yuga.
1899	**ASCENDING BRONZE YUGA – FIFTH ERA BEGINS**
	Two-hundred-year transition into ascending Bronze Yuga is complete.
1840	Sunspots sharply increased and solar activity began climbing to a new high after the Maunder Minimum and mini ice

	age. Bronze Yuga transition.
1816	Year With No Summer after eruption of Tambora Volcano resulted in widespread famine in northern hemisphere.
1780	NASA uses the solar maximum for this period as the standard for a normal solar cycle. Bronze Yuga transition.
1699	Current ascending Bronze Yuga starts 200-year transition.
1650	Maunder Minimum with very low sunspots between 1650 and 1710 is resonant with the Gothenburg Magnetic Excursion in a 12,000-year cycle.
1599	Magnetic field began weakening. Transition out of ascending Iron Yuga.
499 CE	**ASCENDING IRON YUGA BEGINS**

Lowest point in descending Iron Yuga. The Roman Empire collapsed. The Pyramid of the Feathered Serpent (Quetzalcoatl) constructed in Teotihuacan's late classical period.

2701 BP	**DESCENDING IRON YUGA – FOURTH ERA BEGINS**

Upper and Lower Egypt unified; hieroglyphic writing introduced. Epic wars recorded in Vedic *Mahabharata* are fought. Krishna speaks the *word* for initiates. Dark age of descending Kali Yuga begins. Krishna is shot with arrow and dies but resurrects in seven days.

5101 BP	**DESCENDING BRONZE YUGA - THIRD ERA BEGINS**

Feathered Serpent's Long Count begins August 13, 3114

8701 BP	**DESCENDING SILVER YUGA – SECOND ERA BEGINS**

Indus Valley's early settlement begins parallel with the Neolithic culture in the Eastern Hemisphere after glacial floods.

12,001 BP	Construction of Gobekli Tepe begins amid massive die-offs and flooding with the global temperature cooling after cosmic impact 12,800 BP.
12,400 BP	Brief reversal of the magnetic poles for fifty years in the Gothenburg Magnetic Excursion, between 12,400 and 12,350 BP is recorded in the geological record.

12,800 BP Cosmic object scattered molten debris across four continents. The global temperature, which had started rising circa 18,000 BP and end of the ice age, cooled again for 1,300 years, until 11,500 BP. This sudden cooling that reversed the planetary warming trend points to massive volcanic eruptions, food shortages and endemic environmental toxins.

13,501 BP Temperatures warmed with rapid glacial melt amid high cosmic radiation at peak of the last 24,000-year period and beginning of the present one. Galactic core explosions that scientist Paul LaViolette calls Superwaves occur about every 13,000 to 14,000 years for major outbursts and more frequently for lesser events. . . Astronomical discoveries confirm aspects of LaViolette's hypothesis of galactic Superwaves. "For example, in 1985, astronomers discovered that Cygnus X-3, an energetic celestial source of cosmic rays, which is about the same distance from Earth as the Galactic Center (25,000 light years), showers the Earth with particles traveling at close to the speed of light, moving along essentially straight paths. Later, scientists found the Earth is impacted, at sporadic intervals, with cosmic rays emitted from the X-ray pulsar Hercules X-1 (about 12,000 light years distant)." ("Galactic Cosmic Ray Volleys: A Coming Global Disaster," LaViolette)

13,501 BP **DESCENDING GOLD YUGA – FIRST ERA BEGINS**

The Hopi's Fourth World began at the end of lengthy migrations following destruction of the Third World by floods. The most likely period for world-changing floods was between 13,000 and 10,000 BP, matching the Judaic Great Deluge. Using glacial flooding during the zenith of the 24,000-year yuga cycle as a benchmark aligns Hopi prophecy with the galactic-solar model. Hopi tradition advises that fire will destroy the Fourth World before the Fifth World begins. Solar outbursts and galactic radiation both hold potentials of world-changing fire in a number of forms.

Exposure to variable galactic radiation levels explains rampant changes on planets in the solar system since the 1970s: Venus was rotating six and one-half minutes slower in 2012 than it was in 1996; Jupiter's mysterious red spot shrank and slowed down to the same rotational speed as Venus in 2012; and in the same year Saturn's rings were disappearing.

The species of Earth are more active or sluggish during cyclic periods of the Sun's rhythmic journey around the Great Center. The organic brain, polarized with the physical world, awakens with virtue during the Sun's day of 12,000 solar years in an ascending cycle. It sleeps during the night of 12,000 solar years of the descending cycle. States of planetary wakening and slumbering relative to magnetism explain variable potentials for mental virtue that Sri Yukteswar describes.

Consistency of calculations for the 24,000-year planetary, solar, and galactic cycles by the ancients points to advanced science and mathematics. The periods predict a continuing decline of civilization for the 12,000 years of descent into galactic night, which ended in 499 CE. The transcendent Feathered Serpent emerged with a full collar of feathers in Mexico at Teotihuacan in the late Classical period, between 300 and 700 CE. The Feathered Serpent's emergence parallels the end of a 12,000-year descent and beginning of an ascending cycle.

Superwaves of high-energy radiations and cosmic rays periodically emitted from the core of the galaxy, which systems theorist Paul LaViolette documents in ice cores and tree rings, affects the entire galaxy[4] Cosmic rays are subatomic particles that LaViolette posits travel near the speed of light and then breakdown with quantum interactions to produce gamma rays and other radiations. He finds evidence of large superwaves approximately every 13,000 to 14,000 years, with smaller ones in shorter intervals. A large superwave can continue for hundreds of years and smaller ones for briefer periods. La Violette finds a superwave about 5,300 years ago, or just before the beginning of the Feathered Serpent's long count.

Stone Sages

An ancient relationship between Egypt, Mexico, and India's far-reaching empire is shown with intentional placements of complexes at Teotihuacan and Angkor Wat relative to the Great Pyramid, showing movement with a radian of 57°2', a function of pi. Engineers use radians to calculate rotation. In this case, the angle of a radian is stated as degrees in the circumference of the Earth. Working in large stones, the megalith builders adapted measures to their medium. They used 3-1/7 for pi, derived by dividing 22 by 7, and truncated numbers to one decimal.

- The difference between Teotihuacan's distance from the Great Pyramid Complex in Egypt and Angkor Wat's is a radian of 57°2'.

- The distance between Teotihuacan and Angkor Wat is 157°2', or a factor of a radian.

- It is 130° from Great Pyramid Complex to Teotihuacan.

- It is 72°4' from Great Pyramid Complex to Angkor Wat.

Great Pyramid
31°1' E, 29°5' N

Angkor Wat
Cambodia
103°5' E
13°2' N

Teotihuacan
Mexico
98°5' W
19°4' N

Krsanna Duran © 2014

Modern science posits the solar system makes a complete orbit through the spiral arms of the Milky Way Galaxy in approximately 250 million years.[5] In its long, long journey through the galaxy, the solar system travels through myriad cycles while simultaneously orbiting with its larger center that TimeStar posits is Arcturus, based on Babylonian astronomy. Modern scientists estimate that the solar system moves above or below the galactic mid-plane, or equator, in undulating serpentine motion approximately every 26 million years. Increased gravitational pull when the solar system is aligned with the galactic equator excites comets in the Oort Cloud, creating greater hazards from comets and asteroids. At the same time, increased activity is induced in the Earth's core, resulting in large volcanic eruptions and mass extinctions[6] The hypothesized impact of Kingu's debris and volcanic eruptions that killed off the dinosaurs were within the 26 million-year cycle of alignment with the galactic equator. These followed several earlier off-cycle impacts and suggest that if Kingu (Maldek) was destroyed by hydrogen weapons, it may have destructed as early as 75 million years ago and debris was ejected in several waves. The final ejection of debris coincided with gravitational pull during the solar system's alignment with the galactic mid-plane in a periodic 26 million-year transit 66 MYA.

Long-range galactic cycles of this order cannot be observed with either the naked eye or small telescopes in any single life. They are extrapolated with advanced mathematical theory and calculations, which were embedded in the allegory of the Hindu Vedic verses, or sutras.

Plato wrote in "Timaeus" about the Great Year: "And so people are all but ignorant of the fact that time really is the wanderings of these bodies, bewilderingly numerous as they are and astonishingly variegated."[7]

Ancestors' Gateways

A galactic-solar cycle derived with identical ratios of a 360° circle in diverse cultures separated by vast distances point to ancient global connections. Zero and thirteen dot-bar numbers observed with cyclic world eras were used in both Mexico and India, with measures of 1/20th of a circle. In Greece, Plato measured a Great Year of 24,000 solar years meted with eight stations, corresponding with the Hindu's eight yugas. Anciently, Egypt and Mexico both revered uniquely feathered serpents, called Quetzalcoatl in Mexico and Wadjet in Egypt. At Angkor Wat, dedicated to the Hindu Vishnu, the great Garuda bird carries the naga serpent on his back to elevate the naga identical to those in Mexico and Egypt.

Global culture was diffused through three distant sites interrelated by Feathered Serpent mythos, mathematics, geometry, and cycles of Humankind, Earth, Sun, and the Milky Way. These are mapped in measures of rotation in Stone Sages encircling the globe.

- The Mediterranean Basin with borders on Egypt, Greece, and the Levant with Turkey
- India with borders that anciently included Angkor Wat, and modern borders on China, Central Asia, and the Indian Ocean
- Mexico with borders on North and Central America, the Pacific Ocean, and Gulf of Mexico

Notes

[1] Cruttenden, Walter. 2006. *Lost Star of Myth and Time.* St. Lynn's Press. Pittsburgh, PA pp 44-52

[2] .Yukteswar, Sri. 1977. *The Holy Science.* The Self Realization Fellowship: Los Angeles, CA. pp ix-xi

[3] Yukteswar wrote about the Sun's dual, suggesting a binary solar system. Some indications suggest a special relationship with Sirius, p 138. See Liddington Castle 2010 Crop Circle:

http://www.allstarroundup.com/cc/ccliddington2010.html

[4] LaViolette, Paul. 1997. *Earth Under Fire. Humanity's Survival of the Apocalypse.* Starlane Publications: Schenectady, NY. pp 70-71, 94

[5] . Wethington, Nicholas. "The Milky Way's Rotation." *Universe Today.* January 26, 2009.
www.universetoday.com/23870/the-milky-ways-rotation/.

[6] Cain, Fraser. "Comet Strikes Increase As We Pass Through the Galactic Plane." *Universe Today.* May 6, 2008.
www.universetoday.com/14082/comet-strikes-increase-as-we-pass-through-the-galactic-plane/

[7] Plato, edited by Edith Hamilton and Huntington Cairns. 1980. "Timaeus." *Plato, the Collected Works, including the Letters.* Princeton University Press: Princeton, NJ pp 1151-1211

CHAPTER THREE

America's Mother Culture

A gateway of ancient global civilization between Egypt, Mexico, and Cambodia, construction of the pyramid complex at Teotihuacan in Mexico began circa 200 BCE. It was the first large metropolis in the Western hemisphere, housing as many as 200,000 in the fifth century CE when Rome collapsed. Older pyramids beneath the Sun and Moon Pyramids await excavation to find their construction dates.

As well as maintaining buildings to house visiting tribes, Teotihuacanos established embassies in distant regions and traded iconic incense burners throughout Mexico and Central America.[1,2] The pyramids at Teotihuacan were the home of Mexico's mother culture and initiation center for the Feathered Serpent that followed on the heels of the Olmec's first civilization in America.

An Olmec pyramid at Tampico on the Gulf of Mexico, which former astronaut Gordon Cooper co-discovered, was occupied 5,000 BP (3000 BCE). Cooper reported it contained "celestial navigation symbols and formulas that, when translated, turned out to be mathematical formulas used to this day for navigation; and accurate drawings of constellations, some of which would not be officially 'discovered' until the age of modern telescopes. . . . The Olmec had used the same means of celestial navigation as the Egyptians and Minoan civilization on Crete, and at the same time."[3]

At La Venta, the Olmec carved Mexico's first image of the Feathered Serpent with a satchel identical to those in Gobekli Tepe and Greece, circa 1000 BCE. Jaguars in all guises of living and transforming states were the Olmec's signature totem, which diffused through Mexico and as far as Peru in the south. A serpent, jaguar, and bird were the earliest images for the Feathered Serpent at Teotihuacan, before the serpent emerged with a full collar of feathers on the Pyramid of Quetzalcoatl in the sixth century CE. Along with the feathered serpent's imagery, the only astronomical alignment in Teotihuacan's construction commemorated the August 13 anniversary of the long count the Olmec introduced with zero circa 300 BCE.[4]

Frank Waters described the site, a stunning constellation of art and architecture at La Venta occupied by 1200 BCE, in *The Mexico Mystique*:

> "Here the Olmec constructed a round clay pyramid 420 feet in diameter and 103 feet high with eleven vertical ridges, resembling a petalled flower. They also excavated three huge pits floored with a thousand tons or more of slabs of green serpentine inlaid with mosaic jaguar masks. There were tombs of basalt and columns, a sarcophagus with a lid in the shape of a stylized jaguar, and large stone altars. All the structures were laid out along a central axis.
>
> "If the architectural remains are surprising, the sculpture leaves no doubt that the Olmecs were the first and finest sculptors in Mesoamerica. Tomb ornaments included objects of amethyst, turquoise, obsidian, quartz, magnetite, amber and pyrite. Carving jade with stone tools, they produced exquisite pieces rivalling those of the Shang dynasty in China (1500-1027 B.C.) with which they have been compared: small figurines and statuettes, ceremonial axes, funerary offerings of jewels, ornaments, and anthropomorphic jaguars. Their stelae, monuments of basalt decorated with sculpture, are magnificent. The largest at La Venta, Stela C, stands fourteen feet high and weighs some fifty tons. Yet their monolithic sculptures of giant human heads and altar statues hacked out of coarse basalt are most expressive of their enigmatic genius."

With their long-standing presence in Mexico, colossal head sculptures and astounding mathematics, the Olmec are the prima facie ancestors of Mexico's thirteen-ton Sun Stone. The archetypal alchemical vessel, the head housing the brain is the processing center of intelligence and sentience that distinguishes humanity among creatures of the Earth. The head and brain are the hallmark of human creature evolution.

After the Sun Stone was unceremoniously dredged from a cathedral yard in 1790, it was erroneously called the Aztec calendar for centuries. The Sun Stone emblazoned calendar glyphs the Aztecs acquired when they claimed possession of the Mexico Valley by virtue of conquest in 1325, centuries after designs in the Sun Stone were portrayed in Borgia Codices circa 900 CE.[5]

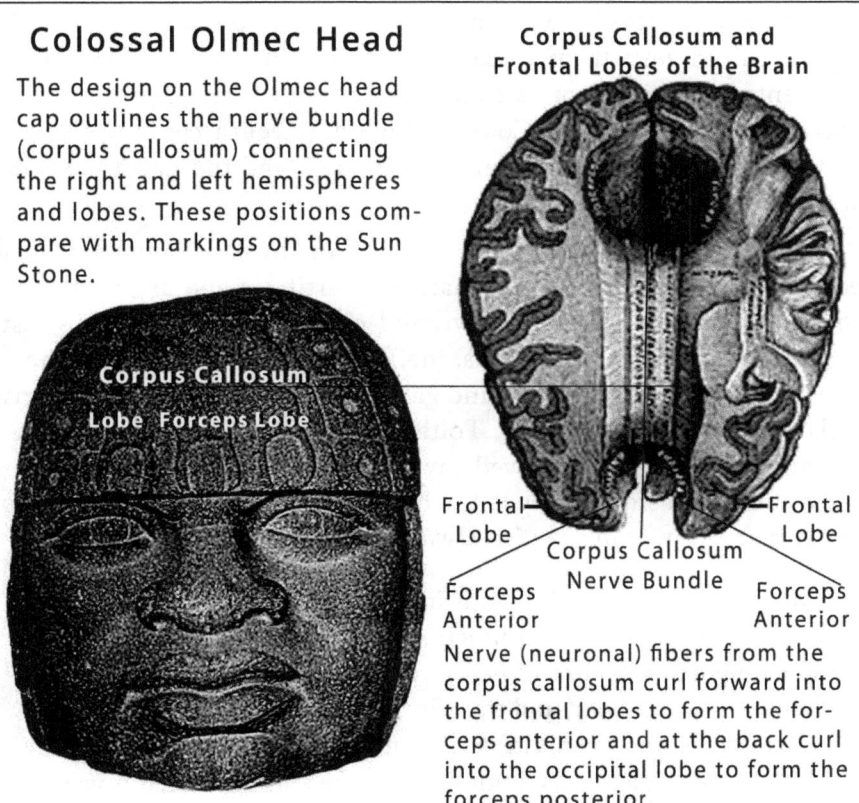

Colossal Olmec Head

The design on the Olmec head cap outlines the nerve bundle (corpus callosum) connecting the right and left hemispheres and lobes. These positions compare with markings on the Sun Stone.

Corpus Callosum and Frontal Lobes of the Brain

Nerve (neuronal) fibers from the corpus callosum curl forward into the frontal lobes to form the forceps anterior and at the back curl into the occipital lobe to form the forceps posterior.

This 5'9" tall sculpture weighing four tons was carved between 3,000 and 1 BCE with anatomical features that were unknown in Europe until the 1700s. It is in San Lorenzo Museo Comunitario de San Lorenzo, Tenochtitlán.   © Krsanna Duran 2016

The gigantic monolith carved in black basalt around a human head in the Sun Stone is characteristic of the Olmec. Their sculptures show that the Olmec had Negroid features with Asiatic eyes. Waters' comments on possible Olmec origins echo influences Le Plongeon identified in the Maya's codices:

> "They recall the anthropological belief in an early mixture of Negroid and predominantly Mongoloid types in India and Indonesia, resulting in a stock which later mixed with Oceanic Negroids. This ultimately produced the Polynesian race which passed through the Malay Archipelago and Melanesia to populate the islands of Polynesia, including Easter Island."[6]

After the Olmec introduced zero with thirteen dot-bar numbers intercalated with twenty glyphs in the Mayan calendar, zero next appeared in Hindu temples with the same thirteen dot-bar numbers. The Arabs acquired zero from India and introduced it into Europe in the tenth century. This history strongly agrees with Le Plongeon's early interpretation of the Troano Codex, which nineteenth-century historians rejected, believing that continents cannot sink and the Earth's axis does not shift.[7]

No direct observers, textual sources, or instructive maps exist for Teotihuacan's builders. Visual analysis of artifacts and art are the only basis for deductions about the pyramid complex. Teotihuacan's visual grandeur is its "canon of symbols, ineffable in import, by which the energies of aspiration are evoked and gathered toward a focus" for tourists, scholars, Rome's army, Aztecs, Toltecs, and local tribes. The silence of Teotihuacan's builders endowed mythic proportions to the message of the pyramids and stones they left behind. Joseph Campbell writes about this evocative power in *Creative Mythology*:

> "The rise and fall of civilisations in the long, broad course of history can be seen largely to be a function of the integrity and cogency of their supporting canons of myth; for not authority but aspiration is the motivator, builder, and transformer of civilisation. A mythological canon is an organisation of symbols, ineffable in import, by which the energies of aspiration are evoked and gathered toward a focus."[8]

Mother Earth, Father Sky, and Cosmos

Names Teotihuacan's builders used for the complex and pyramids in their own language are not known. Esther Pasztory writes about the iconography of the oldest and largest pyramid in *Teotihuacan: An Experiment in Living*:

> "Unlike the arts of most of Mesoamerica that glorified violence and dissension, art at Teotihuacan emphasized harmonious coexistence. As striking as the lack of themes of conflict is the lack of dates. Teotihuacan presented itself as a timeless place, as if it had existed from time immemorial and would exist into eternity, outside of history and historical contingency...
>
> "The most intriguing Teotihuacan deity is the Goddess, who seems especially strongly associated with masks. She is generically related to the various water, fertility and death goddesses of Mesoamerica,

Pyramid of the Sun at Teotihuacan

The largest and first pyramid built at Teotihuacan, which much later was called the Pyramid of the Sun, is reconstructed in a scale model. The pyramid was built with its main staircase aligned to the opening to caves, similar in theme to the hole in the floor of underground Kivas, where the Hopi communed with ancestors. The kiva symbolizes the womb of the Earth and the hole in the floor represents the place where they emerged from the last world to enter the Fourth World. The pyramid was anciently sequestered from mundane traffic on the central avenue by a wall shown in the scale model. Why the largest and most prominent pyramid was not accessible from the public central avenue is among Teotihuacan's mysteries. Walls contructed in the cave beneath the pyramid show that it was used before the complex was closed and abandoned.

but her specific form has no ancestry outside of Teotihuacan, and, with the possible exception of some Xochicalco images, she has no visual descendants. Three colossal statues in Teotihuacan style depict this goddess as a neutral or benevolent power. The representational strategy of Teotihuacan was thus seduction rather than terror. A feminine major deity serves to emphasize cosmic rather than political issues, and a benevolent appearance emphasizes positive values.

"One of the remarkable aspects of the Pyramid of the Sun is that it does not fit neatly into either the plan of the city or the surrounding

An Olmec figure emerges from an underworld cave carrying a transformative human-jaguar baby (were-jaguar) in a sculpture at La Venta, Mexico. A serpent rises over the top of his headdress, which has the Phoenician "X" equivalent to the Greek Tau is carved on it. The Jaguar Priesthood was the guardian of esoteric knowledge at Teotihuacan. Felines guarded occult and hidden knowledge worldwide, and the jaguar symbolized the knowledge of sorcerers through out Mexico and Central America.

landscape. From whatever direction one looks at it, it is a colossal individual monument, self-sufficient on its own, integrated with the other monumental architecture only artificially. It is an anomaly — sitting on one side of the Avenue without a symmetrical structure, without its own avenue leading up to it. (Modern site authorities created such a street with souvenir shops as if unconsciously wanting such an axis.) Only further archaeology will reveal whether it was the first major monument at the site, but I argue that it might have been the first or among the first and that the original ritual purpose of attracting people to Teotihuacan was to build it, as in Millon's hypothesis. (Recently, Millon suggested that an even older structure might be inside the Pyramid of the Moon.) . . . Whatever the reasons and history, the Pyramid of the Sun always remained central but separate and unique visually. This visual uniqueness could reflect the distinctiveness of its cult and function...

"It faces west toward the setting sun, and solar phenomena have been noted in relation to it. Millon and, following him, Clemency Coggins have suggested that the Pyramid of the Sun is associated with a grand concept of time — the idea of the beginning of a cosmic era. They relate this premise to the orientation of the Avenue, 15 degrees 25 minutes east of true north. However, this offset pertains to the site as a whole and not just to the Pyramid of the Sun...But basically, nothing has been found archaeologically that would provide definite deity identification for the Pyramid of the Sun."[9]

The transmuting and transfiguring deities of the new world baffled European religions and scholars. Pasztory commented on difficulties of attempting to transfer European-schooled classificatory methods of natural science to Mesoamerican humanities and social science:

"The first scholar to tackle this Mesoamerican system methodically was Eduard Seler, and his work was both brilliant and problematic: brilliant because he developed the first coherent interpretation of the iconography of sixteenth century codices, and problematic because not only did he not come to terms with the problems presented by the system of mixed messages, and his method is still the unquestioned canonical approach of most of those who write on Mesoamerican iconography. To create his classification of deities and attributes, Seler relied on two strategies: the substitution of one motif for another and the principle of association. Thus, "water" could be signified by water, a water-creature like a frog, or green precious things like jade and feathers. So far this approach is in line with Mesoamerican thinking. An Aztec father would have called his daughter a "green stone" or a "feather" to signify "preciousness," which was also the epithet of "water"...

"Because Seler correctly noticed the multivalent thought and image system of Mesoamericans, he did not see the extent to which he was manipulating the system to come up with a classification that meant something to him and to us Westerners. His classificatory system is surprisingly close to the Classical paradigm of individual deities and clear spheres of action. It is also close to other nineteenth-century systems of classification in the sciences based on the identification of key characteristics and interrelationships. Seler was thus a part of the great classificatory approach of the nineteenth century, brought over from the natural sciences into the social sciences and humanities.

"Motifs of the underworld, centrally important in ancient sites and ritual, are representative of the primordial womb, the place of gestation that ends with birth into the world as an individual. Caves are archetypal symbols of profound dwellings of the unconscious and emergent life, implicit in the Hopi's passage to the surface through an opening in the floor of the Fourth World." [10]

Alignment of sophisticated architecture and engineering to caves, as was done at Teotihuacan, shows their symbolic importance. The main staircase of the sun pyramid is built at the opening to a cave system, and cloverleaf-shaped walls built in the cave beneath the pyramid show it was used. Located on the east side of the central avenue, the sun pyramid's staircase faces west, toward the Pacific Ocean where the motherland Mu once thrived. Climbing out of the cavern opening at the sun pyramid the initiate's head emerges first, as it did at the birth into the physical world. Ritual emergence from the cave represents birth from the womb of the Earth.

The central avenue at Teotihuacan that divides the complex into equal west and east sides is one of the three earliest and largest structures. It extends from the plaza in front of the moon pyramid for over a mile to a ceremonial square in the south at Pyramid of the Feathered Serpent. With no access to the central avenue from the underground opening, the initiate must climb the main staircase to the temple at the top of the pyramid, or symbolically walk the path of life, to reach the summit.

The only astronomical alignment found at Teotihuacan is a sight line between the sun and moon pyramids for observing the setting sun's meridian on August 13 each year, the anniversary of the long count's beginning on August 13, 3114 BCE.[11] Father Sky metaphorically gazes from the moon pyramid to the goddess of fertility, Mother Earth. She carries and nurtures life represented with each initiate that climbs the summit after emerging from the cave. Father, mother, and child are the essential trinity, commemorated with homage to Father Sky, Mother Earth, and the tree of life.

Serpent Reptilian Brain	Dog Mammalian Brain	Death Extinct Early Human	Human Homo Sapiens: Parietal Lobe	Eagle Crown Chakra & Vital Energy

Feathered Serpent Timewave

A serpent, jaguar, and bird were the earliest representations of the Feathered Serpent in his initiation center at Teotihuacan in Mexico. Called *Quetzalcoatl* among the Toltecs and *Kukulkan* by the Maya, the Feathered Serpent first emerged with a full collar of feathers in the sixth century CE at Teotihuacan. Portraits of the alchemical vessel the head symbolizes, from reptilian to soaring eagle, encapsulate brain evolution in the Human-Earth Calendar of the Dresden Codex. The only head portraits in the calendar, each corresponds with a phase of brain development in species. The reptilian brain regulates autonomic functions with base life energy, or kundalini. The mammalian brain engages emotional states and responses. The parietal lobe integrates sensory information and language.. The governing meridian along the spine, neck and head distributes vital energy in subtle bodies with chakras.

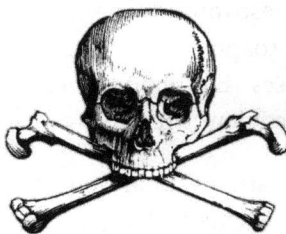  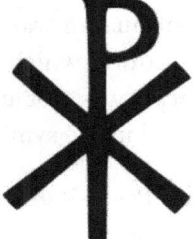

Skull and Crossbones of the Knights Templar

Human head is set into the center of the Movement glyph on the Sun Stone, the pivot of balance and center of power

Chi-Rho (XP) first two letters of Greek for "Christ;" origin in solar ecliptic path 360 BCE (Plato)

Solar Cross Astronomical symbol for Earth

Phoenician Tau carved with oldest image of the Feathered Serpent in Mexico

Icon for Lemuria, T-pillars at Gobelki Tepe & Greek Tau

© Krsanna Duran 2015

Sun, Moon, and Venus

Venus is the guiding star throughout Native America and the ancient world, with indications that measures for the Sun, Moon, and Venus were encoded in the megaliths in Great Britain and Europe and the Great Pyramid in Egypt.[12]

The Native American Church of North America ritual, which originated in central Mexico, is timed with the bright and shining morning star. The teepee or ceremonial setting, with an earthen altar in a crescent moon shape, is oriented to the east, and aligned to provide a view of Venus as it rises. The service lasts from dusk until dawn. The first two rounds of songs continue until Venus rises, and then prayers are offered with midnight water. *Midnight* in this sense is the midpoint that pivots (crosses) from the night to the morning with Venus rising.

Cycles of the sun, moon, and Venus painted in the ball court at Chichen Itza have striking similarities to Teotihuacan. A Toltec tribe that had first settled near Teotihuacan, and then built Tula, migrated to Chichen Itza by 950 CE. Mayan and Teotihuacan-style architectures and art are harmoniously integrated at Chichen Itza.

"Teotihuacan was the only pyramid center in Mesoamerica lacking a ball court, which caused some archeologists to posit that Teotihuacan was not used for astronomical purposes. Ball games were central in the symbolic and mythical worlds of ancient Mexico.

"The *Popul Vuh's* accounts of the game of ball attests its antiquity. The Game of Ball, *Juego de Pelota*, the *Tlachtli*, seems to have been played throughout Mesoamerica. In almost every ruin is found a ball court. The one at Chichen Itza is perhaps the largest and best restored. It is in the shape of a rectangle 272 feet long and 200 feet wide, flanked on each side by high stone walls, with a temple or stand at each end and platforms for spectators. The acoustics are remarkable; a person speaking in a normal voice from one end can be heard at the other. In the center of each flanking wall is imbedded a large stone ring, the *tlachemalacatl*. The game was simple and dangerous. The opposing members of each team played a hard rubber ball back and forth, the object being to knock it through the stone ring. The use of their hands was not permitted. They could strike the ball only with their elbows, knees, and hips and over these they wore protective covers. Death was the reward of the loser. This is dramatically shown in a low relief sculpture on the lower side of one wall. Players of both teams are facing each other, separated by a disc in which is carved the head of death. The first player on the losing team has one knee on the ground and his head has been cut off. Opposite him is standing one of the winning players, holding in one hand a large stone knife and in the other the decapitated head. From the neck of the headless loser a stream of blood is spurting in the form of serpents, while the central stream becomes

The Sun Stone depicting the cycles of Suns, or Worlds, correlates with the Hindu Yugas in a 24,000-year cycle. Buried in a cathedral yard after the Spanish stripped casings from pyramids at Teotihuacan to build cathedrals, it was discovered in 1790. Origin of the 24-ton basalt monolith is unknown. The central axis formed by human heads at the base and the top glyph at the crown is proportionately scaled with structures on north and south ends of the central avenue. Elements of its design were depicted in the Borgia Group of codices centuries before the Aztecs entered the Mexico Valley. Virtually all the tribes in central Mexico used designs copied from Teotihuacan in calendars and pyramids built after Teotihuacan's unidentified builders abandoned the complex circa 700 CE.

the stem of a plant bearing fruit and flowers. "Surely this scene portrays the symbolism embodied in the Game of Ball.

"Its meaning is astronomical, according to Seler: the sudden changes in the moon that alternately loses and wins in the game. "It loses when it begins to approach the morning, the Sun, and then dead, it ends up by becoming the new moon; it wins when it appears in the western sky changed into a young god, when it recovers a form which gets round and rounder until it at last shines in all the splendor of the new moon." There is justification for this interpretation in the *Borgia* where there are depicted structures resembling ball courts, notably in paintings 35 to 40; and figures which he identifies as Quetzalcoatl and Yohualtecuhtli wearing protective hide on their hips and putting out their buttocks to catch and bounce the ball. . . .

"The notable exception is the great ruin of Teotihuacan where no vestige of a ball court has been found. This is strange. Can we account for it by the fact that the birthplace of Mesoamerica's greatest civilization was almost wholly concerned, not with the moon, but with Venus' identity with Quetzalcoatl, whose mythical meaning did not require a structural and astronomical illustration? But how do we account for the depiction of ball courts in the *Borgia Codex* which so superbly and pictorially recounts the Quetzalcoatl myth? Perhaps because the *Borgia* paintings may have been made far later by artists in the Mixteca-Puebla region, based on the religious beliefs of Teotihuacan."[13]

Sun Stone Signature

A cap on the head in the center of the Sun Stone monolith is reminiscent of the Olmec's colossal head sculptures. Positions of the frontal lobes, corpus callosum, and pineal gland beneath it are marked on the cap. The Olmecs commonly emphasized brain structure with designs on emblematic caps.

Frank Waters noted that Olmec heads "are a psychological record of an early state of mankind when consciousness was beginning to emerge from the unconscious. No necks, no bodies. Just huge heads emphasizing the new significance of the head-center."[14]

Concentric rings carved in the Sun Stone are melded with Teotihuacan's signature triangular shield, and were recorded in a ninth century codex from the highlands, the *Borgia* group of codices. The Sun Stone is scaled to fit proportionately over a map of Teotihuacan's preplanned design. The head fits directly above a temple platform in the middle of the central avenue. Two human heads facing each other at the base of the Sun Stone fit over the large ceremonial square on the south end.

Serpent kundalini rises from the base of the Sun Stone, the same place it does in every esoteric system in the world. A serpent body emerges from the heads facing each other at the bottom of the Sun Stone. The left and right sides of the human sympathetic nervous system mirror each other in the same fashion as the heads at the bottom of the Sun Stone. Flames erupt from each serpent body as it rises to the crown at the top, where they form a unified circle ringing the outer edge of the Sun Stone. The Feathered Serpent pyramid is on the south end of the central pyramid in a square; the entire ceremonial area is below street level in two tiers. Small temples surrounding the Feathered Serpent's pyramid on three sides are laid out with the key numbers of Native America's calendar — thirteen and fifty-two, encoding the mathematical logic of the Mayan calendar. The Feathered Serpent appeared with a full collar of feathers for the first time on the facade of this pyramid. In the earliest images, the serpent appeared with only one, then two or three feathers. The Feathered Serpent's iconography that spread throughout Mexico originated and evolved at Teotihuacan.

The brain is permeated with microscopic particles that are magnetized by electrical current generated by the body. These electric and magnetic currents interact as electromagnetism, imaged in a variety of ways, including Magnetic Resonance Imaging (MRI). The body and brain are marvelous instruments of intelligent mind that characterize the human species.

The central avenue at Teotihuacan divides the pyramid complex into equal west and east sides, comparable to the hemispheres of the brain. As the corpus callosum connects the hemispheres of the brain, the central avenue connects the two sides of the complex. This pattern is repeated in the Sun Stone, where separate hemispheres in the outer ring are unified in a circle at the crown of the stone, which the Toltecs and Aztec tribes call *Reed*. The glyph's central position and function at the top of the Sun Stone is similar to the crown energy center, or crown chakra, associated with the pineal gland in Eastern traditions.

Directly across the central avenue from the ceremonial area of the Feathered Serpent's pyramid, is another large square area free of structures. It was undoubtedly used for community purposes, possibly for an open-air market.

Corpus Callosum Connects Left and Right Hemispheres of the Brain

The bundle of nerves that comprise the corpus callosum compare to the central avenue that connects the two sides of the pyramid complex at Teotihuacan. The fissure between brain hemispheres at the top compares to the Plaza of the Moon at the north end of the avenue. The lower right brain hemisphere above the cerebellum compares to the ceremonial square with the Pyramid of the Feathered Serpent on the south end of the avenue. Lower left hemisphere compares to the open public square facing the Feathered Serpent's pyramid on the opposite side of the avenue.

| Open public square at south end of the avenue. | Feathered Serpent's Pyramid in large ceremonial square |

Like a spinal cord correcting the crowning vision of the stars at Teotihuacan with its root in the earth, a road sprawls from the south end of the avenue into the countryside.

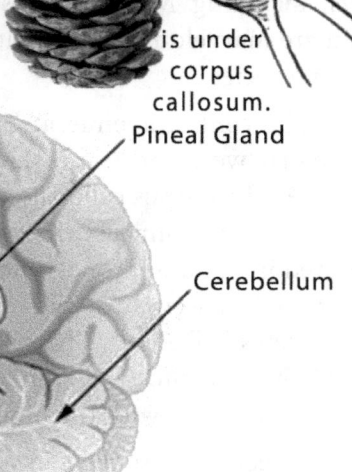

Pineal gland is under corpus callosum.
Pineal Gland

Microcosmic Portrait of Macrocosm
Head and Rim of Flames on Sun Stone Overlaid on Body of Pyramid Complex at Teotihuacan (Map)

Avenue is oriented 15.25 degrees east of true north.

North

Moon Pyramid

Sun Pyramid
Heart, Life
Soul, Earth,
Great Mother

San Juan River

Ceremonial square, "The Citadel"

Open-air platforms across from ceremonial square

Central Avenue

Feathered Serpent Pyramid in ceremonial square

The central avenue dividing the pyramid center at Teotihuacan into two equal sides -- east and west or left and right -- forms the spine of the complex. It compares with the central nadi (psychic nerve), the Sushumna, aligned with the spine in Tantric Buddhism, Indian Yoga and Chinese medicine and the corpus callosum that connects the left and right hemispheres of the brain. The head, center of the Hawaiian kahuna's middle self, fits over a platform in the center of the avenue on the above map proportionately sized with the Sun Stone. The kahuna's high self, located about five feet above the head, aligns with the crown glyph at the top of the Sun Stone. Two human heads that meet on the rim of flames at the base of the spine/avenue compare to the Ida and Pingala nadis. Frank Waters observed that the Olmec were similar to a Polynesian racial group that had migrated through India and Malaysia.

Reconstruction of central area after Millon, Drewitt and Cowgill 1973. © KDuran 2015

The two large squares at the south end of the central avenue face each other in parallel relationship with the two human heads at the base of the Sun Stone.

The crown fits over the Plaza of the Moon at the base of the Pyramid of the Moon. The serpent heads at the base fit over the ceremonial squares at the south end of the central avenue. The basket on the brow in the Sun Stone fits over the only temple platform built inside the central avenue. All other temple platforms and pyramids are built beside the avenue, but not in it. The precise planning of the pyramid complex before it was constructed required builders with extraordinary skill, capable of memorializing a design theme with the only platform featured inside the central avenue. When the Sun Stone and map are proportionately sized, the human head in the Sun Stone's center fits over the central platform in the central avenue.

Microcosmic Portrait of Macrocosm

Among the many amazing features of Teotihuacan is that the city's design was preplanned before construction began. Aerial mapping conducted by archaeologist Rene Millon, published in 1967, found that Teotihuacan's symmetry could have been achieved only by pre-planned design.[15,16] Most perplexing is that the three largest structures -- Pyramid of the Sun, Pyramid of the Moon, and the central avenue -- were constructed by an unidentified work force circa 200 BCE, before a larger population moved into the twelve-square-mile complex. By the time Teotihuacan's population boomed with new immigrants 400 years after it was built, or 200 CE when volcanic eruptions abated, the Olmec had departed the region by the first century CE.

Exterior casings from the pyramids were stripped to build Catholic cathedrals in the sixteenth century, and all information that may have been encoded on the pyramids was lost. Like the Great Pyramid in Egypt, where the outer casing also was stripped, measures of the pyramids and their relationships in the complex continue to convey crucial information in universal languages with mathematics and geometry. An extensive study conducted by American engineer Hugh Harleston found markers for orbits of all the inner planets in the solar system indicated with placements of pyramids and platforms on the central avenue. Numerous platforms and pyramids are configured in 3-4-5 Pythagorean triangles, and other key Pythagorean geometries in the gestalt of structures.

Stone monuments with signature measures in geometric constellations are messengers of true human intelligence that have survived tyranny and time. Teotihuacan's place in an ancient global network is shown in "Stone Sages" in "The Ages of Humankind."

Extreme volcanism prevented continuous settlement in the Mexico Valley for thousands of years before construction commenced on the

The **Sun Stone**, carved from black basalt in bas relief on a larger surface, was roughly cut away from its backing, leaving jagged edges around the circular carving. The 24-ton monolith was found buried face-down in a cathedral yard in 1790, after the Spaniards stripped exterior casings from the pyramids at Teotihuacan to build cathedrals in the sixteenth century. The Sun Stone's origin remains unknown, but its colossal size featuring a head is typical of Olmec sculpture. Concentric rings of glyphs and images are melded with Teotihuacan's emblematic triangles with curled footings. The broad body of the "Lizard" glyph closely resembles crocodiles found in southern Mexico and coastal areas the Olmec inhabited. The unpainted basalt above is enhanced for printing.

largest structures at Teotihuacan. A round stepped pyramid complex at Cuicuilco near Teotihuacan, buried in successive layers of volcanic lava, was excavated to a strata dating to the third millennium BCE in 1920, but neither the pyramid's foundation nor the pavement beneath it were penetrated before lack of funding ended the project. The archaeologist who conducted the excavation, Byron S. Cummings, estimated debris had accumulated around the pyramid for 6,500 years, which poses a date for the complex's abandonment of 4,500 BCE.[17] A date for Cuicuilco's construction has not been determined, but Cummings found that after the builders abandoned the pyramid site, it had been occupied by a succession of groups. Cuicuilco was repeatedly abandoned following volcanic eruptions that again covered the site with younger layers of lava. As happened at Gobekli Tepe, the earliest construction at Cuicuilco was the finest quality. Crafting declined over time, with the most recent occupants presenting cruder work than earlier occupants. Deepening descent of the yuga cycles and environmental deterioration may account for this cross-cultural phenomenon of declining craftsmanship in Turkey and Mexico.

In 1941, a congress of the Sociedad Mexicana de Antropologia passed a resolution affirming that "mistaken views identifying the Toltecs with the Teotihuacans have been proved wrong." The Toltecs migrated into the Mexico Valley by 600 CE, centuries before the Aztecs arrived, and commingled with Teotihuacan's builders before they departed.

After 800 years of unparalleled prosperity, the pyramid complex at Teotihuacan was abandoned as inexplicably as Gobekli Tepe in Turkey.

Toltecs, Aztecs, and Rome

The first of the Nahuatl migrations, the Toltec, arrived and settled in the Teotihuacan region by 600 CE and commingled with the pyramid builders before they departed. After a brief but bloody war, the Aztecs declared themselves the rulers and heirs of the Mexico Valley in 1325. By the time the Aztecs arrived, Teotihuacan had been abandoned for 500 years. The complex was completely covered with brush and debris, and the Aztecs never inhabited it.

Natives of the Mexico Valley said that when they lived in darkness, the Feathered Serpent gave them letters and numbers at the dawn of civilization. Teotihuacan's signature symbols spread throughout central Mexico. The Borgia group of codices, which the Spanish took from the area north of the pyramid complex, is the sole surviving literature most closely associated with Teotihuacan's builders. In contrast to Mayan codices, which were largely almanacs, cosmology and ritual are topics of the *Borgia Codices*.

A nomadic tribe with no ancestral home, the Aztecs declared themselves the heirs of Mexico Valley's rich heritage after a brief, bloody war with the Toltecs in 1325. They adopted the peaceful Feathered Serpent from Teotihuacan into the Aztec pantheon beneath the god of war, *Huitzilopochtli*.

With no experience in formalizing and measuring domains, as the Egyptians and Greeks did, the Toltecs and Aztecs called the broad-leafed vegetal design at the top of the Sun Stone *Reed*. A tall thin-stemmed grass, reeds bear no resemblance to the crowning glyph on the Sun Stone. *Toltec* means *People of the Reeds*, and tribal legend asserts they had once lived in a great city. The name of the city *Tollan* translates as *Place of the Reeds*, but reeds do not grow there. After a lengthy search for reeds at sites the Toltecs inhabited, Frank Waters was not able to locate a site in Mexico fitting the description of their ancestral home.

The Toltecs and Aztecs gave the complex and pyramids at Teotihuacan names from their own language, reflecting their cosmology. *Teotihuacan* is a Nahuatl word meaning *City of the Gods*, because the Aztecs imagined that only gods could have built the immense pyramids in the abandoned complex they inherited by conquest. Frank Waters summarized the Toltecs who first settled near Teotihuacan and then built Tula, before migrating to Chichen Itza:

> The Toltec-Tula culture, in short, was that of a semi-barbaric militaristic society built upon the ruins of the high religious culture of

Teotihuacan whose elements it adopted but failed to assimilate. Its importance lies in the influence it exported to Chichen Itza in Yucatan, and that as a transitional military culture it opened the way for the domination of Mexico by the aggressive Aztec.[18]

Soon after Cortes conquered Mexico in 1519, newly arrived, enterprising clergy gathered information from the native people. These included Franciscan friars Diego Duran and Bernardino de Sahagun, who also began teaching Mexicans to write in their own tongue using the Latin alphabet.

"From such sources...the friars learned that the Mexica were members of an Aztec tribe which had only recently entered the Valley of Mexico in the middle of the thirteenth century and had established themselves on an island in the great Texcoco Lake [Mexico City] at the beginning of the fourteenth century...

"According to the Aztec tradition, the Toltec leader Quetzalcoatl had fallen on evil days and been obliged to depart eastward about A.D. 950 of our era. Thereafter the Valley of Mexico was invaded by less civilized Indians from the north, among the last of which were the Aztecs, who burned their own records and rewrote their history to bury their obscure origins and pass themselves off as true descendants of the indigenous noble Toltecs."[19]

The Spanish Conquistadores perpetuated and compounded confusion about Mexico and its history. Diego de Landa, who arrived in Mexico in 1549 at the age of twenty-five, was charged with bringing Roman Catholic faith to the native peoples. The violent abuse Landa exerted to enforce conversion shocked even Catholic clergy. The crown had previously exempted indigenous peoples from the authority of the Inquisition, but Landa was convinced an underground network led by native leaders jealous of the Church conspired to overthrow it and seize power. He claimed to have discovered idolatry, as well as human sacrifices, even after one of the alleged victims was found alive and well. After seeing sacred Maya writing in books, Landa believed the astronomy and sciences in Mayan codices were proof of evil, and wrote:

"These people [Maya] also make use of certain characters or letters, with which they wrote in their books their ancient matters and their sciences, and by drawings and by certain signs in these drawings they understood their affairs and made others understand and taught them. We found a large number of books in these characters and, as they contained nothing in which were not to be seen as superstition and lies of the devil, we burned them all, which they regretted to an amazing degree, and which caused them much affliction."[20]

Landa burned five thousand native religious images and at least twenty-seven painted books filled with glyphic images relating to traditional religious practices and beliefs. Only four pre-Columbian codices, containing rare examples of Mayan writing, survived. Landa rose to the position of Bishop of the Yucatan in 1573. Landa's manuscript about Maya religion, land, culture, and writing systems, *Relacion de las cosas Yucatan,* influenced Eurocentric interpretations of the Maya and their calendar for nearly 400 years.

As well as dismantling the Aztec pyramids for materials to build cathedrals, the Spaniards razed facings with any information they contained from pyramids at Teotihuacan. The Sun Stone could not be burned, but it could be dragged. It was given a proper Christian burial, face down in the yard of a cathedral in Mexico City, where it was exhumed during construction in 1790. Imagery on the Sun Stone depicting five Suns may have given the monolith priority on Rome's list for elimination. Thousands of artifacts and documents were shipped to Europe after conquest, and the only codices spared from the Inquisition's flames were those that had already been shipped.

Scholars relied on Landa's flawed manuscript for centuries, until J. Eric Thompson deciphered the Mayan calendar codices in 1950. Landa's contributions to confusion and misidentification in Ancient America are summarized in Thompson's comments about the Mayan hieroglyphs:

> "That Landa's system per se cannot be used to read the glyphs is too well known to need comment. (I omit the question of modifications and expansions which various authors have suggested in recent years as not pertinent to the discussion.)"[21]

Notes

[1] Cowgill, George L. "Teotihuacan and Early Classic Interaction: A Perspective from Outside the Maya Region." Braswell, Geoffrey E., editor. 2004.

The Maya and Teotihuacan. University of Texas Press: Austin, TX. pp 328-335

² Ibid pp 10-11

³ Cooper, Gordon with Bruce Henderson. 2002. *Leap of Faith: An Astronaut's Journey into the Unknown.* HarperTorch: New York, NY. p 212-214

⁴ Malmström, Vincent H. 1997. *Cycles of the Sun, Mysteries of the Moon: The Calendar in Mesoamerican Civilization.* Austin, TX: University of Texas Press. pp 102-104

⁵ Pastorzy, Esther. 1974. *The Iconography of the Teotihuacan Tlaloc.* Dumbarton Oaks: Washington, DC. p 6

⁶ Waters, Frank. 1989. *The Mexico Mystique: The Coming Sixth World of Consciousness.* Ohio University Press Books: Swallow Press. pp 31-32

⁷Nothing that survived the doctrine of Manifest Destiny in the USA compares with Mexico's ancient pyramid culture. American Indian reservations and Christian boarding schools that conditioned Indian children with Eurocentric values were the Protestant weapon of choice against the "savages" in the USA. Indian children were not allowed to speak native languages or practice their culture in Christian schools where they were boarded until the age of 18. With brutal inquisitions, the Catholic Church exercised torture and executions but didn't confine Indians to reservations and mandate removal of children to boarding schools at the age of five. A cathedral briefly surmounted the Pyramid of the Sun at Teotihuacan, but the pyramid was too mountainous to easily dismantle as the Catholics had done with the Aztec pyramids. The Mexican Revolution in 1910 was largely a conflict between religious authority and the state, when Mexicans began reclaiming their culture. Indian culture entered the twentieth century very differently in Mexico than in the United States and, while the two cultures stem from shared indigenous roots, they no longer equate in the terms they did in pre-Columbian America.

⁸. Campbell, Joseph. 1978. *Creative Mythology.* Penguin Books: New Yok, NY. 5-6

⁹. Pasztory, Esther. 1997. *Teotihuacan: An Experiment in Living.* pp 83-85

¹⁰ Ibid. pp 64-65

¹¹. Barrios, Carlos, translated by Lisa Carter. 2009. *The Book of Destiny.* Unlock-

ing the Secrets of the Ancient Mayans and the Prophecy of 2012. Harper One, an imprint of HarperCollins Publishers. p 211

Although the Maya's complex timekeeping system included accurate astronomical counts, an astronomical basis for the long count has never been proven. The basis for the long count is outside classical Western models of astronomy. See "The Ages of Humankind," Chapter Two, for the long count's correlations with Hindu yugas and beginning and ending dates. A number of extraordinary historical events approximating the 3101 BCE date in the Timeline demonstrate this was a period of extreme change in human affairs worldwide. I argue that extraterrestrial factions reached an accord that ended a war between Atlantis and Mu, when Upper and Lower Egypt were unified in approximately 3100. Dates of the accord were memorialized in the long count and the anniversary noted at Teotihuacan.

[12] Knight, Christopher and Alan Butler. 2004. *Civilization One*. Watkins Publishing: London, UK. pp 219-225

[13]. Waters, Frank. 1989. *The Mexico Mystique: The Coming Sixth World of Consciousness*. Ohio University Press Books: Swallow Press. pp 158-159

[14] Ibid p 33

[15] Stanford University Humanities Lab. "Reconfiguring the Archaeological Sensibility: Mediating Heritage at Teotihuacan, Mexico" http://humanitieslab.stanford.edu/teotihuacan/1497

[16] Tompkins, Peter. 1976. *Mysteries of the Mexican Pyramids*. New York, NY: Harper & Row, Publishers, Inc. pp 226-229, 241

[17] Hapgood, Charles S. 1966. *Maps of the Ancient Sea Kings*. Reprinted by Adventures Unlimited Press: Kempton, IL. pp199-204

[18]. Waters, Frank. 1989. *The Mexico Mystique: The Coming Sixth World of Consciousness*. pp 61-66

[19]. Tompkins, Peter. 1976. *Mysteries of the Mexican Pyramids*. pp 20-23

[20] Clendinen, Inga. 1998. *Ambivalent Conquests — Maya and Spanish in the Yucatan, 1519 — 1570*. Cambridge University Press: Cambridge. p 70

[21]. Thompson, J. Eric S. "Systems Of Hieroglyphic Writing In Middle America and Methods Of Deciphering Them." *American Antiquity*, Vol. 24, No. 4,

1959 pp 349-364

CHAPTER FOUR

Cosmos

Few strands of the true human story that escaped editors' knives survived information wars of gods and oligarchs who claimed divine right to rule the Earth. In their relationship showing rotation, the Great Pyramid, Teotihuacan, and Angkor Wat memorialize information that surpasses the vanity of gods and rulers. Their undiluted message is shaped in geometries and measures that informs the mind of the species.

Human

A microcosmic human face in the center of Mexico's Sun Stone peers into the expanding spheres of the macrocosm. Orbits of the sun around a great center give impetus to ascending and descending virtue in periods of 24,000 years of Hindu yugas. Human experience in physical, psychic, awareness, and spiritual time was discussed with Ida Kannenberg and time travelers in an unpublished manuscript.[1]

"Time Travelers: You are living on four levels of being at once. What we tell you is true on one level, but misleading on others.

"Ida: Four?

"Time Travelers: Yes, you know them. In your writing, you called it four dimensions of time.

"Ida: . . . Let's see, I said physical time, emotional time, mental time and spiritual time.

"Time Travelers: Good. Only you are not too clear about it. What you call emotional time is really psychic time. That is your major error. And what you call mental time is best called awareness time. Time dimension is only one of the attributes.

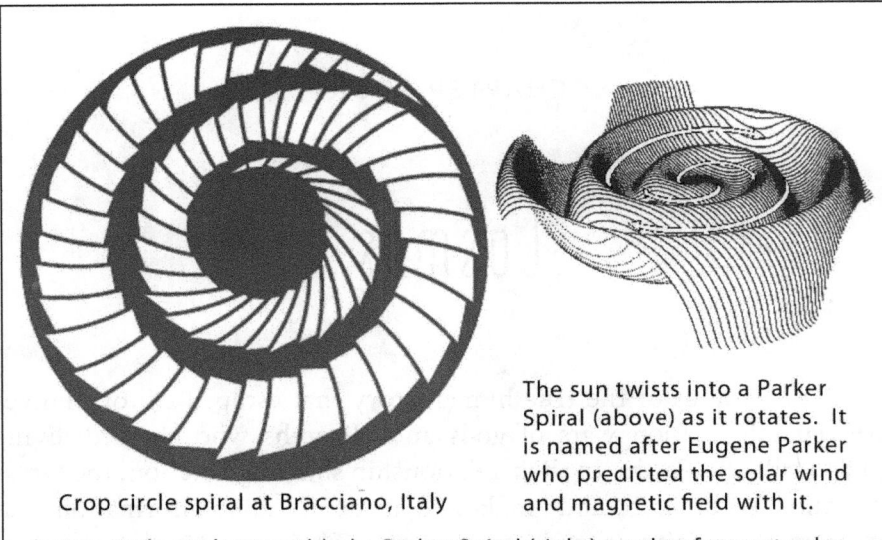

Crop circle spiral at Bracciano, Italy

The sun twists into a Parker Spiral (above) as it rotates. It is named after Eugene Parker who predicted the solar wind and magnetic field with it.

A crop circle circle resembled a Parker Spiral (right) used to forecast solar activity at Bracciano, Italy on May 20, 2012 (left), following an unpredicted interplanetary shock wave. A large earthquake shook Italy 100 miles northwest of the crop circle hours after it formed. Brisk solar winds with low numbers of sunspots and solar flares followed the crop circle.

"Ida: You told me recently the sun was the key! Now if the psychic world and the spiritual world are two different things, in no way connected, then obviously the sun is too limited to be the center of the spiritual world or connected with it as a key, then the sun must be the center of the psychic world as far as our universe is concerned. Is that the key?

"Time Travelers: . . . The sun is the sensitive center of all psychic activity. Now this of course needs much explanation. The words are not as simple as they sound. The word *center,* for example, the simple word *center.* The center of what? A galaxy, universe, this small cluster of planets and stars you call the universe?

"Ida: I guess I did not mean spatial center, but *center* in the sense of most sensitized or powerful."..

Changing awareness of psi and science has literally shifted the focus of human history since 1899, when a Hindu yuga cycle began. Public interactions of UFOs with the people of Earth in the 1940s coincided with World War II and the drive to develop ever-more powerful weapons, which culminated in the atomic bomb, UFO visits, and birth of the national security state. When UFOs proliferated at nuclear research and

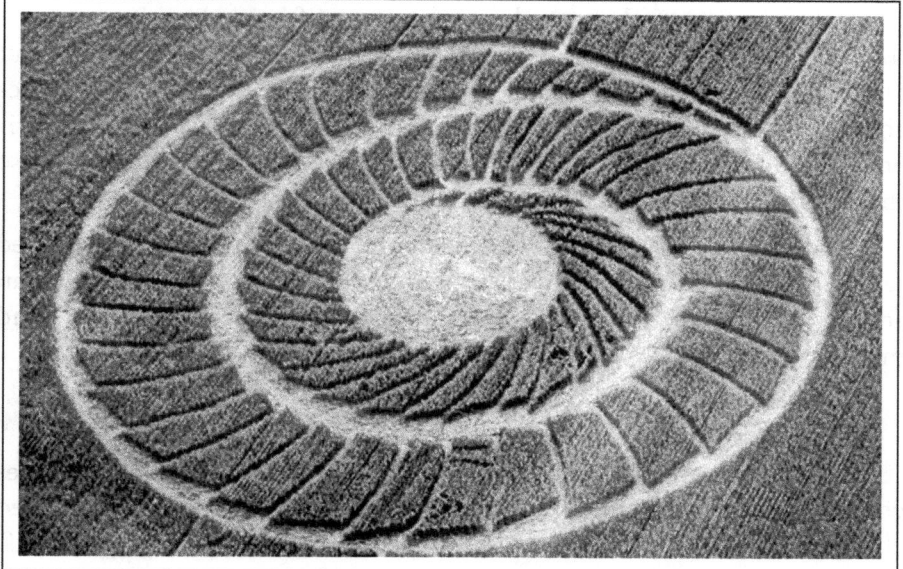

testing sites, the National Security Act was passed to keep the UFO official secrets for the few.

In the early decades of UFO contact, individuals and groups were commonly encountered in outdoor settings or while driving in vehicles.[2] My first conscious encounter occurred while walking on a street in Oklahoma City at the age of fifteen. I was literally picked up in a beam of light after watching a bright light moving above houses at dusk in 1963. After Ida observed what she thought was a full moon in 1940, her husband stopped their vehicle to observe the strange object. In both Ida and my encounters two hours of time were missing after observing luminous UFO.

Denise M. Stoner, co-author of *The Alien Abduction Files: The Most Startling Cases of Human-Alien Contact Cases Ever Reported*, recalls an extraordinary UFO encounter while traveling with her husband on a highway in the 1980s. Their car was elevated over a field and three hours of missing time followed. Both Stoner and co-author Kathleen Marden are seasoned UFO researchers who hold executive positions in branches of the Mutual UFO Network (MUFON) in their areas.[3] Nuclear physicist Stanton Friedman, who participated in writing the book, has co-authored no less than eleven books and assisted with numerous studies of UFO activity and encounters as well as official records released by military and government authorities. Their research for *The Alien Abduction Files* included an extensive and detailed survey of individuals who report UFO contact.

Stoner reports that people now in their fifties and sixties continue to experience UFO encounters. They are remembering more about UFO experiences and report they receive downloads of information, according to Stoner's study. Although information many UFO experiencers "download" may be inaccessible at present they generally sense they will remember it sometime in the future.[4]

Modalities of encounters and anomalous crop circles associated with UFO paralleled broadly streamed changes of awareness in human activity since 1940. As UFO experiencers remember and understand more, UFO modalities change.

Earth

Booming, trumpeting sounds that vibrated the bones of witnesses could be neither explained nor quieted in 2011. Solar scientists debated changes in the sun, and NASA announced strange solar activity with affirmations worthy of old-time prophets. Geologists watched a tectonic plate fracture for the first time ever in 2012. The electric and magnetic "builders and geometers" had been anticipated in a 1999 discussion with Ida in *My Brother Is a Hairy Man*.[5]

> "Ida, 1/9/99: ...Maez and I were talking about ley lines and that North/South lines are magnetic and W/E lines are of gravitational forces and their interaction with the surrounding "sea of information" which must be electricity of a kind.[6]

> "Tres: So it is. Cosmic electricity.

> Ida: That gives us some form of three of the Great Builders or Geometricians, but the fourth one — the resonating electric-magnetic force — where does that come in?

> "Tres: Indeed, where? Think!

> "Ida: Could it be the person, the living being that stands on the intersecting N/S and W/E lines? Are WE the resonating electromagnetic fields? Well, of course we are! The brain is the electro, the mind the magnetic field.

> "Tres: Welcome home, Ida!

> "Ida: Everyone?

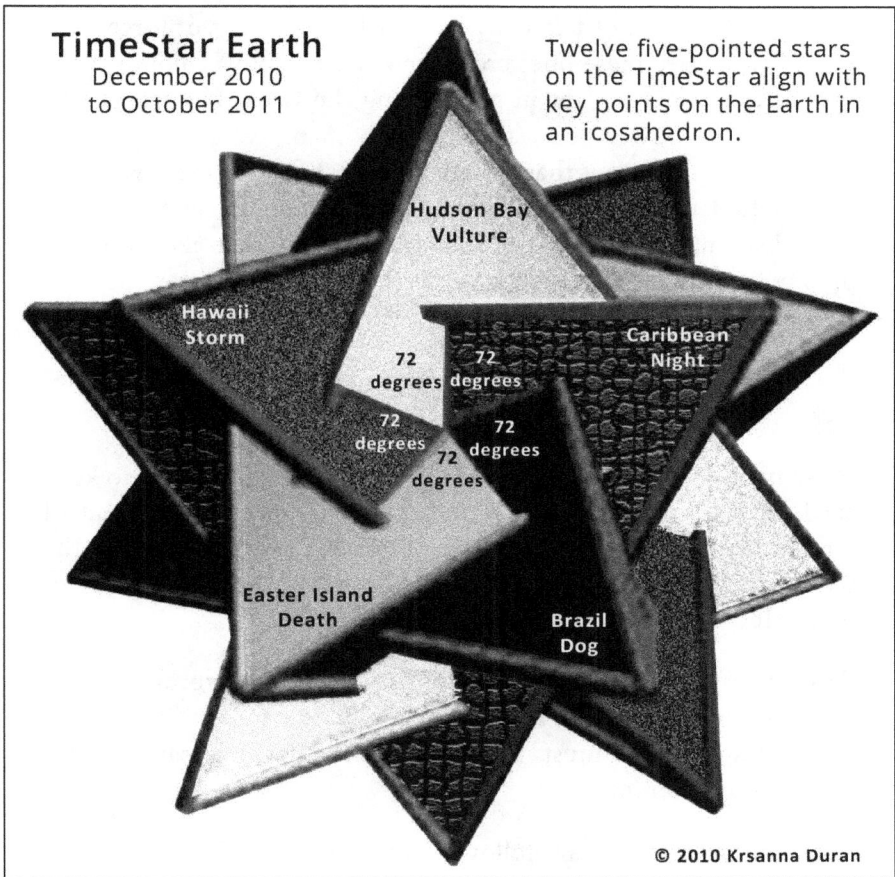

"Tres: To varying degrees. That is, they are able to accept themselves in that aspect in varying degrees, and to that degree use the power it invokes.

"Ida: Power?

"Tres: Believe it!

"Ida: To what do we resonate? Oh. God? . . .

"Tres: To what then?

"Ida: I already said it. To the sea of information — the electric sea of God's consciousness that surrounds us — supra-consciousness.

"Tres: Meditate on that awhile. You've just uncovered a spectacular truth. Now what are you stewing about?

"Ida, 1/10/99, 2:40 P.M.: Telepathy. See you tomorrow.

"Tres to Ida: No, not telepathy, but ley lines or lines of force, N/S and W/E. Since these lines cross each other at power points, your friend Krsanna was right in pinpointing the Great Pyramid as the Earth's major power point as marked by man. Who could better know where to place it than Thoth (Hermes) its architect? Krsanna has found a unique and brilliant use for combining lines of force with the timing of the Maya calendar in a way that allows her to predict coming earth events — earthquakes, volcanoes, storms, floods, etc.

"Let us leave this research to her genius and we shall take another tack.

"Krsanna has taken the map's lines of latitude and longitude to keep track of her prediction points and to point out the placement of crop circles relative to such power points as the great pyramid, the pyramids and other markers at Teotihuacán. A brilliant piece of work. It should (and will) be better known.

"We shall not intrude upon her domain but use our recognition of power points and lines in a different fashion and for a different purpose, although we must necessarily recognize the same major points. But differently.

"The lines of force we are following are magnetic N/S and gravitational W/E. These are not always as stable as the lines of latitude and longitude on a map due to the tilt of the Earth and other erratic things we will discuss later. Yes, this does have to do with Bigfoot, be patient. And they are not as mathematically straight as lines on a map. They seem to wander and waver sometimes due to interfering lines of cosmic force (electricity). We will get into all this as we go along. And it does have to do with the placement of Bigfoot. He is far more important than just being a biologically unique specimen. He has been engineered to do specific work and he does it well."

Magnetic Core, Weakening Field, and Cosmic Rays

Weakening of the magnetic field had been ongoing since the sixteenth century, when magnetic north's pace exponentially accelerated months after a crop circle depicted the magnetic core on May 28, 1993. Markers in the crop circle at Kennewick, Washington pointed to true

WEB OF LIFE AND COSMOS: HUMAN AND BIGFOOT STAR ANCESTORS

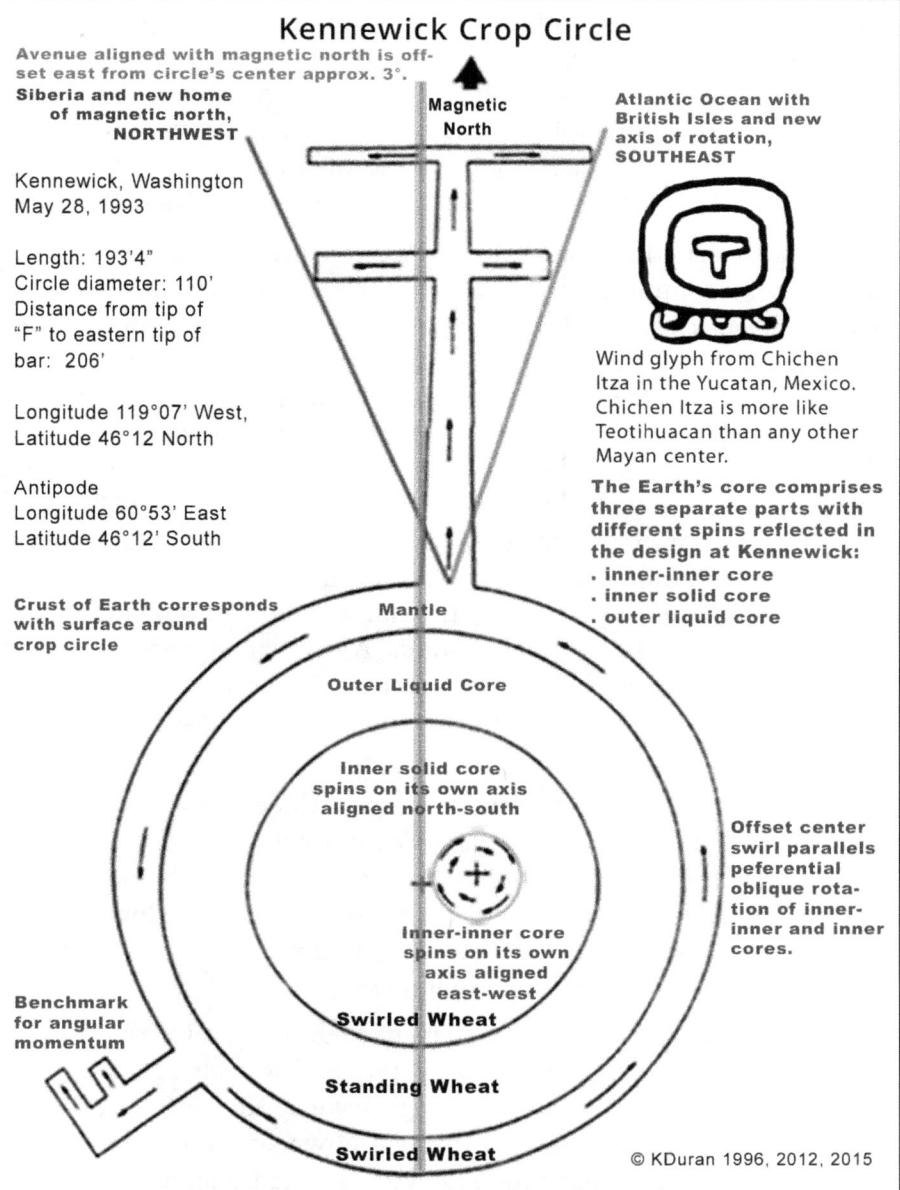

Kennewick Crop Circle

Avenue aligned with magnetic north is offset east from circle's center approx. 3°.

Magnetic North

Siberia and new home of magnetic north, **NORTHWEST**

Atlantic Ocean with British Isles and new axis of rotation, **SOUTHEAST**

Kennewick, Washington
May 28, 1993

Length: 193'4"
Circle diameter: 110'
Distance from tip of
"F" to eastern tip of
bar: 206'

Longitude 119°07' West,
Latitude 46°12 North

Antipode
Longitude 60°53' East
Latitude 46°12' South

Crust of Earth corresponds with surface around crop circle

Wind glyph from Chichen Itza in the Yucatan, Mexico. Chichen Itza is more like Teotihuacan than any other Mayan center.

The Earth's core comprises three separate parts with different spins reflected in the design at Kennewick:
. inner-inner core
. inner solid core
. outer liquid core

Mantle

Outer Liquid Core

Inner solid core spins on its own axis aligned north-south

Inner-inner core spins on its own axis aligned east-west

Offset center swirl parallels peferential oblique rotation of innerinner and inner cores.

Benchmark for angular momentum

Swirled Wheat
Standing Wheat
Swirled Wheat

© KDuran 1996, 2012, 2015

The avenue and top bar reflect the Wind glyph, Greek letter Tau and "T" pillars at Gobekli Tepe in Turkey, iconic symbols for Lemuria and Hyperborea. Standing crop obscured view of the avenue when standing at the center of the circle. When viewed from the vantage of true north, the avenue pointed to the core of the Earth: A gentle reminder of perspective. The Kennewick circle formed an equilateral triangle with the Feathered Serpent's long count home at Teotihuacan and a July 21, 1993 crop circle at Herkimer, New York. Kennewick's opposite point (antipode) is in the Indian Ocean where the magnetic field was strongest in 2014.

north, magnetic north's position in 1993 and Siberia, magnetic north's destination.[7,8] The sudden increase in magnetic north's movement and weakening magnetic field was sandwiched between robust solar maxima in 1989 (Cycle 22) and 2001 (Cycle 23). Anomalous gamma rays permeated the solar system in January 1993, less than two years after the historic July 11, 1991 solar eclipse predicted in the Dresden Codex.

A solar eruption that baffled NASA scientists December 5, 2006, the deep of solar minimum, signaled changes deep in the sun. The heliospheric current circuit and rotating magnetic fields that form the heliospheric current sheet in the solar system were indicated in a crop circle at Bracciano, Italy on May 20, 2012.[9] Named for Eugene Parker who discovered the solar wind, the Parker Spiral is a geometric model for the heliospheric current sheet depicted in the Bracciano crop circle. The current sheet is the surface within the solar system where the Sun's polarity changes from north to south; and the very important interplanetary magnetic field influences all planets in the solar system. The shape of the current sheet results from the Sun's rotating magnetic field on plasma in the interplanetary solar wind. A very small electrical current flows through the sheet, in the field that extends through the Sun's equator in the heliosphere. The resulting current forms part of the heliospheric current circuit.

Systemic changes in the solar system include signs of heating and other changes on numerous planets: Venus' rotation on its axis is slowing, a bright flash on Jupiter was attributed to an impact but neither debris nor a cloud hole were detected; moreover, Jupiter has lost an entire planetary ring that encircled it; Saturn's rotation is slowing, and its predictable storms are earlier and more intense.

In the environment of system-wide heating, bizarre explosive booms and trumpeting sounds were reported worldwide in January 2011. Soon after a 9.0 magnitude megaquake at Honshu, Japan culminated in three nuclear reactors melting down at Fukushima Daiichi March 11, 2011, large numbers of sinkholes began opening around the globe. And geologists reported exponentially high soil liquefaction, according to science journalist Linda Moulton Howe:[10]

"Are Sinkholes Related to Loud, Unexplained Booms?

"Recently I [Linda Moulton Howe in 2013] received an email from a retired communications and electronics expert for several contractors that have done work for Hill AFB in Utah. He has also worked for the Intercontinental Ballistic Missile Strategic Planning Office between 1993 to 2005. In his work, he came to know a geophysicist also working on military contracts for the U. S. Air Force. When the Air Force builds, the ground structure needs to be solid, so geophysicists will do ground surveys. If the Air Force building is going to have underground facilities - perhaps for computer servers and/or missile silos - the geophysicists will do ground readings. The electronics expert who contacted me said he told his geophysicist friend that for some time he has been hearing booms at a distance almost daily, but his windows rattle. So he asked the geophysicist if there was hard bedrock between his house and the Great Salt Lake and over into the Hill AFB bombing range?

"Worldwide Booms - Is Earth's Inner Core Changing?

"The geophysicist surprised his electronics friend when he said that the booms have been becoming more frequent around the world, not just the U. S. He said there have been reports from the Soviet Union, Europe, Africa, China, and Guatemala and that the first report in 1998 was from a deep mine on the Alaska/Yukon border. At that time, miners reported hearing sounds like rocks or sand falling down a metallic tube.

"The geophysicist told the electronics engineer, 'Since 2011, many geologists have noticed almost a 1000% increase in soil liquefaction.' This might explain the more frequent sinkholes, not only in the United States but around the world.

"[Editor's Note: Wikipedia - Soil liquefaction describes a phenomenon where by a saturated soil substantially loses strength and stiffness in response to an applied stress, usually earthquake shaking or other sudden change in stress condition, causing it to behave like a liquid.]

"The geophysicist said he and his colleagues believe something is going on in the inner core of the Earth. They don't know if it's a magnetic pole change; restructuring of minerals within the soil down to the mantle and core. It's becoming more frequent and so has the intensity. They really have no real idea what's going on. He said they don't know if it's a short term, one-time boom phenomenon, or something very serious. They don't know if it's a regular occurrence that happens in cycles on the Earth. So far, there is no explanation for the boom phenomenon."

"Why Inner Earth Core Change Could Cause Sinkholes and Booms?

"The geophysicist also told his electronics friend that the increasing sinkholes might be related to the core, mantle and crust changes because sound frequencies are involved. He emphasized they are aware of pretty steady infrasound that the human ear cannot hear, but dogs and other animals can - which would explain why dogs have been reported running before a boom occurs.

"[Editor's Note: Wikipedia - Infrasound, sometimes referred to as low-frequency sound, is sound that is lower in frequency than 20 Hz (Hertz) or cycles per second, the "normal" limit of human hearing. Hearing becomes gradually less sensitive as frequency decreases, so for humans to perceive infrasound, the sound pressure must be sufficiently high. The ear is the primary organ for sensing infrasound, but at higher intensities it is possible to feel infrasound vibrations in various parts of the body.]

"So what is the physics when people can hear the loud booms and even be jolted by them at least in a localized area? The electronics expert said the geophysicist used the analogy of the Earth's crust acting like a large speaker diaphragm, projecting sounds, some of them going through the atmosphere and out through the ionosphere and some returning as audible sound that the human ear can hear.

"Why Government Silence On Unexplained Booms and Light Flashes?

"When I asked the electronics expert why our government does not simply say all this to the American people, he answered from his conversation with the geophysicist: "Panic. Strictly panic. That's all I can tell you. The government and political system is afraid of panic."

"I also asked the electronics expert about the bright white flashes of light associated with the loud boom phenomenon.

"He said it's like a very large static electric discharge associated with the apparent huge stress emanating from the inner and outer core to the liquid mantle beneath the Earth's crust. He said he understands there has been a change in the speed with which the mantle is moving so now the mantle is moving faster. The mantle flow increase sets up new vibrations from the magnetic conductivity created.

"I asked the electronics expert what the geophysicist says could be the worst-case scenario if the booms and light flashes persist - or even grow in frequency and intensity?

"He said, "The geophysicist said the worst case would be that there are more cracks that could appear in the main continental plates. So instead of having one huge plate more or less from the East Coast of Japan down through Indonesia and back up to South America and up the coastline through California - what would happen if that big plate bulged in the center and created cracks? They know they've got something causing these core to mantle to crust vibrations that releases huge, sudden, quick energy in the focused booms. But what it is? And what scale could it affect, they don't know."[11]

TimeStar posits increasing numbers of booms and explosions that began proliferating in 2011 result from rising levels of high-energy cosmic rays that induce electrical discharges. Native Americans associated periods of high-energy cosmic radiations with the Thunderbird, who came with thunder and lightning. After reaching a fifty-year high in 2009, cosmic ray levels continued to rise as Earth's magnetic field weakened in the presence of declining solar activity. During the weakest solar maximum (cycle 24) in 200 years, booms, explosions and light anomalies steadily increased to new highs in 2015, paralleling continual decline in the magnetic field and solar activity. The presence and absence of the Thunderbird corresponds with cosmic rays, ambient electrical force and declining solar activity. TimeStar forecast this trend in 2012, along with increasing electrical force and appearances of the Thunderbird.

Sun

One of the largest solar flares in thirty years that unexpectedly erupted in 2006 was among the first signs of a shift in the solar phase. Solar physicists initially predicted the solar maximum that began in 2008 would peak in 2012 with the most intense activity in fifty years, based on the "conveyor belt" theory. Sunspots, visible tangles of magnetic forces on the sun's surface, should have been at record high levels in 2012, according to a NASA solar storm warning in 2006:

> "Solar physicist David Hathaway of the National Space Science & Technology Center (NSSTC) explains: "First, remember what sunspots are — tangled knots of magnetism generated by the sun's inner dynamo. A typical sunspot exists for just a few weeks. Then it decays, leaving behind a 'corpse' of weak magnetic fields."
>
> "Enter the conveyor belt.
>
> "'The top of the conveyor belt skims the surface of the sun, sweeping up the magnetic fields of old, dead sunspots. The 'corpses' are dragged down at the poles to a depth of 200,000 km where the sun's magnetic dynamo can amplify them. Once the corpses (magnetic knots) are reincarnated (amplified), they become buoyant and float back to the surface." Presto — new sunspots!
>
> "All this happens with massive slowness. "It takes about 40 years for the belt to complete one loop," says Hathaway. The speed varies "anywhere from a 50-year pace (slow) to a 30-year pace (fast)."
>
> "When the belt is turning 'fast,' it means that lots of magnetic fields are being swept up, and that a future sunspot cycle is going to be intense. This is a basis for forecasting: "The belt was turning fast in
>
> "'1986-1996,' says Hathaway. 'Old magnetic fields swept up then should re-appear as big sunspots in 2010-2011.'
>
> "Like most experts in the field, Hathaway has confidence in the conveyor belt model and agrees with Dikpati that the next solar maximum should be a doozy. But he disagrees with one point. Dikpati's forecast puts Solar Max at 2012. Hathaway believes it will arrive sooner, in 2010 or 2011.
>
> "'History shows that big sunspot cycles 'ramp up' faster than small ones,' he says. 'I expect to see the first sunspots of the next cycle appear in late 2006 or 2007 — and Solar Max to be underway by 2010 or 2011.'
>
> "Who's right? Time will tell. Either way, a storm is coming."[12]

Then something remarkable happened. With the very low number of only forty-three sunspots visible on the surface, an enormous X9-class flare erupted.

"The event occurred on Dec. 5, 2006. A large sunspot rounded the sun's eastern limb and with little warning it exploded. On the "Richter scale" of flares, which ranks X1 as a big event, the blast registered X9, making it one of the strongest flares of the past 30 years.

"NASA managers braced themselves. Such a ferocious blast usually produces a blizzard of high-energy particles dangerous to both satellites and astronauts. Indeed, moments after the explosion, radio emissions from a shock wave in the sun's atmosphere signaled that a swarm of particles was on its way.

"An hour later they arrived. But they were not the particles researchers expected.

"NASA's twin STEREO spacecraft made the discovery: "It was a burst of hydrogen atoms," says Mewaldt. "No other elements were present, not even helium (the sun's second most abundant atomic species). Pure hydrogen streamed past the spacecraft for a full 90 minutes."

"Next came more than 30 minutes of quiet. The burst subsided and STEREO's particle counters returned to low levels. The event seemed to be over when a second wave of particles enveloped the spacecraft. These were the 'broken atoms' that flares are supposed to produce — protons and heavier ions such as helium, oxygen and iron. 'Better late than never,' he says.

"At first, this unprecedented sequence of events baffled scientists, but now Mewaldt and colleagues believe they're getting to the bottom of the mystery."[13]

The sun's strange behavior deepened. Instead of an intense sunspot cycle with a steep climb to solar maximum as 2010, as Hathaway had anticipated, sunspots had virtually disappeared by 2009 as the solar minimum deepened.

"The sun is in the pits of the deepest solar minimum in nearly a century. Weeks and sometimes whole months go by without even a single tiny sunspot. The quiet has dragged out for more than two years, prompting some observers to wonder, *are sunspots disappearing?*

"'Personally, I'm betting that sunspots are coming back,' says researcher Matt Penn of the National Solar Observatory (NSO) in Tucson, Arizona. But, he allows, 'there is some evidence that they won't.'

"Penn's colleague Bill Livingston of the NSO has been measuring the magnetic fields of sunspots for the past 17 years, and he has found a remarkable trend. Sunspot magnetism is on the decline."[14]

The familiar solar cycle had changed completely by 2010, with a record-breaking solar tsunami that was even more surprising than the unheralded X9-class flare in the solar minimum. NASA News reported in December 2010 a global eruption that had rocked the sun on August 1.

"On August 1, 2010, an entire hemisphere of the sun erupted. Filaments of magnetism snapped and exploded, shock waves raced across the stellar surface, billion-ton clouds of hot gas billowed into space. Astronomers knew they had witnessed something big. It was so big, it may have shattered old ideas about solar activity.

"'The August 1st event really opened our eyes,' says Karel Schrijver of Lockheed Martin's Solar and Astrophysics Lab in Palo Alto, CA. "'We see that solar storms can be global events, playing out on scales we scarcely imagined before.'"[15]

Gigantic eruptions in 2006 and 2010 that stirred NASA's fervor were peculiar to the sun's phase shift that TimeStar predicted in 2002, and the solar maximum fizzled. After spectacular eruptions inspired scientific prophecies of dramatic activity to come, solar activity dwindled to extraordinary low levels and the sun's magnetic poles failed to reverse in2014. NASA issued a baffling news release in June 2014 announcing that the solar maximum had finally arrived based on the number of sunspots. NASA did not comment on the magnetic field and poles in the cryptic news release on June 10, 2014.[16]

NASA's predictions for future solar activity range from reserved to silent. None of its scientists commented on the possibility of a radical change in a solar phase shift, which TimeStar posits could extend to a total change in the sun's magnetic poles. The Sun could shift from a dipolar (a north and a south pole) star to quadrapolar (two magnetic north and two magnetic south poles).

Milky Way

A dense gas cloud called G2 has been approaching the galactic center (GC) on an elliptical orbit since 2006. Initially predicted to approach the GC in July 2013, new observations now predict the cloud to approach the GC in March 2014. Paul La Violette writes about the G2 cloud and an energetic superwave in his blog:

> "I have looked at literature that has been published about this cloud, have considered all aspects carefully, and have reached the conclusion that this encounter could very well initiate an energetic flare from the Galaxy's core as astronomers predict, but that this will likely not be powerful enough to produce a superwave. That is, it will not be sufficiently energetic to launch a cosmic ray volley that could locally overpower the interstellar magnetic field and allow long-range flight of the cosmic rays out of our Galaxy's nuclear bulge. Also, if it were able to release cosmic rays along rectilinear trajectories towards us and produce a superwave, I don't believe that the consequences would pose any kind of health hazard. Although there is a rather remote possibility (which I cannot presently rule out) that such a superwave may be a Magnitude 1 superwave that carries an electromagnetic pulse (EMP) and geomagnetic disturbance similar to a Carrington solar flare event, one that would be able to disrupt our electrical grid and satellite communication systems. Also a magnitude 1 event could possibly cause significant seismic activity similar to the December 2004 tsunami event that struck two days before our satellites registered the largest Galactic gamma ray burst in modern history. But these more serious EMP and gravity wave consequences should occur only if the G2 cloud break-up and consumption occurred quickly, as we will discuss below.

> "One question that comes to mind is whether the G2 cloud has been orbiting the GC for some time. Its orbit is observed to have a period of 138 ± 11 years and we see that no unusual cosmic or auroral effects took place on Earth back in 1875. However, it seems that astronomers have come to conclude that it is making its first pass toward the Galactic center and that this cloud somehow originated for the first time around 1944 in the vicinity of the ring of blue giant

stars that orbits the Galactic Center. So this may be the cloud's first close encounter with the GC. Whether there have been similar close encounters in the past centuries or millennia is left to speculation. Our ability to track such objects in the vicinity of the GC came into play mainly in the past decade. This G2 cloud was first discovered in 2006."[17],[18]

As greater reach into the galaxy is made with advancing technology, Western science assigns unique names and language to newly observed phenomena, even though observations may be identical to those the ancients made. Solar cycles and climate radically changed in the twentieth century, after the Maunder Minimum mini age ended in the mid-nineteenth century. Changes in the solar cycle and climate continued to climb to new levels with the end of the Mayan Long Count in 2012. The Hindu yugas posited profound changes in energetic potentials as the solar systems moved closer to the great center in 1899. Western science raced to keep pace with theory to explain the changing solar cycle and observations of the galaxy. Although the Maya and Hindu had predicted much that Western science observed, Westerners prefer their own language applied to the precepts and concepts they like.

Advanced galactic-solar astronomy is implicit in ancient calendars associated with ancestors from the stars, as extrapolated in "Ages of Humankind," Chapter Two. The ancient scientists that seeded and tended early life on Earth had mastered sciences that enabled them to settle and evolve life systems on distant planets. They communicated to the younger species on Earth with symbolism and allegory that integrated complex systems with principles that spanned multiple levels of understanding.

To tap the benefits that humanity's ancestors passed forward — the inheritance of modern civilization — we must meet them by understanding the worldviews and motives that guide them. These are embedded in the whole cloth of indigenous sciences that bring together designs of human and planetary life as it is experienced on the Earth.

Notes

[1] When Ida Kannenberg planned in 1998 the books she would compile in the coming ten years, she sent to me a box of notes she had made in three decades of contact with the time travelers, but did not think she would

need. Among the notes were the explanation of the levels on which humans experience time and an extraordinary explanation of holographic projectors dated in 1977, in the infancy of holographic technology. Ida had never heard of a hologram and suspected the time travelers were playing a joke on her, when she sent the notes to me in 1998. After her death in 2010, I retrieved the chapter on the brain and holographic projectors and restored it in correct chronological sequence in her book, *Time Travelers from Atlantis*.

[2] Marden, Kathleen, Denise M. Stoner and Stanton Friedman. 2013. *The Alien Abduction Files: The Most Startling Cases of Human Alien Contact Ever Reported.*" Pompton Plains, NJ: Career Press, New Page Books.

[3] Marden, Kathleen and Denise Stoner. 2013. *The Alien Abduction Files.* pp 45-70

[4] Stoner, Dennis M. Special interview on Dreamland radio. June 21, 2013. www.unknowncountry.com

[5] Kannenberg, Ida M. 2013. *My Brother Is a Hairy Man: The Search for Bigfoot.* Atlantis Phoenix Books: Missoula, MT. pp 82-84

[6] Maez is the Arcturian monitor for Bigfoot on Earth, who contacted Ida Kannenberg when began working with an investigator seeking physical evidence for the species. In their discussions, Maez explained Bigfoot's origin and purpose to monitor conditions on Earth. Survival of the endangered species was Maez's overriding interest in the contact.

[7] Duran, Krsanna. 1994. "Magnetic Change Mapped in Kennewick Crop Circle." *All Star Roundup.com: Crop Circles.* www.allstarroundup.com/cc/cckennewick.html

[8] Duran, Krsanna. 2012. "America's East Coast." *All Star Roundup.com: Crop Circles.* www.allstarroundup.com/cc/ccohio9-2012.html

[9] Duran, Krsanna. 2012. "Bracciano Crop Circle: Solar Wind and Earthquake Spree." *All Star Roundup:.com Crop Circles.* www.allstarroundup.com/cc/ccbracciano5-20-12.html

[10] All attributions to Linda Moulton Howe are documented in her database available to subscribers at Earthfiles.com.

[11] Howe, Linda Moulton. "Persistent Sinkholes and Unexplained Booms."

Earthfiles.com
www.earthfiles.com/news.php?ID=2087&category=Environment

[12] NASA News. "Solar Storm Warning." March 10, 2006.
science.nasa.gov/science-news/science-at-nasa/2006/10mar_stormwarning/

[13] NASA News. "Solar Flare Surprise." December 15, 2008.
science1.nasa.gov/science-news/science-at-nasa/2008/15dec_solarflaresurprise/

[14] NASA News. "Are Sunspots Disappearing?" September 3, 2009.
science1.nasa.gov/science-news/science-at-nasa/2009/03sep_sunspots/

[15] NASA News. "Global Eruption Rocks the Sun." December 13, 2010.
science.nasa.gov/science-news/science-at-nasa/2010/13dec_globaleruption/

[16] NASA News. Solar Mini-Max. June 10, 2014.
http://science.nasa.gov/science-news/science-at-nasa/2014/10jun_solarminimax/

[17] La Violette, Paul. 1997. *Earth Under Fire*. Starlane Publications: Schenectady, NY. pp 150-152
_____"Close Approach of Cloud G2 Around July 2013. Starburst Foundation. starburstfound.org/superwaveblog/?p=246

[18] Gillessen, S., etal. "A gas cloud on its way towards the super-massive black hole in the Galactic Centre." Nature journal. December 14, 2011. 10.1038/nature10652

CHAPTER FIVE

Mystery Ancestors

Mystery humans spiced up ancients' sex life.
Nature international weekly journal of science[1]

Security in one's place in the scheme of life and cosmos is so important to the human mind that every clan, tribe, and civilization has a creation story to explain its existence. As a creational motif, the leaps that Charles Darwin took in his theory of evolution served the same psychological need in science as Spider Woman did for the Hopi. Darwin and the Hopi observed the world within their perceptual spectrum and articulated explanations for context. His creational motifs filled the need to explain human existence in the vast web of life and cosmos that was acceptable to Darwin's peers, as the Hopi had done in another era. A Victorian notion of libido in the guise of natural selection pinned down Darwin's theory. Rapid acceptance of his theory is a measure of the social mind in Darwin's day.

New discoveries and improved science have rocked scientific theories about human origins since 2008, when the Denisova species was discovered in Siberia.

> "The ancient genomes, one from a Neanderthal and one from a member of an archaic human group called the Denisovans . . . suggest that interbreeding went on between the members of several ancient human-like groups in Europe and Asia more than 30,000 years ago, including an as-yet-unknown human ancestor from Asia. . . ."we're looking at a *Lord of the Rings*-type world — that there were many hominid populations," says Mark Thomas, an evolutionary geneticist at University College London . . ."[2]

The Denisovans, as it turns out, are relatives of a 400,000-year-old species discovered in Europe, the oldest known immediate human ancestor, or hominin. Discovered in the Sima de los Huesos cave in Spain and studied at the Max Planck Institute for Evolutionary Biology, the Sima fossil was likely related to an ancestor shared by both Denisovans and Neanderthals. Alternatively, a third group — a mystery ancestor — introduced the Denisovan-like genes into the Sima group.[3]

In an epic science chase, Dr. Melba Ketchum and The Erickson Project announced in 2012 that Sasquatch, also known as Bigfoot, is a novel human species with a mystery ancestor. (See the Erickson Project's press release in the notes.) Collecting Bigfoot DNA samples ranged from difficult to very difficult until recently. A wildlife biologist with The Erickson Project established trust with a juvenile Bigfoot he called Matilda in recent years, and obtained both DNA samples and videos to document them. These were among 111 samples that forensic DNA lab director and veterinarian Melba Ketchum used in the landmark study.[4] As with the Denisovans, she found the human genome in Bigfoot's maternal line, the mitochondrial DNA (mtDNA). Bigfoot's ancestral daddy is dramatically missing from all known genome sequences.

A storm of protest arguing that Bigfoot is sheer myth, an ape, or the relic of an extinct species followed at virtual warp speed. Caught in controversy over unauthorized early announcement of the study conducted in her DNA lab, Melba Ketchum answered questions and spoke about the study's protocols in radio interviews in 2012. She explained the study had not been officially released when an enthusiastic Russian scientist prematurely broke the news.

Dr. Ketchum's Bigfoot's DNA findings based on next generation sequencing are in-line with discoveries about mystery human ancestors. Validation of her findings by outside labs and universities didn't save the project from scathing criticism. After a science journal reviewed and accepted the study, the publisher informed Dr. Ketchum that an attorney had advised him not to publish it. Sounding a louder alarm, the attorney threatened to quit the journal if it published the Sasquatch study. Dr. Ketchum purchased the journal and renamed it *DeNovo Accelerating Science*, then published the study in its inaugural issue on February 13, 2013.[5] Review of the DNA study by other scientists continued, and Larry H. Swenson, Emeritus Professor and Chair of Chemistry at Saginaw Valley State University in Michigan, affirmed the study's findings:

> "I went over the manuscript by Melba Ketchum on Bigfoot genomics. My desktop had difficulty with a blast analysis of the consensus sequences. It helped me understand more about the project.

This collaborative venture has done a huge project that taxes me to fully grasp. I see interesting homology with a standard human sequence with 99% match for mitochondria. From my abbreviated study, the nuclear genome seems to have human and nonhuman sequences. My opinion of the creature is that it is a hybrid of a human mother and an unknown hominid male, just as reported. For all practical purposes, it should be treated as human and protected under law."[6]

With verified dates for early human ancestors and DNA for a mystery ancestor identified to fill the "missing link" gap, we can compare what is now known with non-traditional data.

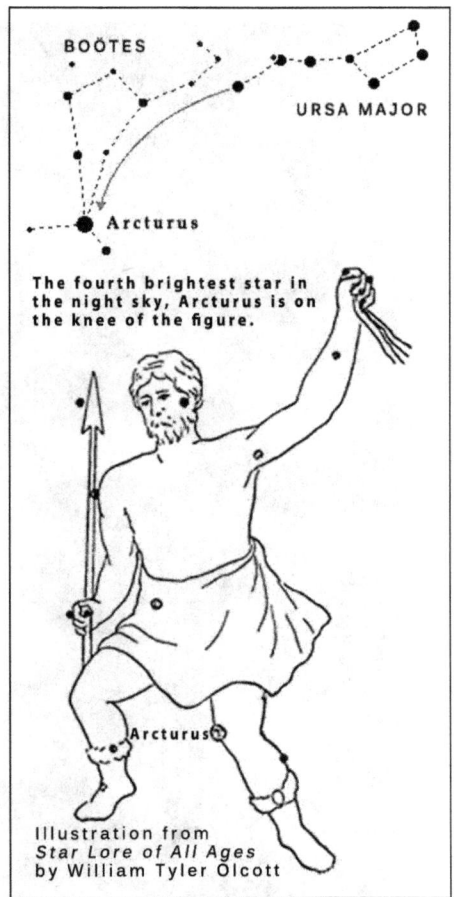

The fourth brightest star in the night sky, Arcturus is on the knee of the figure.

Illustration from *Star Lore of All Ages* by William Tyler Olcott

Arcturian Genesis

In post-modern UFO contacts, Arcturus emerges as the home of true human ancestors. The proto-human genes of Arcturus were mixed with other species for seeding early human species that include Bigfoot, which were the first intellectualized species of Lemuria. Arcturians were among the founders of Lemuria, and subsequently mentored time travelers from Atlantis to move in time directly to the nexus for the twenty-first century.

Located in the Boötes constellation, Arcturus is fourth brightest star in the night sky, with a long and bountiful history among indigenous peoples. The constellation was commonly called Arcturus in the ancient Near East, honoring the orange giant star only 36.7 light-years from Earth. Arcturus is named the "yoke," or Shudan, in the Babylonian Star Catalogue. The Sleeping Prophet Edgar Cayce named very few stars

Bigfoot rendering by Hartmut Jager.

in 14,000 readings, but he described Arcturus as the center of the Sun's orbit and a star gate several times.[7] Arcadia, the pre-Greek home of the Orphic mysteries, knew Arcturus as the "guardian of the bear," who protected its founder, Arca. Polynesian navigators knew Arcturus as "the star of joy" (Hōkūle'a) and used it to navigate the Pacific.

In communications with Ida Kannenberg between 1998 and 2000, Maez, Bigfoot's Arcturian monitor, explained the reasoning for introducing their human strain on Earth.[8] Ancestors from Arcturus anciently lived on Earth, and, when considering returning, they bred Bigfoot to test and monitor planetary conditions. Soon after Bigfoot, they introduced Neanderthals, who interbred with other human species and are forebears of modern humans. The Denisova inhabited a cave in the Altai Mountains in Siberia circa 40,000 years before present, which Neanderthal and modern humans also inhabited.

New discoveries about mystery ancestors expand the potentials of human and Bigfoot genesis that Maez had revealed to Kannenberg. The Arcturian explained mystery ancestors, human and Bigfoot genesis, and capabilities fifteen years before the Max Planck Institute and Dr. Ketchum announced their findings in 2013. The paradigm-changing studies affirmed points the Arcturian had explained. Very importantly, no scientific discovery since 1998 directly contradicts Maez's talking points in dialogs with Kannenberg.

Maez's rendition is a viable contender for explaining human genesis. It provides a baseline to compare with known data for a larger perspective that expands the mind of the species. As we humans map new dimensions of our genesis, we expand the species' mind with knowledge and experience that activates deep potentials inherited from the star ancestors.

November 1998

"**Maez to Ida:** However, you are right that Bigfoot was developed on a base of *Australopithecus africanus*. Then he was genetically engineered with genes of the Arcturian Masters to develop the several variations of Bigfoot alive in the world today. There are only small differences in Bigfoot in various countries to adapt them to the environment in which they live. Their adaptations to various climatic and environmental conditions have further distinguished them from one another, but all come from the same original base of *Australopithecus africanus* [abbreviated to *A.a.*]. Your scientists will presently reorganize their identification base as new discoveries are made.

"Bigfoot was engineered to live in remote and undeveloped areas. His greatest safety device is the speed and ease with which he can change location and his ability to live off the environment wherever he might find himself. This means no possessions to load him down in transit and no permanent home to tie him to a location that might be discovered and staked out for capture. You may well envy Bigfoot his complete freedom, his blending with his environment, and his ability to concentrate on the basic values of life.

"The first Bigfoot was brought to Planet Earth before there were any *Homo s.* or *neanderthalensis*. His purpose was to discover if such modern men could live here. That is why he was given *Homo s.*' characteristics, genes, brain capacities, intuition, and sensitivities. He is, in essence, borderline human.

"Yes, we Arcturians were instrumental in bringing a race of *Homo s.* to Earth, but let us save this story for another time. We want you to understand, accept Bigfoot first, while there is still time to save this unusual and rare species from extinction on Earth. He has served well and earned the right to be protected and aided in his current problems and distress.

"Learn to accept and live with him.

"Yes, Sitchin's stories of the origin of modern man are 90% correct.[9] Any embroidery was in the texts from which he copied, but there are correlative facts which have not yet been revealed and in which we played a major role. Do not discount Sitchin. He wrote courageous and bona fide books. . . .[10]

"**Maez to Ida:** So we have been discussing the possibility of *A.a.* being the more "animal" base of Bigfoot. Believe me, he was, though how you guessed that I'll never know.

"Yes, your scientists have some specimens of *A.a.*, which they believe are about 3 million years and others they date at 1,000,750. Some believe this latter was the first real tool-maker. As I said before, as more specimens are discovered there will be some minor changes in their opinions. Probably some major ones, also.

"We (Arcturians) began the use of *A.a.* a million and a half years ago. No, not I personally. Yes, we had the equivalent of *Homo sapiens sapiens* (abbreviated to *Homo s.s.*) to use, not an Earth species. Your present *Homo s.s.* did not originate from earth species. It is a mixture of various forefathers.

"We are the man-makers of Earth. Read your own book, *Project Earth*, the last few pages, and Sitchin also to see how varied the ancestry of present day Earth man really is!

"As long as a million and a half years ago our scientists were mixing and matching genes and DNA and other life requisites. Let's not get more deeply involved in this now. Enough for today . . .

"**Maez to Ida:** A bit more about the manufacturing of Bigfoot. Even this kind of genetic experimentation takes a long, long time. We started a million and a half of your years ago and continued hundreds of thousands of years before present. Experimental creatures were allowed to live out their long life spans, but gradually we learned how to overcome certain problems in their reproduction cycles. We wanted them to be able to reproduce themselves before we sent them to Earth ***and other planets***. [Emphasis added.]

"Slightly less than three hundred thousand years ago our perfected species was sent to Earth to check out the living conditions. There are energies being emitted from the Earth itself that you are not yet aware of. Some of them are detrimental to your welfare. You will eventually learn how to protect yourselves. Places where there are sulphur springs are the most evident.

"Our Bigfoot took to Earth like a duck to water, and he and his descendants have been there ever since.

"The engineered Bigfoot lived thousands of years. They did not have a built-in obsolescence. After their Earth-born offspring were well established, we brought the original back to Arcturus. Unfortunately, they had been engineered for different climate and environmental living conditions and one by one they succumbed. The Bigfoot on Earth live two or sometimes into their third hundredth year. The increasing crud in your air shortens their lives unmercifully now. They are in actual danger of becoming extinct. Your people hunting them down and creating living problems for them does not help

"You ask where did we get the *Homo s.* species to cross with Bigfoot? The same place we got it to develop *Homo s.s.* on Earth. It was for the latter that Bigfoot was developed to test the Earth. *Homo s.s.* is from ourselves. Did we not tell you once that "our roots are the same"? A great deal of what was told to you and which you printed in your book *Project Earth* referred to us. All the information that Hweig & Co. read off to you so patiently and which you copied down so patiently was prepared by myself and my helpers. Arcturus is the Planet X as you labeled it. Tea Elsta was a name Hweig gave it, since you insisted on a name. It is not our original one. Your star map calls it Arcturus in the Boötes constellation.

"Now you ask, how does this fit in with Sitchin's story of the origin of Earth people? Neatly, very neatly. I don't want to spend time on this now, but your question deserves an answer. The Annunaki of the Twelfth Planet established their Adamic race in what you call to-

Mother of Gods

Mother Goddess at Teotihuacan, with a human head emerging from her midsection and displaying four hands, echoes a totem at Gobekli Tepe in Turkey, the oldest ritual center in world. The Gobekli Tepe totem displays a human head inset into her midsection, four hands, and a serpent rising on each side of her body. At Teotihuacan, serpents drape the mother of gods' body, which is netted in a web that was a signature design at Teotihuacan. Kali, the Black Earth Mother of the indigenous Tamil in India, had four arms in her earliest incarnation but was later depicted with ten arms.

Kali, the Great Divine Mother with four arms, empowers with primordial cosmic energy, or shakti, in Hinduism. She represents dynamic forces that move through the entire universe. She is encircled by a ring of flames and her skirt is tied with serpentine forms that extend on each side of her body in the above statue. She holds a trident that her consort Shiva displays at Benares, one of the most sacred and oldest continuously occupied cities of in the world. Revered by the indigenous Tamil peoples, she was known as the Black Earth Mother in her earliest incarnation. Calcutta in the Bengal district is Kali's namesake. (Statue by Lotus Sculpture.)

Gobekli Tepe Totem

A human head surmounted by four arms is set into the mid-section of a totem at the oldest ritual center in the world at Gobekli Tepe in Turkey. A serpent rises on each side of the totem to cradle the human head between the flattened heads of the serpents in a protective position, which was seen with the Buddha 7,500 years after Gobekli Tepe was inexplicably abandoned circa 10,000 years ago.

day "the Middle East" — Sumeria (today's Iraq) and the lands between there and Egypt and into Africa.

"We, the Arcturians, established our race in the West. You call it Lemuria and the western areas of the United States, although it spread rapidly into what is now Canada, Mexico, Central and South America.

"East is East and the West is West but it is time the twain get together peaceably and stop killing each other.

"We sent the original Bigfoot throughout the whole world but sent our developed strain of *Homo s.s.* to Lemuria and the West. There is not much point in writing much about this until your people are ready to accept the reality of Lemuria. (James Churchward should also be taken very seriously.)

"Let us get back to our subject, Bigfoot as developed from Earth's *A.a.* and our own strain of *Homo s.s.*

"Our scientists felt that to persevere in the wild conditions of Earth against large animals and severe climatic conditions Bigfoot should be very strong physically, large and bulky as you see him today (when you do). Since he does not use tools other than sticks or stones or make permanent shelters other than rocky crevices or clumps of trees or bushes, he must be nearly impervious to cold or immersion in water and other conditions that would quickly kill a man. His extraordinary physicality coupled with a very large brain keeps him alive. He is extremely intelligent, but innocent. His lack of sophistication and an awareness of that fact make him wary of close contact with humans. He just doesn't understand your ways of double-dealing. They are entirely foreign to him.

"**Ida to Maez:** I am confused. You said you chose the finest of the anthropoid line to begin your genetic experiments that eventually led to *Australopithecus* and Bigfoot and still later to us. Yet you say we did not evolve from the ape. That leaves me confused.

"**Maez to Ida:** ...From 1.5 million to 150,000 before present, we the people of the Arcturus system, worked on problems of genetic engineering. We nearly engineered ourselves out of existence. When we woke up to what we were doing there were only a few thousand of our original kind of people left but many experimental types of cyborgs and those we used as workers. Slaves would be a more exact designation but that word always sends you into a moral fit, so we will call them workers.

"We had drawn a great deal of the animal component of our biological structuring from Earth, for which we had a special intention. That is why your people have indeed seen reptilian and other animalistic creatures.

"We soon discovered that *A.a.* was the most promising of the evolutionary strain advancing toward a rational self-thinking creature, so we used him in many ways. By crossing him with our master genes we came up with Bigfoot. The original was a cross of "true man" as we consider ourselves (using your terminology) and the "not-yet" man or *A.a.* It was a long and tedious experiment to find a perfected specimen that could not only explore Earth from one end to the other over millennia but could intelligently report back in such a manner that we could use the information we had sent him to collect. Bigfoot had enough of Earth inheritance to make his explorations there feasible, and enough of our intelligence to make his observations pertinent to our needs.

"We saw it would be greatly to our advantage if Bigfoot could reproduce himself on Earth once we had perfected the exact type of creature that we needed. Reproduction problems proved a great time devourer, just as trying to get your mules to reproduce their own kind would prove to you. Genetic engineering was not a feat handed to us. We had to work it all out for ourselves over many hundreds of years.

"The original Bigfoot had inbuilt communication abilities as well as extensive "psychic" talents that the earth-born gradually lost. We have to use implants with them now just as we do with you. Perhaps the greatly truncated life span of these latter (a couple hundred years compared to the original several thousand) is the reason their psychic abilities do not fully develop. Each succeeding generation of the Earth-born will recapture more of these abilities but it will be a slow inch by inch process. No doubt there will be a "genius" Bigfoot born now and then who will break through the time wall and show unusual psychic abilities, just as happens in your own race. It is a projected inheritance from the past for both of you. Let's not dig deeper into such technicalities now, there is too much else to report and it must be revealed in logical and understandable sequence. You have been given too many incoherent bits and pieces up to now. It will only seem "real" or at least "possible" when you see it altogether in proper order...

"...'There is a time for sowing and a time for reaping'? This is the time to put together for you a coherent picture of what we have been about.

"This is as good a place as any to explain Hweig's description of Bigfoot to you as it appeared in *Project Earth,* page 163.[11]

"**Hweig:** Sasquatch is indeed their (Planet X's) creatures let out upon Earth to test energies from the ground on Earth itself. We do not recognize these energies although they work upon us, sometimes quite detrimentally. Sasquatch is not an ape and not human, but a biological creation about halfway between the two, with no biological connection to either. It is not a missing link. The creatures are mild unless

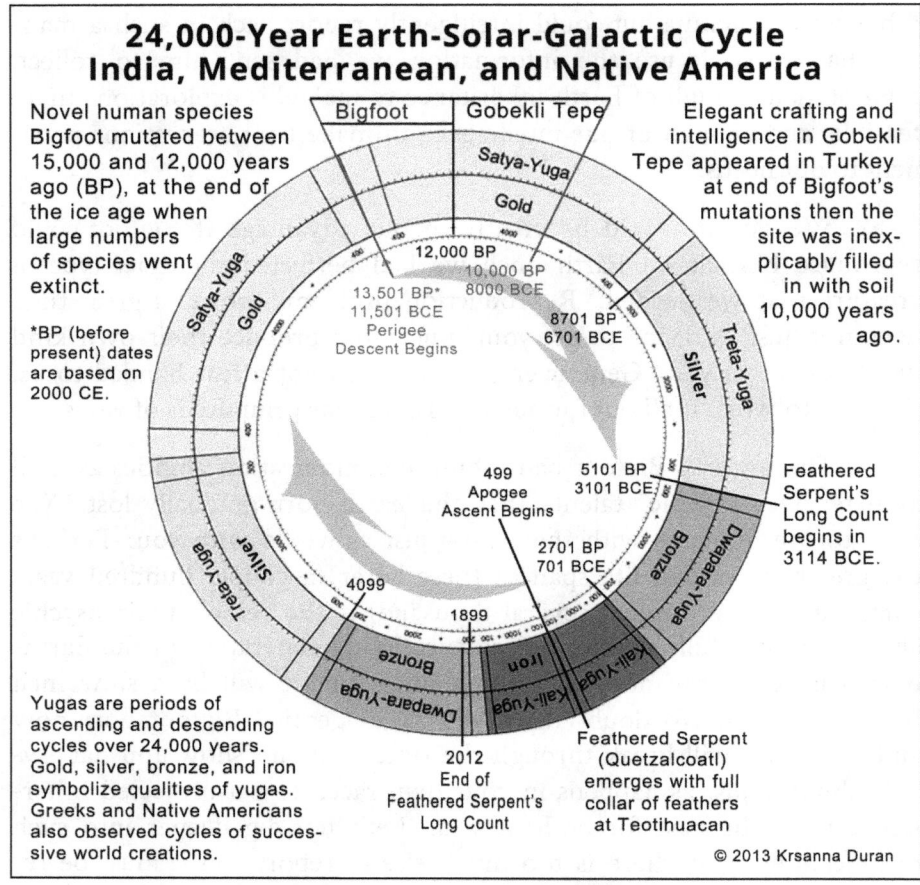

startled when with their young. They have been unloaded here for years, and now have acclimated and orientated themselves. They do have offspring, but rarely. They are monitored by pictorial telepathy."

"**Maez:** When Hweig reported that there was no biological connection to either ape or human, he was referring to the fact that the first Bigfoot was generated hundreds of centuries before your-kind of human existed on earth although you and Bigfoot were built from our genes which we consider "true humanity". Only a small fraction, twenty percent, of Bigfoot's genes was ours - the genes of you of Earth were given a much greater portion. About eighty percent of your genes are from the Arcturian source...

"A million and a half years seems a very long time from your viewpoint but it was scarcely enough from ours to create our Bigfoot person from the genetic elements of *A.a.* and our own genes. Yes, we think of him as a person for he has intelligence and personality befitting a human inside that hairy animalistic exterior. Yes, of course he has a soul!

"Less than 300,000 years ago — your time — we had perfected our creature enough to send him to Earth on the mission for which he was created. The original lived several thousand years *and we kept on perfecting and issuing improved stock.*

"Our purpose was to find good living areas on Earth that would support our original human type, which is similar to your *Homo s.s.* of today. There is perhaps an eighty percent similarity.

"Bigfoot was sent to every area of Earth, most of which was considerably different than it is today. There have been innumerable and great changes.

"Long before 200,000 B.C. (your time) we sent our first true human representatives to Earth on the now-sunken continent you call Lemuria.

"All our first true human explorers were androgynes. They observed the matings of Earth's various creatures and decided to increase their own numbers by propagation. There were so few left on the home planet they did not want to risk all those lives in the unprecedented adventure.

"As androgynes they had no experience in mating or birthing, although they had the necessary requisites. They now divided themselves, not by splitting physically, but by each choosing to differentiate himself by sex, male or female. Since most chose the male role, not many births resulted. So they also chose to mate with the "fairest" of the proto-humans they found on Earth.

"At first they tried to keep their own race pure, but gradually it inter-mixed with the secondary strain that resulted from mating with the Earth stock.

"The more nearly pure strain eventually resulted in Cro-Magnon. The proto-human mixture led to Neanderthal.

"In the meantime Bigfoot continued his task of investigating the four corners of the Earth and reporting.

"So now we had three strains of nearly fully Earth humans: Bigfoot, a borderline human; *neanderthalensis* [Neanderthal], a *Homo sapiens*, and Cro-Magnon type *Homo sapiens sapiens (Homo s.s.).* These three were all together on the continent you call Lemuria.

"Most of the cross-bred humans were brought back to Lemuria as their original purpose had been to help us colonize our new country. These new "citizens" were mostly from the Levantine corridor and were several strains in the neighborhood of *Homo erectus*.

"We selected their young carefully for further inter-mixing and in a few generations had handsome and intelligent members of our expanding communities. Our rejects were taken back to the Levantine corridor and allowed to inter-breed there.

"Where else would the rapid advance in brain size and body stature come from than an outside source? In less than a hundred thousand years, an advance in human evolution occurred that had never been equaled in millions of years. Why else the sudden spurt?

"No more now on the human evolution. Your next book will carry that subject forward. Let us get back now to Bigfoot although their histories do intertwine.

"Bigfoot continued to carry out his original task of reporting environmental conditions and other facts as time went on. He became, in fact, a super-spy on the fast increasing human population. His abilities were too useful to us to free him entirely from our supervision. We have continued to rely on him to this day. He reports on every new logging or mining enterprise and on all new sports resorts that bring many people into the forests and wilderness areas. We have other means of gaining knowledge of industrial and urban activities, but for the wild country Bigfoot is indispensable. *Yes! We consider the Western Hemisphere our property!*

"And we watch with growing concern and impatience what is happening to it! As long as it was occupied by the people we brought into it, the land and its creatures were cherished and treated with respect. When it was flooded with newcomers from the East — well, there went the neighborhood! . . .

"**Maez to Ida:** The mating with the "fairest daughters of the Earth" took place — on our part — among those occupying the Levantine corridor. Yes, even around the country where Jesus was to be born, though that has no particular significance here that I can see.

"These 'girls' were a mixture of various evolutionary advances toward *Homo erectus*. The genes of our adventurers simply speeded up the processes of development toward Neanderthal and *Homo s.*, our own pure offspring stayed in the Western Hemisphere.

"You ask, 'how did the mixture get to Lemuria from the Levantine?' We were not without aerial transportation. We had craft that would go through the air or under the water with equal ease; these were not space ships. We will soon go into an explanation of these; for now just accept them as fact.

"Transport anywhere in the world was easy. Yes, even during the ice age."[12]

APPENDIX

The Erickson Project
Sasquatch the Quest

PRESS RELEASE

Through the years, the Erickson Project has collected and funded testing of a number of Sasquatch DNA samples from various geographical areas of North America at a variety of DNA labs in Canada and the United States. Even though the results of those mitochondrial tests all came back human, namely 'Eastern European' Adrian Erickson and Dennis Pfohl were convinced that the samples were from Sasquatch and not 'contaminated' by humans.

When yet another scientist related to Erickson that a different sample tested at the University of New York (one of the labs the Erickson Project had also used) also came back as 'Eastern European' the scientist dismissed it as human. At that point, however, Erickson knew he was on the right track and needed to test further. He contacted and started to collaborate with Dr. Ketchum and provided her with his samples and the previous DNA results in order to continue testing. As the study expanded Erickson supplied much of the initial funding of Dr. Ketchum's study, which was more in-depth and involved nuclear DNA. This study was completed after five years.

The Erickson Project is a contributor of six Sasquatch DNA samples to Dr. Ketchum's study, all from diverse areas, one of those samples was used to sequence a complete Sasquatch genome in Dr. Ketchum's study. Specific information on the role of The Erickson Project will be released when her manuscript is published; this will be posted on this website.[13]

UPDATES

Dr. Ketchum's press release about upcoming publication of her manuscript:

'BIGFOOT' DNA SEQUENCED IN UPCOMING GENETICS STUDY

Five-Year Genome Study Yields Evidence of Homo sapiens/Unknown Hominin Hybrid Species in North America

DALLAS, Nov. 24 [2012]

A team of scientists can verify that their 5-year long DNA study, currently under peer-review, confirms the existence of a novel hominin hybrid species, commonly called "Bigfoot" or "Sasquatch," living in North America. Researchers' extensive DNA sequencing suggests that the legendary Sasquatch is a human relative that arose approximately 15,000 years ago as a hybrid cross of modern Homo sapiens with an unknown primate species.

The study was conducted by a team of experts in genetics, forensics, imaging and pathology, led by Dr. Melba S. Ketchum of Nacogdoches, TX. In response to recent interest in the study, Dr. Ketchum can confirm that her team has sequenced three complete Sasquatch nuclear genomes and determined the species is a human hybrid:

"Our study has sequenced 20 whole mitochondrial genomes and utilized next generation sequencing to obtain 3 whole nuclear genomes from purported Sasquatch samples. The genome sequencing shows that Sasquatch mtDNA is identical to modern Homo sapiens, but Sasquatch nuDNA is a novel, unknown hominin related to Homo sapiens and other primate species. Our data indicate that the North American Sasquatch is a hybrid species, the result of males of an unknown hominin species crossing with female Homo sapiens.

Hominins are members of the taxonomic grouping Hominini, which includes all members of the genus Homo. Genetic testing has already ruled out Homo neanderthalis and the Denisova hominin as contributors to Sasquatch mtDNA or nuDNA. "The male progenitor that contributed the unknown sequence to this hybrid is unique as its DNA is more distantly removed from humans than other recently discovered hominins like the Denisovan individual," explains Ketchum.

"Sasquatch nuclear DNA is incredibly novel and not at all what we had expected. While it has human nuclear DNA within its genome, there are also distinctly non-human, non-archaic hominin, and non-ape sequences. We describe it as a mosaic of human and novel non-human sequence. Further study is needed and is ongoing to better characterize and understand Sasquatch nuclear DNA."

Ketchum is a veterinarian, whose professional experience includes 27 years of research in genetics, including forensics. Early in her career she also practiced veterinary medicine, and she has previously been published as a participant in mapping the equine genome. She began testing the DNA of purported Sasquatch hair samples 5 years ago.

Ketchum calls on public officials and law enforcement to recognize immediately the Sasquatch as an indigenous people:

"Genetically, the Sasquatch is a human hybrid with unambiguously modern human maternal ancestry. Government at all levels must recognize them as an indigenous people and immediately protect their human and Constitutional rights against those who would see in their physical and cultural differences a 'license' to hunt, trap, or kill them."

Full details of the study will be presented in the near future when the study manuscript publishes.

Notes

[1] Callaway, Ewen. "Mystery humans spiced up ancients' sex life." *Nature international weekly journal of science.* 19 November 2013.
doi:10.1038/nature.2013.14196
http://www.nature.com/news/mystery-humans-spiced-up-ancients-sex-lives-1.14196

[2] Ibid

[3] Matthias Meyer, Qiaomei Fu, Ayinuer Aximu-Petri, Isabelle Glocke, Birgit Nickel, Juan-Luis Arsuaga, Ignacio Martínez, Ana Gracia, José María Bermúdez de Castro, Eudald Carbonell, Svante Pääbo. "A mitochondrial genome sequence of a hominin from Sima de los Huesos." *Nature international weekly journal of science,* 4 December 2013; DOI: 10.1038/nature12788
http://www.nature.com/nature/journal/vaop/ncurrent/full/nature12788.html

[4]. The Erickson Project: The Sasquatch Quest
www.sasquatchthequest.com/.

[5]. Ketchum, M. S., P. W. Wojtkiewicz, A. B. Watts, D. W. Spence, A. K. Holzenburg, D. G. Toler, T. M. Prychitko, F. Zhang, S. Bollinger, R. Shoulders, R. Smith. "Novel North American Hominins, Next Generation Sequencing of Three Whole Genomes and Associated Studies." *The*

DeNovo. Special Edition. Volume 1, Issue 1, February 13, 2013. http://sasquatchgenomeproject.org/

[6]. Review posted on the *Sasquatch Genome Project* website.

[7] Mullaney, James. 2007. *Edgar Cayce and the Cosmos.* Virginia Beach, VA: A.R.E. Press. p 4, 24

[8] Kannenberg, Ida M. 2013. *My Brother Is a Hairy Man: The Search for Bigfoot.* Missoula, MT: Atlantis Phoenix Books. 114-120

[9] Zecharia Sitchin translated ancient Sumerian texts in a series of books entitled *The Earth Chronicles*. He extrapolated advanced science and technology displayed in Sumer with twentieth-century sciences and concluded the earliest Sumerian settlers were extraterrestrial colonists who mined gold on Earth.

[10] Sitchin, Zecharia. 1976. *The Twelfth Planet.*

As a young boy, Zecharia Sitchin encountered discrepancies between literal meanings of the Hebrew languages and euphemisms that denied literal meanings. *Nephilim* literally means *those who descended*, for example, but is commonly interpreted as *the giants* in Genesis 6. Sitchin was chastised for using the literal meaning of Nephilim as a schoolboy.

Sitchin made good on his objections to Hebraic translations after retiring and wrote the *Earth Chronicles*, first published in 1976, after UFO experiencers had introduced ancient astronauts who reported they were parent races of humanity. He was neither a UFO scholar nor experiencer. Sitchin wrote about Hebraic and Eastern cultures within the context of his Hebraic and Semitic education, with the ancient astronaut theme. Sitchin did not have any significant knowledge of Native America, its culture or the ancient Arcturian presence. He either overlooked or did not know the culture and history of Native America in an ancient global culture that existed long before Sumer.

[11] Kannenberg, Ida M. 2013. *Project Earth from the Extraterrestrial Perspective: Species and Mind.* Atlantis Phoenix Books: Missoula, MT. p 163

[12] Kannenberg, Ida M. 2013. *My Brother Is a Hairy Man: The Search for Bigfoot.* Atlantis Phoenix Books: Missoula, MT. pp 17-28

[13]. The Erickson Project: The Sasquatch Quest www.sasquatchthequest.com/

CHAPTER SIX

Web of Life

Delicately gossamer to the eye, Spider Woman's web is woven in stupendous power from the depths beyond common human sight. Mountains that appear solidly fixed in space and time to the human eye shear to emptiness with quantum observations.

"When you drill down into the core of even the most solid-looking material, separateness dissolves. All that remains, like the smile of the Cheshire Cat from Alice In Wonderland, are relationships extending curiously throughout space and time. These connections were predicted by quantum theory and were called 'spooky action at a distance' by Albert Einstein. Quantum mechanics approached the cardinal mystery of existence — the puzzle of how patterns of neuronal activity become transformed into subjective awareness — with ever smaller measurements. One of the founders of quantum theory, Erwin Schrödinger, dubbed this peculiarity entanglement, and said 'I would not call that one but rather the characteristic trait of quantum mechanics." (Dean Radin) [1]

The web that Spider Woman spun from her own substance to create life is a profoundly entangled weave of quantum interactions beyond the range of human vision. Deep connections of the web of life that all peoples recognize in some way or guise are explained with quantum physics in Western science. Observations of quantum mechanics made in numerous experiments lead the edge of discovery. In greatly simplified terms, quantum mechanics shows that the universe is an information network that is distinguished by four primary properties.[2]

Mother Goddess at Teotihuacan

A spider dances on a tree woven in a web design above the head of the Mother Goddess at Teotihuacan in the Tepantitle complex. She is plumed with a bird head and water flows from her human hands. The bird, jaguar and serpent were the first representations that evolved into Teotihuacan's Feathered Serpent with a full collar of feathers during the late Classical period. These three symbols were anciently used together worldwide. The bird represents elevation with flight, the feline represents secret knowledge, and the serpent is base physical energy of life that rises with enlightenment. The shamanic triad of bird, jaguar and serpent were used in Peru, before they appeared at Teotihuacan, according to George Kubler. The Olmec introduced the Feathered Serpent at La Venta circa 1000 BCE.

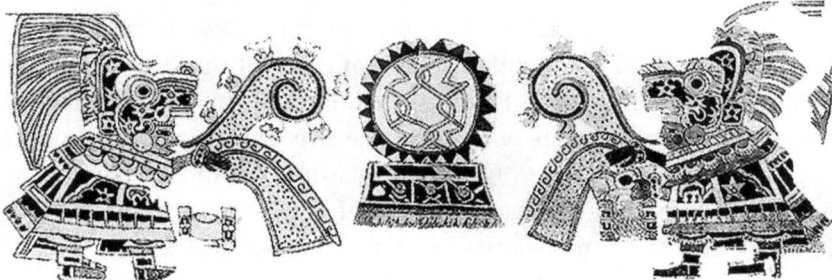

A netted web center mirroring the spider-filled tree surmounting the Mother Goddess at Teotihuacan. It is set in a disk surrounded with twenty-four rays. The five pointed star on the plumed headdresses emblemized the Feathered Serpent, from a Classic period Teotihuacan III.

Properties of the Quantum Web

Entanglement is the principle that subatomic particles that have been connected remain connected, or entangled. If something happens to one particle, regardless of how distant it is from an entangled particle, the other one immediately responds.

Coherence is alignment of particles or waves with each other. Focused laser light is coherent, for example, in contrast to light from random sources that is not coherent.

Non-Locality is instantaneously transportation of information between entangled particles, regardless of location. This challenges Einstein's idea that information does not move faster than the speed of light, but quantum mechanics has proven this is not true.

Resonance is the tendency of a system to move, or oscillate, at a certain rate or frequency. This results from the function of the wave, comparable to other waves such as water waves.

The ancients observed and espoused principles embodied in modernly emerging quantum mechanics in numerous theologies and geometries. In classical Eastern philosophy quantum mechanics expounds on the foundational principle and paradox of the universe, the *Tao*, observed by Lao Tzu in the *Tao te Ching*.[3]

> The Tao produced One; One produced Two; Two produced Three; Three produced All things. All things leave behind them the Obscurity (out of which they have come), and go forward to embrace the Brightness (into which they have emerged), while they are harmonised by the Breath of Vacancy.
> What men dislike is to be orphans, to have little virtue, to be as carriages without naves; and yet these are the designations, which kings and princes use for themselves. So it is that some things are increased by being diminished, and others are diminished by being increased.
> What other men (thus) teach, I also teach. The violent and strong do not die their natural death. I will make this the basis of my teaching.

The Theology of Arithmetic by fourth-century neo-Platonist Iamblichus, for example, employs propagation using ten numbers similar to the way the *Tao-te Ching* uses three numbers.[4] Plato, an initiate of the Egyptian mystery school, employed discourse, allegory and geometric metaphor. His contributions are as timely today as they were when his genius kindled the Rebirth of Europe in the sixteenth century. *Logos*, which Plato used in the gnostic sense to mean "the word remaining within" and the Stoics used for the generative or productive principle of the universe, remains pivotal to theories of intelligent design and observations of quantum mechanics.

Knowledge of ancient origins was lost with expansion of Rome's empire, which first consumed and then discarded memories of indigenous cultures. When Rome collapsed, indigenous infrastructures that had sustained local cultures had been dismantled and Europe fell into a Dark Age. When Plato's manuscripts began awakening Europe with the Renaissance, cultures of the indigenous people of Europe were obscured by ruins of the collapsed empire.

Rome's Inquisition against Galileo for finding that the Sun is the center of the solar system, which the Earth orbits, after viewing it with his telescope deeply affected Western science. In a void of indigenous sciences that had viewed the Sun as the governor of life on Earth, early scientists distanced themselves from Rome's religious bias. Science and religion were separated in Europe, which left it bereft of sacred sciences known to indigenous peoples worldwide.

Knowledge of ancestors from the stars was lost in both the religion and science of Europe. Anxiety about humanity's origin and place in the cosmos grew in the void left by lost knowledge.

The atomic bomb and environmental consequences hand-in-hand with the necessity of unifying physics and metaphysics, science and religion, were chief concerns of the earliest UFO contacts in the 1950s.

At UFO conventions George van Tassel sponsored at Giant Rock, California, UFOs made public appearances, "flying midway between the earth and the starry heaven," just as Homer had poetically portrayed Juno's ancient steeds in the *Iliad*. Van Tassel's UFO contactors, identified with the planet Venus, used symbolism of the Feathered Serpent of Mexico with contemporary terms for context of the contact. Van Tassel never discussed or showed awareness of the Feathered Serpent's historical importance in Mexico, but symbolism the UFO contactors used identified them with the Ancestors of Lemuria and Hyperborea. Giant Rock is in the area Lemurians anciently migrated to when their Pacific Islands began subsiding.

Cosmic Fire

The flame that rises in waters of life, cosmic fire is an intermediary between the physical realm and the celestial world.[5] In Hindu stories and legends of the Purânas, *Agni* is the *fire* that conveys the messages of gods. Agni is one of the three main gods of the Vedas that rises in primordial splendor. It is the first word of the first hymn of the first of the four Vedas.

The presence and flow of electric charge is one of Agni's aspects as electric fire. Electricity gives a wide variety of effects — lightning, static electricity, electromagnetic induction, and electrical current. In electricity, charges produce electromagnetic fields, which act on other charges. In addition, electricity permits the creation and reception of electromagnetic radiation such as radio waves.[6]

Memorializing Agni's awesome power, India named its first long-range strategic missile capable of delivering nuclear weapons, with accompanying electromagnetic pulses, Agni. The Electric Universe theory is based on properties of plasmas comprising 99.999% of the visible universe and natural electrical phenomena, e.g., lightning, St Elmo's Fire, etc., which react strongly to electromagnetic fields.

In the Purânas' tales, Agni's three sons represent his sustaining triumvirate:

1. Pavaka is the electric fire,
2. Pavamana the fire produced by friction, and
3. Suchi the solar fire.

Metaphorically these are "Spirit, Soul, and Body, the three great Root groups . . ." explained Helena Blavatsky

> "Every fire has a distinct function and meaning in the worlds of the physical and the spiritual. It has, moreover, in its essential nature a corresponding relation to one of the human psychic faculties, besides its well determined chemical and physical potencies when coming in contact with the terrestrially differentiated matter." [7]

Discussing the intelligence of *"man-bearing planets,"* the adept Koot Hoomi used the substratum of fire to exemplify the one permanent cause of all phenomena in 1882.

"... there is but one element and it is impossible to comprehend our system before a correct conception of it is firmly fixed in one's mind. You must therefore pardon me if I dwell on the subject longer than really seems necessary. But unless this great primary fact is firmly grasped the rest will appear unintelligible. This element then is the — to speak metaphysically — one sub-stratum or permanent cause of all manifestations in the phenomenal universe. The ancients speak of the five cognizable elements of ether, air, water, fire, earth, and of the one incognizable element (to the uninitiates) the sixth principle of the universe — call it Purush Sakti, while to speak of the seventh outside the sanctuary was punishable with death. But these five are but the differentiated aspects of the one. As man is a seven-fold being so is the universe — the septenary microcosm being to the septenary macrocosm but as the drop of rainwater is to the cloud from whence it dropped and whither in the course of time it will return. In that one are embraced or included so many tendencies for the evolution of air, water, fire, etc. (from the purely abstract down to their concrete condition) and when those latter are called elements it is to indicate their productive potentialities for numberless form changes or evolution of being. Let us represent the unknown quantity as X; that quantity is the one eternal immutable principle — and A, B, C, D, E, five of the six minor principles or components of the same; *viz.*, the principles of earth, water, air, fire and ether (*akasa*) following the order of their spirituality and beginning with the lowest. There is a sixth principle answering to the sixth principle *Buddhi*[8], in man (to avoid confusion remember that in viewing the question from the side of the descending scale the abstract All or eternal principle would be numerically designated as the first, and the phenomenal universe as the seventh, and whether belonging to man or to the universe — viewed from the other side the numerical order would be exactly reversed) but we are not permitted to name it except among the initiates. I may however hint that it is connected with the process of the highest intellection...

Tree of Life Fractal

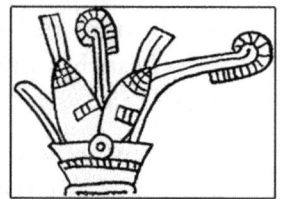

Oval Flint glyphs for Spark or Knife, rectangles used to measure, and wide leaves from the Sun Stone are repeated in branches stemming from tree in the Borgia Codex.

A tree of life formed with glyphs from the Sun Stone comprises a self-repeating fractal. An eagle surmounts the tree that also forms a vertical axis in concentric circles representing cycles of time in the Borgia Codex. On the left the Feathered Serpent (Quetzalcoatl) rises in unison with the Lord of Flowers and Life (Xochipilli) on the right. Concentric rings and glyphs in the Sun Stone were in use at least 400 years before the Aztecs migrated to the Mexico Valley. The Borgia Group of Codices, most closely associated with Teotihuacan, were scribed circa 900 CE. The "T"-shaped tree repeats the House glyph in the Sun Stone, the pillars at Gobekli Tepe and the Greek Tau. After Laurette Sejourne in Burning Water: Thought and Religion in Ancient Mexico.

"Take Fire. D — the primal igneous [fiery] principle resident in X — is the ultimate cause of every phenomenal manifestation of fire on all the globes of the chain. The proximate causes are the evolved secondary igneous agencies which severally control the *seven* descents of fire on each planet, (every element having its seven principles and every principle its seven sub-principles and these secondary agencies before doing so, having in turn become primary causes.) D is a septenary compound of which the highest fraction is pure spirit. As we see it on our globe it is in its coarsest, most material condition, as gross in its way as is man in his physical encasement. In the next preceding globe to ours fire was less gross than here: on the one before that less still. And so the body of flame was more and more pure and spiritual, less and less gross and material on each antecedent planet... On each globe of the chain there are seven manifestations of fire of which the first in order will compare as to spiritual quality with the last manifestation on the next preceding planet: the process being reversed, as you will infer, with the opposite arc. The myriad specific manifestations of these six universal elements are in their turn but the offshoots, branches or branchlets of the one single primordial "Tree of Life."[9]

Earth's life branches from the sprawling elemental roots of the cosmic tree of life. We are the young tree growing from the older trunk, but sharing the same roots. The roots that sustain humanity are the same ones that sustain galactic races. The cosmic tree of life in fractal expressions are the connecting link of the Ancestors' ancient cultures and modern UFO contacts. Laurette Sejourne commented on this fundamental theme in *Burning Water: Thought and Religion in Ancient Mexico*.

"Meso-american cultures again and again describe the mystic formula expressing union between man and the Whole. The mathematical speculations known to have occupied a very important place in their studies were aimed at calculating the successive phases of union between the individual and the cosmic soul – between Venus and the Sun – phases that must gradually lead to complete Union."[10]

Universal patterns are archetypes that shape growth in continually changing conditions of the expanding universe. Every archetype has an opposite consistent with the duality that brings forth the physical world. These opposites are balanced in vector equilibrium.

In philosophy, Plato first referred to ideal Forms of the perceived or sensible things or types to articulate the concept of an archetype. Plato believed the cosmos itself came into being using as its model the world of Forms, or archetypes.

Carl Jung explains, "The term 'archetype' occurs as early as Philo Judaeus, with reference to the Imago Dei (God-image) in man. It can also be found in Irenaeus, who says: 'The creator of the world did not fashion these things directly from himself but copied them from archetypes outside himself... The term 'archetype' is not found in St. Augustine, but the idea of it is... he speaks of 'ideae principalis,' which are themselves not formed . . . but are contained in the divine understanding."[11]

With each part repeating the same characteristic as the whole, which may be identical at every scale or nearly the same in various scales, fractals are permuting archetypes. They are derived with mathematical sets that require tremendous computing capabilities, and developed simultaneously with DNA science in the late twentieth century.

The fractal nature of DNA with self-similar sets and mutations embodies archetypes of organic life. In the web of life, the divine informs creativity, complexity, and organization in the ever-expanding physical universe. The divine is never limited to the dimensions of energy, space, and time with innumerable organic permutations. It is infinite and located only by its own decision and perception. The Spirit of God hovered over the physical medium of water when the Earth was formless in Genesis 1, after exploding into the asteroid belt between Mars and Jupiter. Spirit was exterior to the water and surface of the darkness when calling forth light.

The divine weaves the organic web with quantum processes and properties – entanglement, coherence, non-locality and resonance. Even with two particles, their connection and function represent a system that is entangled and coherently aligned to exchange information independently of location. Oscillation in the wave function of the two particles generates resonance in the morphic field of their branch of the one primordial tree of organic life.

Mind-soul mediates between the infinite divine and the finite physical in a three-way partnership that expands experience and understanding. A failure of understanding brings pain and disruption when the mind-soul does not align the physical with the infinite divine source. The sacred aligns physical, mental, and soul forces with the divine at all levels of true life. No religion is higher than truth.

Never bound in energy, space, and time, the divine binds and unbinds physical dimensions in continuous quantum processes, timelessly connecting humans, Bigfoot, and Ancestors with all of the web's weavers.

Notes

[1] Radin, Dean. 2006. *Entangled Minds. Extrasensory Experience in a Quantum Reality.* Pocketbooks, a division of Simon and Schuster, Inc.: New York, NY. pp 1, 14-17, 209-236

[2] Mitchell, Edgar with Dwight Williams. 2008. *The Way of the Explorer: An Apollo Astronaut's Journey Through the Material and Mystical Worlds.* Franklin Lake, NJ: The Career Press, Inc.

[3] Lao Tzu, translated by James Legge. 1891. *The Tao-te Ching.* Internet Classics Archive. http://classics.mit.edu//Lao/taote.html

[4] Iamblichus, translated by Robin Waterfield. 1988. *The Theology of Arithmetic.* Phanes Press: Grand Rapids, MI. pp 35-40

[5] Chopra, Deepak. "Cosmic Fire." October 21, 2012. deepakchopra.com/blog/view/910/cosmic_fire

[6] "The presence of charge gives rise to an electrostatic force: charges exert a force on each other, an effect that was known, though not understood, in antiquity. A lightweight ball suspended from a string can be charged by touching it with a glass rod that has itself been charged by rubbing with a cloth. If a similar ball is charged by the same glass rod, it is found to repel the first: the charge acts to force the two balls apart. Two balls that are charged with a rubbed amber rod also repel each other. However, if one ball is charged by the glass rod, and the other by an amber rod, the two balls are found to attract each other. These phenomena were investigated in the late eighteenth century by Charles-Augustin de Coulomb, who deduced that charge manifests itself in two opposing forms. This discovery led to the well-known axiom: like-charged objects repel and opposite-charged objects attract.

"The force acts on the charged particles themselves, hence charge has a tendency to spread itself as evenly as possible over a conducting surface. The magnitude of the electromagnetic force, whether attractive or repulsive, is given by Coulomb's law, which relates the force to the product of the charges and has an inverse-square relation to the distance between them. The electromagnetic force is very strong, second only in strength to the strong interaction, but unlike that force it operates over all distances. In comparison with the much weaker gravitational force, the electromagnetic force pushing two electrons apart is 10^{42} times that of the gravitational attraction pulling them together."
http://en.wikipedia.org/wiki/Electricity

[7] Blavatsky, Helena Petrovna. 1888. *The Secret Doctrine*, Volume 2. Wheaton, IL: The Theosophical Publishing House. p. 247

[8] Buddhi is a feminine Sanskrit noun derived from the same root as the more familiar masculine form Buddha (< budh- to be awake, to understand, to

know). *Buddhi* denotes an aspect of mind that is higher than the rational mind and that is attracted to Brahman (i.e., to "Truth" (*sat*) or "Reality" (dharma)). Unlike *manas,* which is a composite of mind and ego deriving from an aggrandized "I-sense" that takes pleasure in pursuing worldly aims and sense pleasures, *buddhi* is that faculty that makes wisdom possible. (Wikipedia)

[9] Sinnett, A.P., compiled by Alfred Trevor Baker. 1923. Letter "From K.H. to A.O.H. Received July 10th, 1882." *The Mahatma Letters to A.P. Sinnett from the Mahatmas M. and K.H.* Letter No. XV, from Koot Hoomi to A. O. Hume, July 10, 1882 pp 88-99

[10] Sejourne, Laurette. 1956. *Burning Water: Thought and Religion in Ancient Mexico.* Thames & Hudson: London. p 74

[11] Jung, Carl, translated by R.F.C. Hull. 1990 *The Archetypes and the Collective Unconscious.* Princeton University Press: New York, NY. pp 3-5

APPENDICES

APPENDIX ONE

Earth-Human Calendar

Ancients living close to nature intuitively knew the female polarity of the planet interacting with the male polarity generates the resonant field that orders the structure of life, from brain waves to DNA. Mother Earth and Father Sky are ancient America's oldest ancestors. Humanity is birthed and thrives in the electromagnetic frequency generated between the earth and the atmosphere that science calls the Schumann Resonance.

"Resonance is the tendency of a system to move, or oscillate, at a certain rate or frequency. This results from the function of the wave, comparable to other waves such as water waves." ("Web of Life") The frequency of prevailing electrical tension in the earth/ionosphere cavity generated by the earth's negative charge and atmosphere's positive charge is the Schumann Resonance. It influences all living forms within the resonant field so profoundly that the base resonant frequency must be artificially maintained in spacecraft for the well-being of astronauts.

The earth-human relationship is the core of the 260-day "sacred calendar," which ancient Americans variously called the human and earth calendar or the Tzolkin. The calendar's signature number thirteen is memorialized in the ceremonial square with the Pyramid of the Feathered Serpent at Teotihuacan. Although instructive inscriptions were lost when Spaniards stripped casings from the pyramids at Teotihuacan, the calendar's raw numbers were designed into structures in the square. Thirteen stairs on each of four sides of platforms in the square, for a total of fifty-two stairs on each platform (4 x 13 = 52), memorialize the key numbers of the fifty-two-year civil calendar, the *Haab*. Thirteen dot-bar numbers sequence with twenty glyphs (day signs) for the 260-day Earth-Human Calendar (13 x 20 = 260), the *Tzolkin*.

One full calendar cycle of fifty-two years can be projected forwards and backwards into time for millions of years, but the long count is a separate measure with a defined beginning on August 13, 3114 and ending on December 21, 2012. Appended into the perpetual calendar matrix, the long count probably originated with the Olmec. Possessing sophisticated knowledge of celestial navigation, the Olmec had settled in Mexico by 3000 BCE with the means and very likely the job to lay the foundation for civilization there. (Cooper, *Leap of Faith*) The Olmec used the same celestial navigation symbols as those in Egypt, where Thoth, the Egyptian lord of astronomy, also used the signature number thirteen. In Egypt Thoth introduced the 365-day vague solar calendar, which the Maya in Mexico also used.

The Feathered Serpent's long count spanned the 5,126-year period when the solar system was most distant from its dual star in the 24,000-year cycle, and at lowest energy. ("Ages of Humankind") By 2012 the solar system had started ascending towards the dual star and moving into greater energy. The long count began thirteen (13) years before the descending Bronze Yuga in 3101 BCE and ended thirteen plus "100" (13 + 100) years after transitioning into the ascending Bronze Yuga in 1899.

"Thirteen" symbolizes the circle of continuous cycles in the illusory nature of the physical world, or "*Māyā*" in Sanskrit. In modern literature and Vedic texts Maya implies an illusion where things appear to be present but are not what they seem. In an older language, it implied extraordinary power and wisdom. And in Indian philosophies, it connotes "that which exists, but is constantly changing and thus is spiritually unreal," and the principle that conceals the true character of spiritual reality.[1] Correspondence of the Mexican Maya's name with the Sanskrit Māyā is significant to their world view, symbolism, and philosophy. The Maya speak a Sino-Tibetan language that has no relatives in the Americas, and has retained many Tibetan words.

First emerging in Egypt and India, a serpent devouring its tail, the "*ouroboros*," symbolizes continuously regenerating cycles, reflecting the never-ending irrational square root of thirteen. A factor of the 360° circle when truncated to two decimals, the square root of thirteen is 3.60 in a 1:100 ratio with 360°. The square root is the inner base for propagating a number, hidden from peripheral view unless one knows how to look and find it.

In Harvey and Victoria Bricker's decades-long study of the Maya's codices they tracked how the night sky would have looked to the Maya, and translated complex codex writing to see what the Maya timekeepers believed was most important. They found astonishing astronomy in the codices. Chichen Itza's calendar codex dating to 1000 CE accurately predicted the historic solar eclipse visible in Mexico on July 11, 1991, using a grid of eclipse cycles they periodically updated.

Feathered Serpent and Ibis-Headed Thoth

An Olmec is cradled in the curves of the Feathered Serpent's body while his plumed head rises above the Olmec figure in the identical position the serpent sheltered Buddha during his enlightenment (above). Thoth with the head of an ibis surmounted by a crest showing the three psychic nerves have risen to power chakras in the head (right). The signature number "13" is used by the Feathered Serpent and Thoth and both symbolized elevated base physical energy risen above the head chakras with feathers.

First emerging in Egypt and India, a serpent devouring its own tail, the ouroboros, symbolizes continuously regenerating cycles, reflecting the never-ending irrational square root of 13. A factor of the 360° circle when truncated to two decimals, the square root of 13 is 3.60 in a 1:100 ratio of 360°.

"We're dealing with real data," Harvey Bricker said. "They're not just squiggles."

The Maya's writing system started with iconic glyphs that expanded by annotating the icons with markings for a syllabary. The Earth glyph in Chichen Itza's Tzolkin contains a vertical "squiggle" with a "lumpy mass" on each side of it.[2] When the Earth glyph is enlarged and proportionately sized with a world map, the "squiggle" closely aligns with the Mid-Atlantic Ridge. Fourteen of fifteen tiny circles marked in the glyph correspond with islands in the Atlantic and Indian Oceans. Some islands not shown on modern maps were on the Piri Reis map, which was updated with Christopher Columbus' discoveries after his 1492 CE voyage to America.

The Earth glyph shows an island on the west side of the Strait of Gibraltar, which is not on modern maps. A Soviet historian confirmed its ancient emergence. (Zhirov, *Atlantis: Atlantology Basic Problems*) This "island" may have been the mud shoal that formed after Atlantis sank and made navigating the Atlantic Ocean difficult in Plato's "Timaeus." A location for Atlantis is not indicated in the glyph, suggesting it represents a period after Poseidon's island sank, or later than 11,500 BP.

The ancient Maya were apt sailors who had coasts on the Pacific Ocean, Gulf of Mexico and Caribbean Sea, giving them easy access to the Atlantic with the Indian Ocean in the southeast. Astute mapping of water lanes is an essential tool for any sailor, and the Maya undoubtedly mapped the waters surrounding them. Maps that might have been used with the Earth glyph template were burned when the Spaniards, especially incensed by the Maya's science, burned more than 5,000 documents in the sixteenth century. Nonetheless, the Piri Reis map amply demonstrates that the ancient world was mapped with advanced mathematics long before Rome claimed the crossroads of the world for its God. Exploring the unknown is among the human virtues that expands the mind of the species, and the Maya had the means and opportunity to explore the Atlantic and Indian Oceans.

The Earth glyph (*Kab'an*) in Chichen Itza's codex is equivalent to the *No'j* glyph for *knowledge* in the Kaqchikel Maya in Guatemala. Mayan Elder Carlos Barrios compares the vertical axis between the two

WEB OF LIFE AND COSMOS: HUMAN AND BIGFOOT STAR ANCESTORS | 151

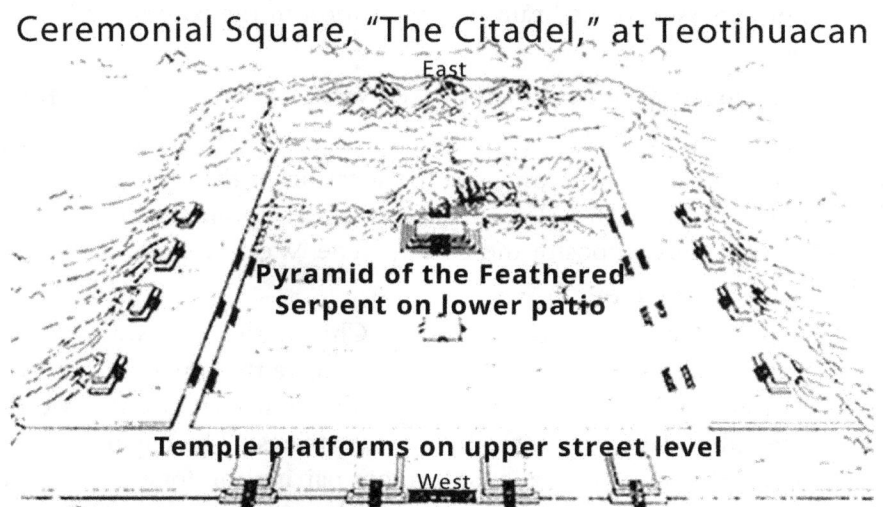

Ceremonial Square, "The Citadel," at Teotihuacan

The Pyramid of the Feathered Serpent dominates the lower patio of a two-level ceremonial square nearly one square mile in size. It was constructed in a recess excavated beneath street level of the central avenue. On the street level, temple platforms with thirteen stairs on each side, for fifty-two stairs on each platform, encode numbers the Maya used with their calendar. The western-facing square is oriented to observe Venus, and temples on the upper level provide sight lines to observe Venus and the Moon in cyclic phases.

Beginning with Mercury near the Feathered Serpent's pyramid and extending north on the avenue, relative positions of all the planets in the solar system are noted with constructions. This context poses the ceremonial square with the center of the solar system with planets in a linear array, resembling the Milky Way's path. The two-tier square with symbolic calendric logic embedded in temples compares with the cube in Johannes Kepler's model of the universe constructed with the Platonic geometries he used to discover the laws of planetary motion.

The lower patio with the Feathered Serpent's pyramid and buried chambers strongly parallels the underworld in earthly context. The entire pyramid complex at Teotihuacan was built to align with the opening to caves that extend throughout the area. Venus and the underworld are consistent cultural themes at Teotihuacan and throughout Native America.

In Greece, where Plato expounded the Great Year, Tartarus is both a deity and place of the underworld. In the more ancient Orphic tradition, Tartarus is the unbounded first-existing entity that gave birth to the Light and the Cosmos. With no Greek roots, Tartarus is a loan word from an unknown language transplanted in Greece.

A puzzling discovery of gold balls covered in magnetic materials, including pyrite (fools gold), in rooms beneath the pyramid in 2013 stymied experts, who expected to find tombs. Symbolically the pyramid and chambers are positioned above the cerebellum in Teotihuacan's cerebral structure.

hemispheric masses to the brain for application in the context of human physiology.[3]

Planet-Changing Fracture Pinpointed with TimeStar Earth Map

The Earth glyph shows compression in the equatorial area of the western hemisphere, approximating the location of the meteor crater at Chicxulub in Mexico 66 MYA. It shows a corresponding bulge in the eastern hemisphere opposite the crater. The West is concave and the antipode in the East is convex.

In a meteor strike like the one at Chicxulub, shockwaves travel through the center of the planet directly opposite the impact to its antipode. A study of forty-five primary hotspots found that twenty-two (or 49%) were antipodal pairs caused by meteor strikes. The paper's author, Jonathan T. Hagstrum, wrote in 2005 about pairings of hotspots: "Monte Carlo simulations indicate that the antipodal primary hotspots' locations and ages are not due to chance at the 99% confidence level. . . . All hotspot pairs include at least one oceanic hotspot, and these are consistently opposite those hotspots related to large igneous provinces and continental volcanism."[4]

Damage at Chicxulub's antipode in the Indian Ocean is estimated to have been as severe as in Mexico. At the time of the impact, India was attached to Madagascar in the Indian Ocean near the antipode. Several studies have been done to discover if the Chicxulub impact uplifted the Indian continent and pushed it northward towards its present location, triggering a series of ferocious volcanic eruptions in the Deccan Traps of India and elsewhere in the Indian Ocean.[5]

Over 66 million years, both the crater and the antipode have drifted northward. India, amid massive volcanic eruptions, moved into its present location at the north end of the Indo-Australian tectonic plate, and left a trail of igneous rocks produced by extreme heat and volcanic eruptions in the Indian Ocean. In its drift, India passed through the area between Madagascar and Malaysia in the Indian Ocean, where Helena Blavatsky reported Mu had existed and Augustus Le Plongeon identified a continent that he deciphered as *"Moo."* Large igneous provinces and mantle hotspots exist in areas both Blavatsky and Le Plongeon identified for Mu using two entirely different sources.

| Earth is represented in the **Ka'ban** glyph from Chichen Itza, in the Dresden Codex. | Hemispheres of the brain are compared to juxtapositioned masses in the **No'j** glyph from the Kaqchikel Maya in Guatemala. |

The active antipodal hotspot for Chicxulub has drifted to Christmas Island off the coast of Java, Indonesia in the region I identified in 1998 as the axis of coming earth changes. The area north of the antipode at 91°East longitude, where the equatorial axis balances, has suffered extreme quakes and volcanic eruptions since 2004.

The megaquake near Sumatra that generated the Asian Tsunami on December 26, 2004 was north of Christmas Island in the region where the Indo-Australian Plate fractured on April 11, 2012.[6] The history-making fracture of the tectonic plate was on 93° East longitude north of the antipode and equatorial axis. Large earthquakes shook every major fault line on Earth in the weeks following the fracture.

Remarkably, the Earth's equatorial axis aligns precisely between the longitudes of the Chicxulub crater (89° West) and its antipode (91° East), which were published with the 2014 discovery of an inner-inner magnetic core.[7] Discovering an inner-inner magnetic core that aligns east-west with the equatorial axis from Chicxulub's longitude, in contrast to the north-south alignment of the outer magnetic core, greatly surprised scientists.

The humble "squiggle" in Chichen Itza's Earth glyph mapped planetary mechanics sufficiently well that I was able to pinpoint in 1998 the region of planet-changing seismicity in 2004 and 2012. After marauding Conquistadores took Chichen Itza's codex in the sixteenth century, it is modernly housed in the Dresden Museum in Germany.

Earth Glyph and America's Coastlines

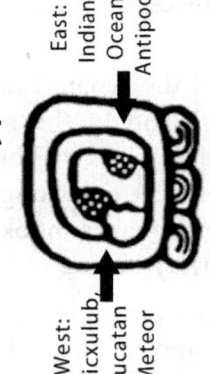

West: Chicxulub, Yucatan Meteor

East: Indian Ocean Antipode

Tilt of Earth's Surface in Polar Wander

Mid-Atlantic Ridge — Iceland
Avalonia
Atlantis Islands
Baltica
Orkney Islands
Celtic Sea
Spain
Africa
South America

An iconic vertical axis in the Earth glyph from the Mayan center at Chichen Itza, now in the Dresden Museum, resembles America's sprawling Atlantic coastline. Greater and lesser detail was included in the glyph, depending on the context in which it was used. The curvilinear line that connects two conglomerate antipodes in the west and east is used in the Quiche glyph from Carlos Barrios, but the Guatemalan glyph does not include the vertical coastal shape. Benjamin Franklin observed in the eighteenth century that coastlines of Africa and South America looked as if they had once been connected, although the Mid-Atlantic Ridge was not discovered until 1872. He also made landmark discoveries about electricity by observing lightning.

What the ancient Maya knew and how they knew it remain mysterious to Western science. The iconic glyph for the Earth in the Earth calendar at Chichen Itza tilts and bulges to the east, opposite an indention in the west where an asteroid impact at Chicxulub resulted in extinction of the dinosaurs 65.5 million years ago. The indented area in the west corresponds with the site of the asteroid impact on 21° North latitude. The bulge in the glyphs corresponding with the Indian Ocean in the east, is in the Indian Ocean. Several studies have examined the mechanism that resulted in the dinosaur's extinction following the asteroid impact focusing on volcanic eruptions at the antipode. A Nature journal article in 2012 examined shifts in the Earth's surface at various angles (above) relative to the rotational axis over long periods.

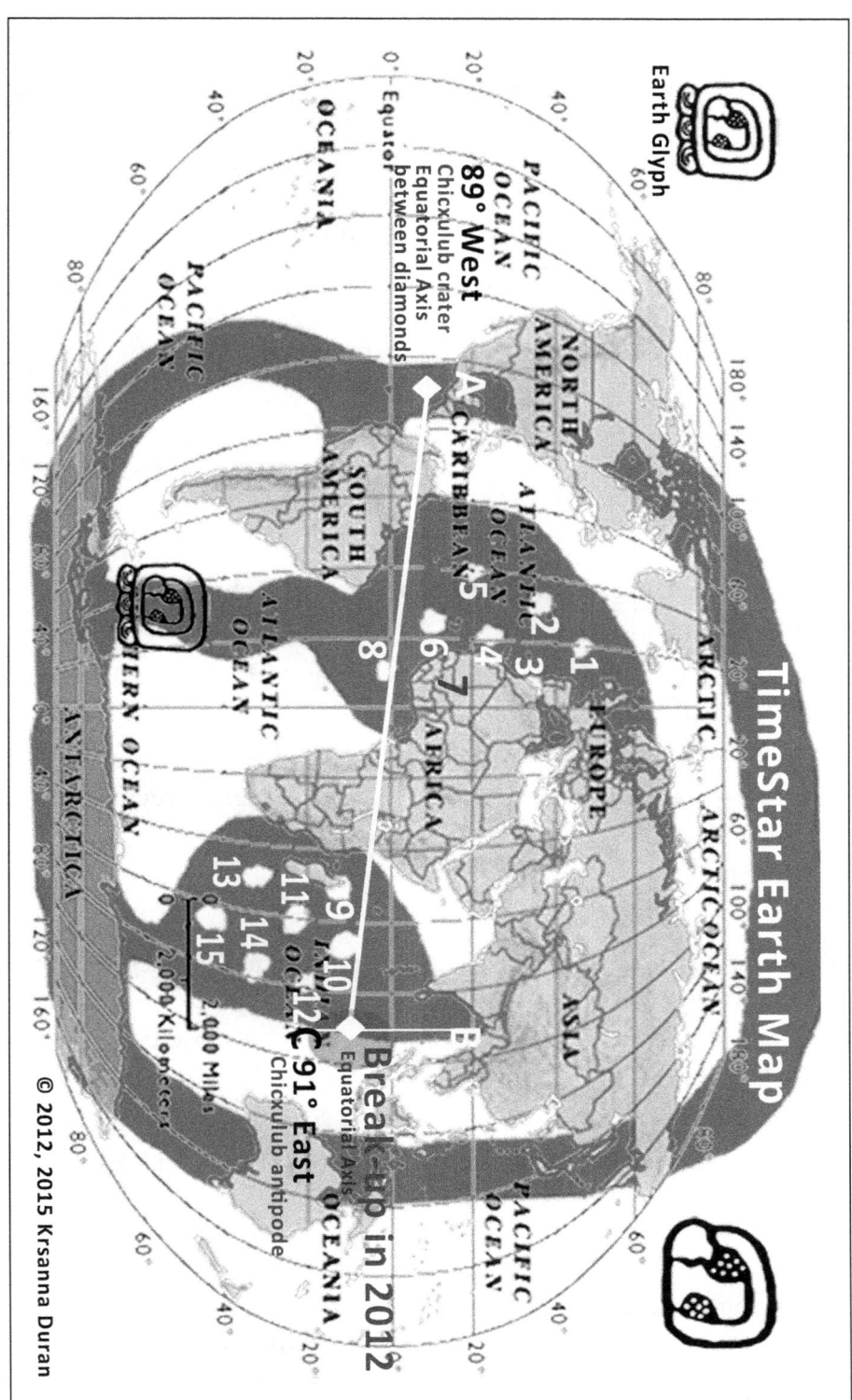

TimeStar Earth Map Legend

A = Impact crater at Chicxulub on the Gulf of Mexico 66 MYA that triggered massive volcanic eruptions worldwide;

B = Opposite point to Chicxulub crater on a great circle on latitude of impact;

C = Antipode of Chicxulub crater through the center of the earth;

1. West of England parallel to Stonehenge, several islands were in this area when the North Sea began forming 12,000 BP. An island may have been above water in this site as recently as 6000 BP;[8]
2. Azores Islands;
3. An island rose in front of the Strait of Gibraltar (Pillars of Hercules) in this location after Atlantis sank, according to Soviet historian B.L. Bogayevsky.[9] The island has again submerged.
4. Canary Islands;
5. Land noted on Piri Reis Map but not presently above water;
6. Cape Verde Islands;
7. Ahaggar and Air Mountains when North Africa was covered with water;
8. Land noted on Piri Reis Map but no longer above water;
9. Providence Island, Farquhar Group and Aldabra Group north of Madagascar;
10. British Territory and Base;
11. Reunion Island;
12. No land is above water at this site very close to the antipode of the Chicxulub asteroid impact;
13. No land is above water south of Madagascar, where water is shown to be shallow;
14. Amsterdam Island;
15. Islands under Port Aux Francais authority, Heard and McDonald Islands.

Mapping with Crop Circles

Anomalous crop circles are a communication medium that embodies symbols from the world's most ancient cultures. African shaman Credo Mutwa wrote about crop formations that mysteriously appeared in fields when he was a boy during the 1920s. (Mutwa, *Isilwane: The Animal*) Crop circle communications with the ancients may span millennia. Communication with the Earth was so important to the ancients that *geometry* literally means *earth measure*, derived from *geo* (*earth*) and *metre* (*measure*).

Crop circles originate from four primary sources and anomalous (authentic) formations tend to appear in sets at sites with high telluric energies, or ley lines, and ancient sites. Their secrets are found by identifying the origin of each formation and its relationship within larger sets of geography, astronomy, physics, sacred sites and geometries, historic and modern landmarks, past and future history, art and crop formation complexes.

Mapping earthian energies is a great application for data gleaned from crop circles. The breakup region of the Indo-Australian tectonic plate that fractured in 2012 is within a triangle formed by three crop circles in 2010 and 2011. Each of the formations conveyed information about the site where it appeared and the breakup region.

The first formation was a circle of burned sunflowers in Argentina, messaging the presence of a potentially undetected extreme heat source in 2010. I databased it to keep an eye on sources of heat. Crop circles first proliferated in the 1970s when planetary temperatures began rising, shortly before the ozone hole was discovered. High heat is a factor in anomalous formations, and may be germane to the circles' message.

A crop circle formed at Java after local people reported sighting a UFO and hearing a strange sound for thirty minutes on January 23, 2011.[10] It was near the world's largest Buddhist temple and sentinel of ancient Mu, the Borobudur temple. I had previously identified Indonesia as the axis of earth changes with the Earth glyph, and carefully watched the area.

A set of simple circles formed north of Teotihuacan on March 20, 2011, following a 9.0 magnitude megaquake in Japan on March 11 that resulted in meltdowns of three nuclear reactors at Fukushima Daiichi. I had first learned about Teotihuacan because of high UFO activity in Mexico City, which led to the discovery that Teotihuacan anchored an equilateral triangle between Kennewick, Washington and Herkimer, New York.

All three crop circle sites were in relatively rural areas with no histories of human crop art for profit. Formations at Teotihuacan and Java were near ancient sacred sites. The one in Argentina was in a rural field with high heat within the circle that had not affected the rest of the field. I noted latitudes and longitudes for the three sites to look for patterns.

Earthquakes shook all three geographically distant areas, virtually simultaneously, on April 26, 2011. I had recently entered their latitudes and longitudes in a database, and they were fresh in my mind when the quakes caught my attention. I drew a triangle between the crop circles in Indonesia, Mexico, and Argentina (MAI) on a world map and looked for what factors might connect the locations. Several volcanoes had erupted inside the triangle soon after the first set of quakes.

Quake and volcanic activity within the triangle was high in 2011-12, and I dug deeper to search for data and expanded my search to outlying areas. The meteor crater at Chicxulub is near the eastern border of the MAI triangle. Sixty-five million years seems like an impossibly long time in the past to be significant now, and the importance of the Chicxulub meteor "sank in" slowly. To my growing surprise, Chicxulub and its antipode in the Indian Ocean have proven to be key factors in at least two history-making tectonic events in 2012 and 2013.

Great quakes measuring 8.6 and 8.2 magnitudes rocked Indonesia north of the triangle's eastern tip simultaneously with quakes at the crop circle sites on April 11, 2012. At that point I realized we were reckoning damage to the oceanic plate and mantle at the antipode of the Chicxulub meteor 66 MYA. I published this conclusion with maps in April 2012. An article announcing that earthquakes that fractured the Indo-Australian Plate were in extinct volcano cones was published in *Nature* journal, September 26, 2012.[11,12]

A new subduction zone that opened south of Portugal in 2013 was a stark reminder that 66 million years is not very long in planetary time. The subduction zone opened in the region where shockwaves from the Chicxulub impact had wasted continental margins in the most probable location for Poseidon's island of Atlantis. Located between Portugal and Africa, Poseidon's kingdom probably extended westerly beyond the Madeira Islands into the Atlantic.

With the many values of crop circles, intrigues surrounding them make rocky roads that one learns to navigate by sheer experience and observation. Some people report that as long as crop art makes them feel good they do not care if humans, UFOs, or Nature's intelligence makes them. Crop art that imitates Nature is entertaining and profitable for modern entrepreneurs. Conversely, authentic crop formations with mysterious origins have conveyed vital information about conditions of the Earth for a long time. Sorting out their truths and pitfalls is well worth the effort.

Islands Rising, Sinking

Signs of new islands rising in the Pacific and Indian Oceans would be evident by 2008 was TimeStar's first prediction in 1996. The 9.1 magnitude earthquake near Sumatra on December 26, 2004 when a tectonic plate slipped signaled processes of change deep within the earth. New islands are rising and anciently emerged lands are sinking. Indonesia, Philippines, and Japan are sinking rapidly since the Indo-Australian tectonic plate fractured on April 11, 2012. Mu's first island, Sweta Dwipa, in the Indian Ocean sank millions of years ago and migrants from Mu moved to new homes in the Indian and Pacific Oceans before going to the inner Earth. Mu is remembered as the mother culture of Native America, Polynesia, Indonesia, Japan, and others. She was the Great Mother, the *Magna Mater*, of Asia as well as Native America. In North America's oldest pyramids at Teotihuacan she is revered as the goddess of the city in union with the wind god, Mother Earth and Father Sky. Long sunken lands of Mu are rising anew in the present time, a rebirth in cyclic renewal.

2013

Three new islands rose, while volcanic activity that will raise an island in the Canary Islands continued, in 2013.

1. A new island rose south of Japan in the Dragon's Triangle November 20, 2013, north of the deepest oceanic trench in the world.

Advisories say that the island is located off the coast of the uninhabited island of Nishinoshima, which is part of the Ogasawara chain or Bonin Islands, just 1,000 kilometers [620 miles] south of Tokyo. On that Wednesday, the coast guard issued an advisory, saying heavy black smoke was coming out of the waters in the area. Then on Thursday, footage showed smoke, ash, and rocks were exploding from the crater. The last time the volcanoes in the area erupted was in the mid-70s, and most of the activity was underwater, thousands of meters deep into the Izu-Ogasawara-Marianas Trench.

The Japanese named the new island Niijima. Another new island formed during the last confirmed eruption of the Nishinoshima in 1973-74. It was extended towards the west by lava flow.

The island emerged at the site of quakes that preceded the 9.0 magnitude megaquake on Japan's coast March 11, 2011. The 2011 quake caused waves in Scandinavia that were documented on videos, but could not be explained with current theory. A theory about "S" waves was quickly proposed to explain the connection.

Maps for November 5, 2013 and March 11, 2011 show a larger pattern. Quakes in the week before the 2011 megaquake are in yellow on the map, and those on the day of the quake are in blue and red. A white rectangle is drawn around quakes on the African and Indo-Australian plate that preceded the catastrophic quake in 2011.

An eerily similar pattern of quakes was seen on November 5, 2013, two weeks before the new island was born. On the 2013 map, quakes shook the area south of Japan near the site where the island rose. Crop circles that spanned the African and Indo-Australian plates in 2012 had focused my attention on that area. The 2013 pattern initially caught my eye because of the spread across the African and the Indo-Australian plates that were included in the crop circles.

Repeated in two different events separated by two years, this pattern — first pointed out in crop circles — suggests profound dynamics that may further explain the waves in Scandinavia after the March 11, 2011 quake.

2. Another new island rose in the Red Sea, discovered October 23, 2013 in satellite images. The underwater eruption that brought up the island started immediately after the 7.8M quake in Pakistan with another new island on its coast September 24. This follows an island that rose in the Red Sea in December 2011 and an island that rose in the Indian Ocean with a 7.8 magnitude quake on September. The map TimeStar posted last April (2013) predicting the sequence that is presently unfolding follows. A good photo of the newest island is not yet available, but it is off the coast of Jebel Zubair.

3. An island rose off the coast of Gwadar, Pakistan on September 24, 2013, immediately following a 7.8 magnitude quake epicentered in the Baluchistan province. It disappeared beneath the waters again two months later, on November 24. It was approximately one-half mile from the shore of Gwadara, between the Sarvestan, Iran crop circle (June 12, 2012) and a TimeStar glyph in the Indian Ocean. TimeStar named the Indian Ocean as a site where islands would rise, based on a crop circle at Kennewick, Washington, which shows a bulge opposite Kennewick's location at approximately 60° East longitude. The new island was at 62°

East longitude, or less than three degrees from the longitude TimeStar named in an April 16, 2013 post. See Kennewick crop circle.

In a sequence with a 7.8 magnitude quake in Pakistan on April 16, 2013, several large quakes shook the West Coast of America along Kennewick, Washington's 119 West longitude, with a 4+ quake at Yellowstone Park. TimeStar predicted the April 16 quake was the first in a sequence that would follow.

A similar pattern of quakes shook America's West Coast, again on Kennewick's 119 West longitude and a 4+ magnitude quake in Yellowstone, on September 22, 2013. Two days later a new island rose off the coast of Pakistan following a 7.8 magnitude quake epicentered in the southwestern province of Baluchistan on September 24, 2013.

2012

The long process of an ancient tectonic fracturing that will eventually produce a new tectonic plate reached a critical state on April 11, 2012, when the Indo-Australian plate fractured. Large earthquakes increased five-fold and some areas of the Philippine Islands sank as much as nine feet in the six months following the fracturing earthquake.

2011

On December 19, 2011, satellites detected sulfur dioxide and a small volcanic plume in the area, and by December 23 a new island had formed in the Red Sea. The island continued to grow in early January, but stopped by January 15th.

New island visible in Canary Islands:

http://abcnews.go.com/International/eruptions-create-island-canaries/story?id=14828261#.UAeihrRcWQo

What would the island be called? And who would own it? Spewing magma and growing in height, an underwater volcano off the Canary Island of El Hierro has captured the imagination of locals in recent weeks. It could eventually rise from the sea to create a new part of the archipelago.

2010

MARIANA ISLANDS: Pilots and seamen in the Commonwealth of the Northern Mariana Islands are being warned to keep away from an underwater volcano which has erupted. The Governor Benigno Fitial declared a State of Emergency at the weekend following the eruption of the volcano south of Sarigan Island. Sarigan is uninhabited, but travellers are being cautioned to keep at least five nautical miles clear. Our correspondent in Saipan, Mark Rabago, says the Emergency Management Office is monitoring the impact but so far little is known. "Current evidence points to a source being the submarine sea mouth, south of Sarigan, that there was a cloud that contained either ash or water vapour that appeared north of Anatahan volcano and now coming towards the CNMI and Guam." Mark Rabago says a team of scientists is expected to investigate the eruption. (May 30, 2010)

2009

A spectacular eruption underwater at Tonga March 19 2009, reported by the Daily Mail.

2006

Near Tonga: A new volcanic island has risen from the South Pacific near Tonga, according to reports from two vessels that passed the area... He said they could see the volcanic island clearly. "One mile in diameter and with four peaks and a central crater smoking with steam and once in a while an outburst high in the sky with lava and ashes. I think we're the first ones out here," he reported. (Published by CNN on November 9, 2006.)

2004

Sumatra-Andaman earthquake: This quake caused the entire planet to ring like a bell and affected the North Pacific area of Alaska by way of the tsunami that followed on December 26, 2004. An event like this has repercussions for at least a decade. The earthquake was unusually large in geographical extent. An estimated 1,200 km (750 mi) of fault line slipped about 15 m (50 ft) along the subduction zone where the India Plate dives under the Burma Plate. The slip did not happen instantaneously but took place in two phases over a period of several minutes.

2002

Amchixtam Chaxsxii Volcano, Alaska: This is the only active underwater volcano in the Aleutians. Discovered in 2002, it will eventually be an island in the Aleutian chain. At the time of its discovery, long and extensive magma flows were present.

2001

Kick'em Jenny is one of the most active volcanoes in the Caribbean and is currently only 190 meters below the surface. It last erupted in December 2001.

[Reuters] For the fourth time in the past ninety years, a small islet off the coast of Trinidad suddenly appeared from beneath the ocean several days ago [prior to May 21, 2001]. Residents of the coastal city of Chatham awoke to find the new territory once again in the Columbus Channel about 1.5 miles (2.5 km) offshore. In the few days since the nameless island has resurfaced, it has already become home to many birds. It has also generated extra income for local fishermen, who are providing boat rides for the curious to take a closer look at the capricious island. However, scientists Jan Lindsay and Kirstie Simpson said the fragile island had formed from a mud volcano and warned people to stay off of it as it could explode in eruptions of mud or emit toxic gasses that could spontaneously combust.

2000

Kavachi, Solomon Island: An international science team has witnessed the dramatic birth of a new volcanic island in the Pacific. Scientists witnessed the rare event during a research expedition to the Solomon Islands on the CSIRO research vessel Franklin. The Franklin is returning to Darwin after two successful cruises looking at volcanic activity and associated mineral formation in the Bismarck Sea and the Pacific. From the first leg of the expedition, scientists are bringing back a world record size "black smoker" chimney from the bottom of the Bismarck Sea. On the second leg of the cruise, scientists found the Kavachi seamount had entered a new phase of island-building eruptive activity after 9 years of apparent dormancy.

1996

Loihi Seamount, Hawaii: The largest earthquakes swarm ever associated with a Hawaiian island started July 17, 1996 and resulted in the collapse of the Loihi Seamount. "We have never witnessed (directly or remotely) a Hawaiian submarine effusive eruption so it is possible that this could be one. The long duration of the swarm event and the moderate magnitude of the quakes are most compatible with either a pit crater collapse or an explosive eruption origin."

Notes

[1] Maya (illusion) Wikipedia: https://en.wikipedia.org/wiki/Maya_(illusion)

[2] Schele, Linda and David Freidel. 1990. *A Forest of Kings: The Untold Story of the Ancient Maya.* Morrow: New York, NY. pp 77-84

[3] Barrios, Carlos, translated by Lisa Carter. 2009. *The Book of Destiny. Unlocking the Secrets of the Ancient Mayans and the Prophecy of 2012.* Harper One: New York, NY. p 211

[4] Hagstrum, Jonathan T. "Antipodal hotspots and bipolar catastrophes: Were oceanic large-body impacts the cause?" *Earth and Planetary Science Letters 236* (2005) 13-27.

[5] Kelly, Morgan. "Massive volcanoes, meteorite impacts delivered one-two punch death punch to dinosaurs." *News at Princeton.* November 17, 2011.

[6] Shen, Helen. "Unusual Indian Ocean earthquakes hint at tectonic breakup." *Nature,* international weekly journal of science. September 26, 2012. www.nature.com/news/unusual-indian-ocean-earthquakes-hint-at-tectonic-breakup-1.11487

[7] Phys.org February 9, 2015. "Earth's Surprise inside: Geologists unlock mysteries of planet's inner core." http://phys.org/news/2015-02-earth-geologists-mysteries-planet-core.html

[8] Zhirov, N. F. 1970. *Atlantis. Atlantology: Basic Problems.* Progress Publishers: Soviet Union, Moscow.

[9] Ibid. p 215

[10] Duran, Krsanna. 2012. "Crop Circles Points to Breakup Region on Indo-Australian Plate." *All Star Roundup: Crop Circles .* www.allstarroundup.com/cc/ccindonesia.html

[11] Shen, Helen. "Unusual Indian Ocean earthquakes hint at tectonic breakup." *Nature,* international weekly journal of science. September 26, 2012. www.nature.com/news/unusual-indian-ocean-earthquakes-hint-at-tectonic-breakup-1.11487

[12] Maps for the April 2011 and April 2012 earthquakes are posted on the All Star Roundup website. www.nature.com/news/unusual-indian-ocean-earthquakes-hint-at-tectonic-breakup-1.11487

APPENDIX TWO

Origins of Crop Circles

Circle and ring designs made by alternating standing and flattened crops began proliferating in Wiltshire, England in the 1970s. Early investigators called the mysterious designs crop circles because initially they were all circular. The name caught on and has persisted despite changing designs. In less than 40 years crop circles have appeared on all continents and more than 200 countries in increasingly complex designs and arrays.

A flood of crop circles involving numerous origins worldwide have been reported since 1970. TimeStar focuses research on crop circles that provide insight into changing conditions of the Earth with a high probability of mysterious origin, which are not humanly made.

Historically, crop circles have been reported for centuries in England, America, and Africa. African shaman Credo Mutwa wrote about crop circles in his book, *Isilwane, The Animal*.

"The sacred fields were ploughed far from the ordinary millet, maize and corn, as they were left unfenced. Over centuries, people had discovered that the star gods sometimes communicated with human beings through these sacred fields. Time and again, strange circular depressions were seen in the centre of these fields. These depressions were called Izishoze Amatongo, the great circles of the gods.

"These circles were an amazing sight to see. The gods never cut the stalks of corn or millet when they form these depressions. It appears as though a great circular, disk-shaped force has descended on the field. It pressed the corn firmly into the ground, without breaking the stalks or damaging the plants. Then the force appears to spin, resulting in the strange spiral appearance of the fallen stalks. Words cannot describe such a phenomenon, which I have seen more than thirty times in the course of my life as a traditional healer. Whenever a circle appeared in the fields, the people rushed to erect a fence of poles around the circle. They would dance and perform other sacred rituals honouring the star gods and the Earth Mother.

"All the kings and chiefs awaited the arrival of these circles. The appearance would be cause for celebrations that lasted several days. Prayers accompanied these celebrations to the gods to watch over the people and to talk to them through the sacred circles."[1]

Crop circles derive from a number of origins, which may combine into complex relationships. For the sake of brevity, formations of mysterious origin with anomalous characteristics in the crops are abbreviated as ACF. Designs made by human crop artists are identified as HCA; and mechanical planking is shortened to MP.

1. Gaia

Signs of high heat in crop circles, also called cereal circles, eerily echo the *Homeric Hymn* to Demeter. The Greek gods Zeus and Hades were Demeter's brothers, and all were the children of the older Titans that Zeus overthrew. While Demeter's daughter Persephone was playing in a field, a magical flower caught her attention. At that instant Hades, in his chariot, descended on Persephone and abducted her to his domain in the underworld. (Hades' underworld had no relationship to the hell that later developed in Judeo-Christian mythology.) Hades was associated with souls of the dead in a domain like any other domain the Greek gods possessed.

Desolate, Demeter, dressed like an old woman and refusing to care for the crops, searched the world of humans for Persephone. She was eventually engaged by a human king to care for his only son, an infant. At night Demeter would place the infant boy in the fire without harm, and he thrived in her care. One night the child's mother came into the room while Demeter held him in the fire, and the mother screamed at the sight. The child started to cry and the mother took him from Demeter.

Demeter told the mother she could have given the boy immortality, but the mother had ruined his opportunity. Bear in mind that Demeter had been holding the boy in the fire when he thrived, and he cried only when his mother burst into the room and took the child away from Demeter.

During the time Demeter searched for Persephone, the crops failed throughout the kingdom. Humans were not able to make offerings to

Zeus without crops, and Zeus was forced to negotiate with Demeter for Persephone's return. When Hades learned that he must return Persephone, he gave her a pomegranate seed to eat. Persephone accepted and ate the seed. The first question Demeter asked Persephone when she returned was if she had eaten anything Hades had given her, and Persephone lied. She said she had not eaten anything. Because Persephone had eaten the seed, she was required to return to the underworld six months of each year, and became a powerful queen of Hades.

Demeter chose to remain in the human world and teach the mysteries of immortality. She founded the first mystery school in the town of Eleusis, where the Elysian Mysteries of immortality were given to humans. Demeter's school was open to all, but initiates into the mysteries were vowed to secrecy.

The fire in which the infant boy thrived is the critical point of the goddess' story. The child was not harmed or alarmed until his biological mother took him from the goddess Demeter; he had the potential to withstand the fire that would have made him immortal, had his mortal mother not taken him back to the mortal world with her. The symbolic seed that Hades gave to Persephone, thus requiring her return to Hades every year, parallels Demeter's fire in terms of quantum entanglement that connects identities beyond mechanical limits of space. Entanglement and non-locality are two key features of quantum mechanics.

High heat applied to crop circles cause changes in vegetation, including crystalline cell changes. It changes heritable traits in future generations of crops. Electrical and magnetic variations are common in crop circles with mysterious origin. Various theories have been offered to explain the heat source that alters the crops, including plasma and balls of light. The sources of heat associated with authentic crop circles remain as elusive as the secrets of immortality that Demeter taught.

Intelligence in Nature that shapes order and form was well recognized in antiquity; in ancient Greece as well as Native America intelligence was recognized as the spirit of the Earth. The Greeks called the intelligent spirit of the Earth *Gaia* and Native Americans revered it as *Mother Earth,* the mother of life on Earth. Greek gods recognized the power of Nature's mind in the intelligent essence that directed the body of a river in Homer's *Iliad*. The spirit they called *Xanthus* and the river's body they called *Scamander*. In the *Iliad*, Homer wrote that Xanthus, the god or spirit of the river, rose up to protest Achilles clogging its channels with corpses he had slain. Achilles agreed to stop throwing bodies into the river but not to stop killing. When he heard the river's plea for help,

Achilles attacked the river. The river dragged Achilles downstream to a floodplain and nearly killed him. Only the gods' setting the plain on fire and boiling the river's water until it released him saved Achilles.

Powers wielded by initiates and masters of all traditions originate in the intelligence of Nature's mind, capable of vast imagery in naturalistic designs that reflect conditions of the phenomenal world. The shapes that emerge from Nature's mind vary as causative factors change, thus they may appear different from older forms, or anomalous. In actuality, what may seem extraordinary or anomalous to humanly constructed perception is newly emerging aspects of Nature's power reflecting changing states.

Small, randomly placed circles called *dragon's footprints* appeared in Wiltshire before the modern crop circle period began. They give a whimsical impression that a dragon might have walked through the field. These are formed entirely from Earthian and non-human intelligence.

A circle is the most powerful shape in nature, and symbolizes not only power but also wholeness. A central circle with four satellite circles was among the earliest crop circle designs in modern England, as well as the most common symbol of ancient Mexico's shamanic culture. This geometry was the basis of the Star glyph from the Mayan calendar at Chichen Itza in southeast Mexico. This symbol was the emblem for both Inanna in Sumer and the Feathered Serpent in Mexico. In ancient cultures, shamans served as intercessors with non-human intelligences in ethereal, or supernal realms. Over generations, Earth's rich shamanic heritage discovered and memorialized Nature's language and transmitted this knowledge to future generations in symbolic systems that transcended written language in oral traditions. Direct experience with Nature, the supernatural and ethereal realms is the threshold of this knowledge.

Intuition, process, and form are the medium and the message of those crop circles that directly originate in Nature. An initiate of the Egyptian mysteries, Plato cautioned in "Phaedrus" about constructions of written language:

"If men learn this [written language], it will implant forgetfulness in their souls; they will cease to exercise memory because they rely on that which is written, calling things to remembrance no longer from within themselves, but by means of external marks. What you have discovered is a recipe not for memory, but for reminder. And it is no true wisdom that you offer your disciples, but only its semblance, for by telling them of many things without teaching them you will make them seem to know much, while for the most part they know nothing, and as men filled, not with wisdom, but with the conceit of wisdom, they will be a burden to their fellows."

Phaedo in Greek means: *"the shining one"* or *"the brilliant one."* It derives from the verb *"faino"*, which itself derives from the word for light, *"fos."*

2. Balls of Light and UFO

Crop pictures with inexplicable phenomena are often associated with balls of light and/or UFOs in the vicinity. The larger designs commonly displaying symbolism from Earth's many cultures comprise the majority of crop circles studied. Their elegance, ingenuity, fluid lay of crop, and electromagnetic anomalies attracted researchers to crop circles before human crop art (HCA) proliferated. Often associated with balls of light and UFOs, anomalous crop circles may represent collaboration of multiple sources and intelligences. A number of unique characteristics distinguish anomalous crop circles from human-made crop art:

- Elongated apical plant stem nodes (stretching of the first node beneath the seed-head) is the most reliable visible plant change documented by the scientific research that indicates a cause other than mechanical flattening.
- Expulsion cavities (holes blown out usually at the lower plant stem nodes) are the second most reliable visible plant change shown by the scientific research to be related to non-mechanically-flattened crop.
- Stunted, malformed seeds and serious germination abnormalities are another scientifically-proven effect of the crop circle energy system.
- Marked bending of plant stems at the nodes — if present immediately after a crop circle has formed — may also be an indicator of authenticity; however, bending can also be caused by natural plant recovery processes, particularly in young, vigorously-growing crop, thus making this visible plant change one that must be very carefully evaluated.

These physical changes to crop circle plants and to the reproductive capability of the seeds from these plants vary among crop formations, due in part to the various species of plant involved, its growth phase and the precise composition and intensity level of the various energies involved.[2]

3. Commercial and Mechanical Planking by Humans

Self-professed hoaxers Doug Bower and Dave Chorley stated they had started the phenomenon in 1978 by making circles in crops with boards and ropes. They proceeded to make a crop circle in one hour after announcing they had come up with the idea while drinking in a pub. Their creation, however, had none of the inexplicable characteristics identified above in the first and second types. They succeeded in crudely flattening crop with boards and gaining notoriety.

Colin Andrews reported an effort to discredit crop circles with Operation Blackbird in the early 1990s. One of the mysteries of human-made crop art is the lack of arrests for damaging farmer's fields. Freddy Silva reports that some artists pay farmers for using their fields. At least one person has been prosecuted for property damage to farmers' crops. Matthew Williams was arrested and confessed to planking and stomping crop circles in the Dave and Doug style. Williams reported that he confessed his crimes to the court and made an agreement. He was able to speak publicly about formations he had constructed because they were covered by his agreement with the court. In 2010 he publicly spoke about crop circles he had made in the 1990s and subsequently launched an internet television channel dealing with human-made crop circles.

Crop circle conferences, tours, clubs, books, DVDs, and calendars boomed. A market demand arose which vendors were able to meet by making their own formations. Some researchers estimated that 95-99% of crop circles made in Wiltshire, England, in 2010 were human fabrications.

Wiltshire took a lead role as the crop art capital of the world, with estimated revenues in excess of 500,000 British pounds in 2010, or approximately $810,000 US. That is a great deal of annual revenue for a cottage industry reportedly dreamed up in a pub! Crafty creatures of the marketplace, some crop art makers also lay claim to special, if not divine, inspirations in their creations. Some say they seek to complete what nature has left incomplete.

Long-time researcher Freddy Silva reported numerous crop circle hoaxes in Wiltshire in an interview about his 2011 book, *Common Wealth: Our Legacy of Places of Power and the Transfiguration of the Human Soul*. He suggests that crop circles as a phenomenon have moved away from Wiltshire and into other parts of the world. Silva reported that after he published information about ACF that appeared on naturally occurring lei lines, hoaxers began to make crop art in the same locations he had named. Crop art makers have improved their skills with experience, and many hoaxed crop pictures are impressive to casual and inexperienced observers; but, with 30 years of experience, Silva reports hoaxing details that casual observers overlook.

Psychic capacities are part of the human experience, and it is well within the realm of possibility that a crop circle hoaxer could receive "channeled" information. The hoaxers' abilities to translate channeling into the physical characteristics of a crop circle, at best, vary on a case-by-case basis. People are inspired with intuition and messages daily, but their execution of inspired information remains within the range of the knowledge, skills, and abilities as a set of human construction.

4. Mechanical Planking after Anomalous Crop Pictures Form

Astronomer Carl Sagan wrote a letter to the United Kingdom's Ministry of Defense about official efforts to destroy real crop circles and create hoax replicas in 1996. Sagan's March 6, 1996 letter was posted on Linda Moulton Howe's Earthfiles.com on December 7, 2012. Dr. Sagan wrote to the U.K. Ministry of Defence:

> "Evidence has been uncovered showing some farmers have been paid considerable sums of money to destroy the real crop circles when they appear, and groups encouraged to then make hoaxed replicas."

Anomalous crop circles that have been altered as Carl Sagan discovered are sometimes found, especially in England. After an anomalous crop circle forms, mechanical boarding may be done over the top of it, additional features that "go nowhere" are hoaxed, or the entire formation may be destroyed and a clumsy replica hoaxed. Signs of overboarding were reported by early crop circle investigators but only suspected in some cases. The June 2, 2010, crop circle at Liddington Castle, Wiltshire, demonstrates the confusion created by overboarding.

Together with other indicators, I used the high precipitation and extreme temperature changes observed at the Liddington Castle crop picture to forecast cooler-then-average temperatures and high levels of precipitation for 2011.

Major floods and snowfall dominated the winter and spring in areas worldwide, notably Australia, Indonesia, and the USA, along with cooler-than-average temperatures in winter 2010 and spring 2011. Rainfall was so high worldwide in 2011 that sea levels dropped with water saturation on land. Similar anomalies were not reported in any other Wiltshire crop circles in 2010. Crop samples were not collected for testing from Liddington Castle, but the correlations between high rainfall and precipitation inside the circle suggest that an ACF was later overboarded at Liddington Castle.[3]

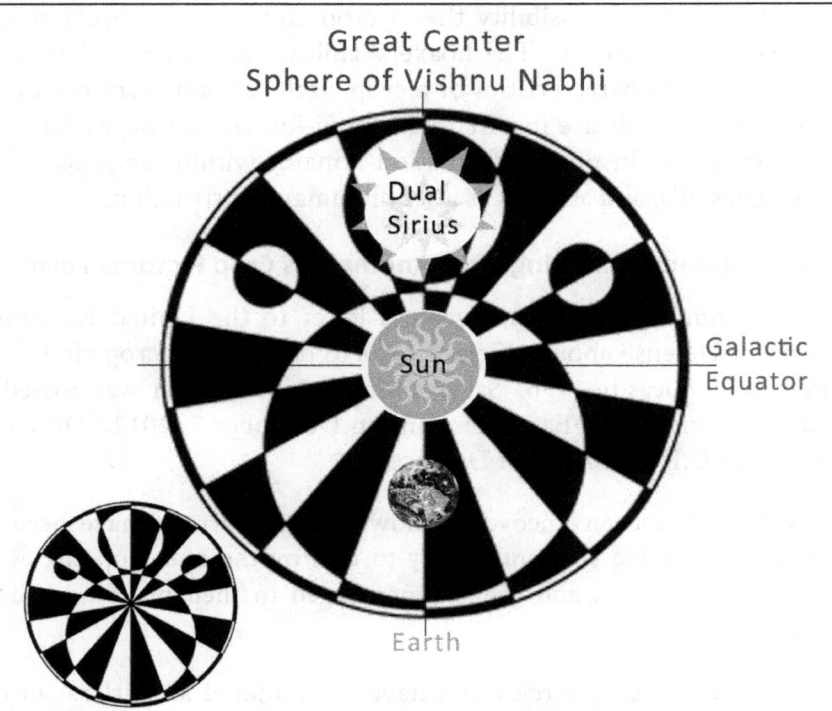

A rare conjunction of Sirius A and B while it conjuncted the Sun and the Earth was conjunct all three in a solar eclipse on July 11, 2010 corresponds with alignments in a crop circle formed at Liddington Castle (above left). The sphere of the galaxy is represented in eighteen increments of twenty degrees each that parallel the Mayan Tun count. The Tun uses eighteen months of twenty days each; thus, each day of the Tun is equal to 1/360th of a 360° circle. At the end of 360 days five extra days are added for a vague solar year of 365 days. This count is the basis of the Mayan civil calendar, the Haab. The crop circle formed June 2, 2010 in Wiltshire, England.

© 2010 and 2013 Krsanna Duran

A crop picture at Oliver's Castle in England on August 16, 2008 demonstrates that information contained in an ACF can be altered and falsified but recovered. The crop circle came to my attention in 2012 when the Mayan Ac Tah published his book on Mayan tradition, *The Night of the Last Katun: 2012 Maya*. Ac Tah wrote about the importance of the lunar eclipse on August 16, 2008, and I searched for crop circles on that date. Information about the Venus cycle gleaned from the formation was highly relevant to the Mayan calendar, but visible lines caused by mechanical planking were blatantly evident in photos. I would have dismissed the crop circle based on the visible planking lines except for two points that could not be easily ignored: The extreme relevance of the Venus cycle to the Mayan calendar and the late-season date in mid-August the crop circle appeared. Most profitable crop circle tours and conferences are completed by early August. Commercial entrepreneurs have little to gain by investing in mechanically made crop circles after the tourists leave. Fortunately, Janet Ossebaard had done an on-site investigation and reported her findings.

Ossebaard found "construction lines (forming the backbone of the formation) but...only bits and pieces!" Humans use construction lines for mechanical planking but they do not appear in ACF where unbroken crop bends with high energy and heat. She also found "more strange and totally unnecessary (from a geometrical point of view) underlying lines that seemed to be going nowhere. Some of these even exceeded the perimeter of the formation!" Some of the unnecessary lines that went nowhere were clumsy and nonsensical, thus discrediting the crop circle's construction and information, but it also contained anomalous features that defied mechanical planking.

In some areas Ossebaard found features of an ACF. "The centre of the formation showed a stunning swirl where the 3 tracks joined together. What struck me was the way the crop had swirled around the centre. This was not necessary for the creation of the inner swirl, the crop could have simply been pushed straight forward to meet in the middle and be twisted into a central bundle. In reality however, the outer right side of the tracks flowed toward the left as they reached the central point, thus creating a river-like flow of 3 streams meeting and swirling into each other as if to form a clock-wise vortex, a twister of stalks and seed heads." She found large downed areas where "the crop had gone down in a hexagonal way, as can clearly be seen on some of my pole shots...The hexagonal shape of the formation itself was repeated in the swirls of the triangle tips, like a hologram or a fractal: repeating itself into the finest details, into infinity..."

Mechanical construction and anomalous features were mixed in the formation. This suggested an effort to destroy and hoax over an ACF after it was discovered, as Carl Sagan had reported in his 1996 letter.

Crop circle profiteers are more likely to invest resources in mechanically constructed crop pictures to bring tourist business to Wiltshire. Altering and defacing an ACF does not serve the tourist industry. Destroying ACF and making clumsy replicas discredits the intelligence and capabilities of the mysterious Circle Makers, thus minimizing competition for loyalty to established authority.

Various sequences of designs and locations of crop circles within specific periods of time appear to relate to each other through conditions of the earth. As earth's conditions change over time crop circles and sets of crop circles change.

Crop Circle and UFO Context

Megalithic Britain

First UFO reports during World War II and then crop circles in fields near Stonehenge caught the British by surprise in a brief thirty years of post-modern history. Winston Churchill dispensed with UFO reports in 1942 by classifying them top secret, with comments about sustaining religious faith during time of war. Decades before secret UFO reports were declassified for public review, bright blinking lights appeared above fields in England where mysterious impressions appeared in crops near the ancient megaliths at Stonehenge in the 1970s.

Crop circles in fields all could see were not as easy to obscure with secrecy as the UFOs had been in 1942. They required masking with deceptions like stage magician Jasper Meskelyne had used to hide British military operations during World War II. The era of humanly made crop art, often overboarded on top of anomalous crop circles, began in the 1980s.

Wiltshire with Stonehenge was ringed with fourteen Army bases by 2006, a measure of the importance the British government placed on the small county of only 1,346 square miles. Do the British plan a military defense of Wiltshire in central England, in contrast to coastal areas where conventional invading forces are more probable? Or does militarization of the Stonehenge area have darker objectives? A landmark UFO cover-up case in Rendelsham Forest, at the Royal Air Force Station Woodbridge 155 miles northeast of Stonehenge in Suffolk near the English Channel, in 1980 continues to be a focus of UFO investigations in England. It is sometimes called "Britain's Roswell," and compared with the UFO crash at Roswell, New Mexico in 1947.

The modern military build-up in Wiltshire is as mysterious as the ancient megalithic builders in Scotland, home of the oldest astronomical observatory in the world that is 10,000 years old. Older megalithic sites from Orkney Island stretching through southern England were erected between 11,000 and 5,000 years ago, with Stonehenge among the newer additions to the megalithic grid. Wooden postholes at the Stonehenge site have been carbon dated to 11,000 years of age (9000 BCE), even though the present-day megaliths were raised about 4,400 years ago (2200 BCE). Construction at Stonehenge had continued for over 6,000 years by unknown builders, between 11,000 and 5,000 years ago, before mysterious crop circles proliferated around them in the 1970s.

Great Britain was connected to mainland Europe by the Dogger land mass in the North Sea until a tsunami resulting from a submarine landslide in Norway separated it from the mainland about 8200 years ago. Islands remained above water between England and Holland 6,000 years ago. Hunter gatherers, the ancestral peoples of Western Europe, populated the British Isles 14,000 years ago. DNA sampling shows that Great Britain's population is consistent with others of Western Europe, but none of them had permanent settlements 11,000 years ago. Great Britain was among the last areas of Europe to develop agriculture, because of slower warming there at the end of the ice age. Analysis of burials from the first phase of Stonehenge found minerals from Switzerland in the enamel of teeth 5,000 years ago. A settlement at Durrington Walls east of Stonehenge is carbon dated to 4,600 years before present (2600 BCE), or the last phases of Stonehenge when megaliths were raised. Much of England was settled during the Nordic Bronze Age between 1700 and 1100 BCE and then later by Germanic tribes. The earliest Celtic culture in central Europe appeared about 3200 years ago (1200 BCE), and the Celts appeared in Ireland between 600 and 400 BCE, or 2,600 years ago.

The identity of the megalithic builders with complex astronomy in Scotland 10,000 years ago, when hunter gatherers wandered Western Europe before agriculture remain as mysterious as the origin of anomalous crop circles and the UFOs that appear with them. Signs of high heat expression with anomalous electric and magnetic fields are characteristics of mysterious anomalous crop circles. In this historical landscape human crop artists began imitating authentic crop circles of mysterious origin in the 1980s, a decade after crop formations of mysterious origin began appearing near Stonehenge. Although appealing to the eye, human-made crop art does not display signature heat, electric and magnetic characteristics of anomalous formations. The English deceived the Germans with Jasper Meskelyne's stage magic during World War II, but they deceive only private citizens with staged crop circles.

Anomalous crop circles -- authentic ones -- continue to appear on every continent of the Earth, while the majority of crop circles in Wiltshire are made within days of profitable crop circle tours and conferences. A small number of crop circles formed in England in early 2014, but the number suddenly escalated during paid tours of crop circles and conferences that were advertised months in advance. After paid tours and conferences ended, the number of crop circles in England rapidly declined.

Brilliantly laid crop circles in Holland formed in surprising alignments with the megaliths that predated Stonehenge when portions of Doggerland were above water. Anomalous crop circles continue to proliferate on ancient sacred lands of indigenous peoples worldwide.

Notes

[1] Mutwa, Credo. 1996. *Isilwane, The Animal.* Struik Publishers: Cape Town, South Africa. p 24

[2] BLT Research www.bltresearch.com/

[3] Duran, Krsanna. 2011. "Liddington Castle Crop Circle." All Star Roundup.

http://www.allstarroundup.com/cc/ccliddington2010.html

APPENDIX THREE

Symbols and Communication

"If men learn this [written language], it will implant forgetfulness in their souls; they will cease to exercise memory because they rely on that which is written, calling things to remembrance no longer from within themselves, but by means of external marks. What you have discovered is a recipe not for memory, but for reminder. And it is no true wisdom that you offer your disciples, but only its semblance, for by telling them of many things without teaching them you will make them seem to know much, while for the most part they know nothing, and as men filled, not with wisdom, but with the conceit of wisdom, they will be a burden to their fellows." (Plato, "Phaedrus")

Communication between two different systems, whether they are physical, mental, or cultural systems, requires a medium of exchange to negotiate differences. In the simple communication of ideas between you and me through the written word on this page, we must have a point of exchange for your ideas and mine, the exchange between the reader and the writer. As much as Plato did not like to rely on "external marks" for remembrance, printed words and images are a medium we commonly use for exchanging between personal and cultural viewpoints.

Broad spectrum communication with modulated differentials is achieved with tensor technology in UFO contacts. Tensors translate differentials between sets of coordinates. If, for example, a city is laid out with streets and cross streets in an area eight miles long and two miles wide, the eight mile by two mile grid of streets is its coordinates. Another city laid out in circles has a different set of coordinates. Each city has different points of tension and stress inherent in its layout. A tensor translates correspondences and parities between coordinates for the square city and the circular one.

Humans intuitively use tensors to communicate on multiple spectra of living. Symbols are natural tensors of mind and consciousness, both within an individual's personal perception and intuition (remembrance within self) as well as with other selves. Each living human is a composite biosystem of body, mind, and spirit with unique coordinates in time and space and energy. The sum of all coordinates of consciousness within a social-cultural system comprises its collective consciousness, its construction of time and space as expressions of existence. UFOlk are professionals in communicating with a wide range of civilizations in various states of development and have fine-tuned these processes to science and technology. Mysteries of time and space that UFOs display are part and parcel of the enigmatic UFO intelligence, which embraces tensor applications and rich symbolism.

"What we call a symbol is a term, a name, or even a picture that may be familiar in daily life, yet that possesses specific connotations in addition to its conventional and obvious meaning. It implies something that is hidden from us.... [It] is never precisely defined or fully explained. Nor can one hope to define or explain it. As the mind explores the symbol, it is led to ideas that lie beyond the grasp of reason..." (Jung, *Man and His Symbols*)

Allegory

Representing an abstract or spiritual meaning through concrete or material forms is allegory. In this passage from Genesis, water is a metaphor for an incorporeal form not yet existing in physical experience but is in process of acquiring structure. "And God made the firmament, and divided the waters which were under the firmament from the waters which were above the firmament: and it was so." In making the firmament God gave structure with the "under" and the "above," to separate with defined structure that which had been formless and void, thus giving definition to that which had not been defined. This defining process extrapolated with the metaphor of water is allegory.

"Allegory is an extended form of metaphor in which objects, persons, and actions in a narrative are equated with meanings that lie outside the narrative itself." An abstraction is made in the guise of a concrete form. Ideas are represented with concrete forms in allegory.

The absence of a material island in the Atlantic Ocean where Plato said Atlantis had existed prompts some to view his narrative about Atlantis as allegory pertaining to the ideal government. Other readers view Plato's narrative about Atlantis as a literal account of the island's demise. In this instance, Plato may have taken advantage of Atlantis' disappearance to extrapolate allegory about the ideal government.

Analogy

An analogy compares two different things to show how they are similar, but extends beyond a figure of speech or symbolism with a logical argument. By showing how two things share similar characteristics, an analogy invokes a logical conclusion that they are similar in other ways as well.

Archetype

A universally understood symbol, term, or pattern upon which others are copied, patterned, or emulated is an archetype. Carl Jung states: "The term 'archetype' occurs as early as Philo Judaeus, with reference to the Imago Dei (God-image) in man. It can also be found in Irenaeus, who says: 'The creator of the world did not fashion these things directly from himself but copied them from archetypes outside himself... The term 'archetype' is not found in St. Augustine, but the idea of it is... he speaks of "ideae principalis," 'which are themselves not formed... but are contained in the divine understanding.'" (Jung, *The Archetypes and the Collective Unconscious*)

Archetypes are used to illuminate personality and literature. They are universally meaningful, non-literal elements that can include scenes, plots, and characters. The familiar and comfortable haven is the archetypal opposite of the wilderness. Every archetype has an opposite consistent with the duality that brings forth the physical world. In philosophy, Plato first referred to ideal Forms of the perceived or sensible things or types to articulate the concept of an archetype. Plato believed the cosmos itself came into being using as its model the world of Forms, or archetypes.

A symbolic archetype is a symbol that signals direct association with an archetype. The Homo genus of primates that walk upright on two legs is an archetypal evolution on Earth. Although the genus has numerous variations in skull sizes and prominences, a skull that depicts the general features of the skull of the Homo is a symbolic archetype if it signals shared attributes of the archetype. The skull may be Homo sapiens, Homo erectus, or some other rarer species if it embodies archetypal attributes of the genus.

Metaphor

Something that is used to represent something else is a metaphor. It may be a symbol or a figure of speech that is not literally applicable in order to suggest a resemblance. Cosmic water and seas are metaphors anciently used for incorporeal mediums, depicted in both narrative and graphics. Plato had lived in Egypt as had Moses before writing Genesis, and they shared a cultural frame of reference that used water as a metaphor for an incorporeal entity.

All Egyptian cosmology held that the world had arisen out of the lifeless primordial waters of chaos. In its ancient meaning "chaos" was a chasm, a gap, or a void, in contrast to the modern meaning of disorder. The account of how the world was created from primordial waters differed from city to city, depending on the god most closely associated with the city. Egyptian creation stories all involved eight primordial gods in varying orders of importance, collectively called the Ogdoad. In Moses' creation story he used the Hebrew plural form, in the sense that it is both masculine and feminine, of the word for "Gods," or "Elohim." The Hebraic text of Genesis still uses the plural form of gods in the beginning of creation, but Vatican scholars who translated the Bible changed the text to read in the singular, or "God."

> 2. And the earth was without form, and void; and darkness was upon the face of the deep. And the Spirit of God moved upon the face of the waters...
>
> 6. And God said, Let there be a firmament in the midst of the waters, and let it divide the waters from the waters.
> 7. And God made the firmament, and divided the waters which were under the firmament from the waters which were above the firmament: and it was so.
> 8. And God called the firmament Heaven. And the evening and the morning were the second day. (Genesis 1 King James Version of the Bible)

Plato compared the incorporeal form of water with a twenty-sided geometry, an icosahedron, in "Timaeus." "If the Form of Water is an incorporeal entity, it is difficult to see what it would mean to insinuate phenomenal properties into it. Once we see the definition of the elements separated from the hypothesis that explains the phenomenal properties of their cosmic images we can see that it is the Demiurge who is made responsible for matching up a geometrical structure with a type of phenomenal property and for establishing their necessary connection... Nothing in the nature of the geometrical structure of water entails that cosmic water feel watery to us as opposed to fiery. This is why a definition of phenomenal water is a definition of an image needing to be supplemented by a definition of the Form of Water; that is, by a mathematical definition [in the case of Plato]." (Gerson, *Aristotle and Other Platonists*)

As planets go, the presence of water as a phenomenal substance is relatively rare. But, water as a Perfect Form in potential, or archetype that abides with planets, planets that are presently waterless amid the primordial waters of the cosmos possess the potential of water that will develop as Plato's Perfect Form unfolds in planetary life.

Sign

A sign is something that stands for something else. A sign has finite and discrete meaning, such as the letters of the alphabet with specific and limited sounds associated with them. The sounds of letters form words that are written to specify discrete and limited meanings. The word "tree" represents the tree, which you may climb or chop down. The word "run" stands for an action, which you may perform, or perhaps the place where you keep your dog.

It is the recitation of literal meaning of written language as signs that stand for other things to which Plato referred when he said, "...they will cease to exercise memory because they rely on that which is written, calling things to remembrance no longer from within themselves..."

This pitfall of written language is the liability of rote recitation, but it is the necessary evil that has freed the common person from reliance on single-pointed authority that doles out knowledge at discretion. Translating the Bible into English freed the Protestant Revolution to understand the "word" as it was written in contrast to how it was interpreted by one or another authority.

A word has a general meaning, its "dictionary meaning." For almost all words, the dictionary meaning is actually a range of meanings, which can differ widely. A word's dictionary meaning is nonspecific; it does not refer to any particular thing or experience. When used in a specific context, a word has a specific meaning. The word "tree" has a number of meanings, ranging from "a tall, woody plant" to a diagram showing family lineage; "tree" can also be a verb meaning to force someone into a difficult position.

A symbol and a sign each invoke distinct and unique modalities of the mind. Well utilized, a symbol calls forth non-linear intuitive thinking. A sign employs linear discrete thinking to the task of interpreting the meaning that best suits its application and context.

Symbol

A symbol means more than it literally says and has more than one layer of meaning. The more profound the symbol, the greater the complexity of the layers of meaning. The symbol itself may be simple, like the universally recognized tree of life that may be depicted with simple line drawings. The level or levels of meaning of a symbol are revealed in the way it is used.

A symbol may have three main levels of meaning and often will have all three:

Personal symbols have associations unique to an individual's experience. We all give meaning to things in our experience, beyond their immediate practical uses. A child's fond memories of his mother's uniquely shaped face and head as she told bedtime stories may hold the shadows cast by a woman's head and face as personal symbols of magical tales and loving intimacy. The head is a powerful cultural and universal symbol, but the personal experience shared by child and mother in the glow of a bedside lamp conjure a personal association within the larger matrix of the symbol's layered meanings.

Cultural symbols have unique attributes within a defined group of people who often share language and beliefs that project special meaning. Symbols may have different meanings in different cultures. The Skull and Crossbones symbol is used in various ways by different cultures. It marks Spanish cemeteries. Some militaries use it. The Skull and Crossbones Society at Yale University is culturally recognized within America for its members who joined the ranks of number of powerful and elite leaders after leaving the university.

Universal symbols apply to all humans and are recognized for their transpersonal, transcultural meanings. Jungian psychology argues that some symbols have universal meaning derived from the collective unconscious. Jung reminds us that the head or skull served as the transmuting vessel for the alchemist. For the Greek alchemists, the same equivalence existed between the "Stone-brain," i.e. the Philosopher's Stone and the "Stone which is not a stone", i.e. the brain.

Jung clarified that the hermetical vessel is of the highest importance: "For the alchemist the vessel is something truly marvelous...it must be completely round, in imitation of the spherical cosmos...It is a kind of matrix or uterus from which the filius philosophorum, the miraculous stone, is to be born". ("Psychology and Alchemy," Collected Works, Vol. 12) The vessel is as important as the prima materia, which, in turn, is assimilated to the outcome of the Philosopher's Stone. We may thus understand why the head, the spherical body is, at one and the same time, the Philosopher's Stone: head, and hence spirit. In fact, the alchemical treatise Artis Auriferae reminds us that the brain is the space where the Royal Marriage is realized and consummated. (Arturo Schwarz, "Ofer Lellouche and the Alchemical Skull")

APPENDIX FOUR

UFO Communication and Technology

Without a single television interview on *Good Morning America* or the *Tonight Show* UFO communications have spread far and wide. All public sightings of UFOs have been at sufficient distances to preclude direct contact with the physical craft. A UFO has never landed on the White House lawn or any public venue for open house inspection. Metal samples have never been offered for public viewing.

Communication about UFOs and extraterrestrials has arisen from the grassroots level of individual witnesses and experiencers as well as investigators and onlookers. When establishing communication with an individual contactee or abductee, UFO contactors invariably demonstrate telepathy in-hand with a wide range of technology.

The distant nature of UFO activity since the *Shoot Them Down!* era in the 1950s poses a variety of problems that require human experiencers to learn the ropes one step at a time. Communication is of the essence in a scenario of this kind. Of course, the subtleties of face-to-face communication and body language humans use intuitively are limited in remote UFO contact.

In its essence, communication comprises signals containing information with one or more observers, or points of observation. Information may arise from the mind, the psyche, or the body, or any combination of these planes. Signals are sent, received, and understood for good communication. Signals may arise from and be perceived and understood with any of the five physical senses — sight, sound, smell, taste, and tactile — as well as paranormal senses. Steadily repeated signals represent coherence, or alignment, in communication.

Exchanging communication involves

1) receiving and understanding signals that contain information and

2) responding to information transmitted in a way that's coherent with the originating signal.

In order to be understood a signal containing information must be comprehensible at the point at which it is received. Once a signal is received and understood, a response must be comprehensible at the point to which it is sent. If, for instance, a cat meows to signal hunger, a coherent human response is to feed the cat. If, instead, a human sprays the cat for fleas and leaves the cat hungry communication breaks down and coherence is lost.

An unidentified object hovering in full view of 1.25 million people for thirty minutes at the Battle of Los Angeles signaled the presence of mystery with technological power. A UFO crash near the Roswell Army Airfield where the Enola Gay was launched to carry the first atomic payload signaled that the Army was not alone in the desert. A spree of intelligently guided fireballs between Sandia and White Sands in 1948 signaled the ability and willingness to act expeditiously. Visual presence of previously believed impossible shapes, speeds, and technologies is a powerful communication.

The American government responded to the steady signals sent by UFOs by creating the CIA, Department of Defense, and a stand-alone Air Force that could chase down UFOs without informing the Army. The CIA formulated a policy of blocking all information about UFOs to the media and the public. The Air Force carried out the policy with maximum security without alerting the Army, which was, after all, a land force. UFOs called for an Air Force.

With communication blocked at official levels of government and military, UFOs increased appearances to make them more visible to the public. Comprehensible signals that could be understood by the public and a means of disseminating information that bypassed the official machine that blocked communication with the American public was the challenge for intelligently controlled UFOs by 1952. By ignoring the steady signal UFOs sent, even though intelligent bystanders could clearly observe the signal, the official machine created a blockage of power that threatened to overload the bureaucracy that created it. It was only a matter of time.

Informing the public of his official activities with the Air Force after his retirement, J. Allen Hynek filled the need for a hero. The official machine's self-serving gratification and missile envy had created a demand for a hero from within its own ranks. After retiring from professional duties with the Air Force, Hynek founded the J. Allen Hynek Center for UFO Studies. He publicly conceded that astronomers and the Air Force do, in fact, see UFOs. The unspoken dictum of official policy after the Robertson Panel made its recommendations was not to inform the media about UFOs. Hynek charted the wilderness with classifications for communicating about a variety of UFO activities. These included daylight discs, nocturnal lights, radar sightings, and Close Encounters of the first, second, and third kinds. Close Encounters of the fourth and fifth kinds were later proposed.

The CIA was more concerned with reports about UFO than it was with the UFOs. Official policy dictated that unidentified flying objects never be called UFOs. They were to be called a balloon, a meteor, an aircraft, or anything the public would accept as long as it was not officially called a UFO. As an Air Force consultant Dr. Hynek released the now-famous swamp gas explanation. The media was deliberately and meticulously omitted from the communication lines of UFO reports.

The Phoenix Lights remain the premier nocturnal lights event yet reported. A triangular formation of lights traveled in the night-time sky across the U.S.A. states of Arizona and Nevada and the Mexican state of Sonora on March 13, 1997. Observed by millions of people, the light formation was visible for 106 minutes. A second series of stationary lights, which some witnesses described as a huge carpenter's square-shaped UFO containing lights, was visible over the Phoenix, Arizona, area. Fife Symington, then governor of Arizona, witnessed the Phoenix lights and called the object "otherworldly." The U.S. Air Force identified the stationary lights in the Phoenix area as flares dropped by aircraft at the Barry Goldwater Range.

William F. Hamilton, one of the most experienced UFO researchers in the United States, started his study of UFOs as a teenager with George van Tassel at Giant Rock in 1953. At the Giant Rock conventions Hamilton made first-hand observations of many UFO flybys at low altitudes in Close Encounters of the first kind (CE-1). He participated in George van Tassel's communication with extraterrestrial intelligences in Close Encounters of the fifth kind (CE-5). He was acquainted with many UFO contactees who reported Close Encounters of the third kind (CE-3). He was the youngest member to join Dan Fry's "Understanding" organization. Hamilton was transported aboard a UFO in 1992 in a Close Encounter of the fourth kind (CE-4), where he encountered a tall Gray that met him with a sense of universal love. While Hamilton was aboard the UFO his wife awaited his return in an altered state, representing a Close Encounter of the second kind (CE-2). In a CE-2 a UFO is observed with associated physical effects, including, but not limited to, heat or radiation, damage to the terrain, paralysis, interference with engines or TV or radio reception, or lost time.

The Giant Rock Spacecraft Conventions that George van Tassel hosted from 1953 to 1978 provided the venue for Close Encounters of the first kind (CE-1). While thousands gathered on the California desert at Giant Rock clearly structured UFOs commonly flew directly into observers' view, well within the 500 yards that define a CE-1. UFOs' appearances during conventions that van Tassel planned and advertised in advance endowed these with special features of a Close Encounter of the fifth kind (CE-5), as Steven Greer of the Disclosure Project proposed. Close Encounters of the fifth kind are joint contact events produced through the conscious, voluntary, and proactive human-initiated or cooperative communication with extraterrestrial intelligences.

Contactees and Abductees

Lone individuals reporting face-to-face contact with UFO occupants are also a direct source of information. Contactees, those who experience conscious face-to-face meetings with UFO occupants, provide the most reliable information accepted by popular standards. Contactees are few and far between since the flying saucer air wars of the '50s, when President Harry Truman ordered the Air Force to shoot down any UFO that refused to land. Contactees discuss with UFO occupants numerous topics, ranging from science, history, biology, and evolution to personal matters. The presence of military personnel has never been reported in conscious physical UFO contacts. Daniel Fry and George van Tassel typify Close Encounters of the third kind (CE-3) as well as Close Encounters of the fifth kind (CE-5).

After numerous face-to-face contacts with UFO occupants in the '50s, reports of abductions that had been blocked from memory began proliferating in the '60s. As with all organic organizing principles, these guidelines are not absolute in strict linear terms. A small number of abductions occurred as early as 1940, if not earlier. Some abduction scenarios parallel ancient accounts of angels, fairies, *little people*, and mystical lore that are well documented within metaphysics, beyond classical physics.

In contrast to contactees with direct physical encounters in a waking state, abductions commonly occur during sleep. Sightings of physical UFOs are sometimes made before or after abductions. Abductees commonly describe transportation through physical objects, such as walls. In rare instances, implants that have been inserted into their bodies are recovered. ET interests in human genetics, pregnancies, and interrupted pregnancies are common scenarios. Some abductees report military personnel present during abductions. A small number of abductees report childhood experiences with mind control projects involving the military, and almost always when a family member is in the military. Whitley Strieber and Betty and Barney Hill typify abductees in Close Encounters of the fourth kind (CE-4).

Profiles of both contactees and abductees include psychic functions that heighten as anomalous contact experiences increase. Psychic abilities, skills, and awareness in broad social terms increased throughout the twentieth century, and included private and military experiments, studies, and publications. Not a single scientific study of extrasensory perceptions was published in the nineteenth century, when five senses — sight, sounds, smell, taste, and tactile — were the scientifically accepted modes of perception. Numerous well documented scientific studies of the paranormal were published in the twentieth century, when renowned psychic and remote viewer Ingo Swann spoke at the United Nations about seventeen perceptual modes. Scientific interest in abilities and perceptions beyond the five senses continues to climb in the 2first century with theories and proofs of quantum mechanics.

Tensor Technology

Tensor communication employs a beam similar to microwave that is attuned to the frequency of the nervous system of the person to whom it is directed, according to Richard Miller in *Star Wards*. In some cases, the frequency of a tensor beam can be set to include more than one person, as was done with George Hunt Williamson and Richard Miller. Stevens reported that he witnessed Hunt Williamson and Miller channel the same message word-for-word in perfect stereo while both were in altered states.

In some instances a person at a compatible frequency with a tensor beam may actually hear the transmission as it is sent and before the channel articulates the words. A person with a frequency dissonant to the tensor beam may even experience a slight "shock" when walking into or interrupting the beam in transmission to the channel. With experience and sensitivity tensor technology can be recognized as distinct from psychic channeling.

Mediums

Introductory statement from the Ministry of Universal Wisdom, George Van Tassel's official organization, founded in 1952:

"Our organization is in no way correlated with Ashtar Command or their personality of their Ashtar. "Ashtar Command" was started by a man named Robert Short (or also known as Bill Rose), an Editor of a 1950s UFO magazine — "Interplanetary News" and at one time friend of George Van Tassel. Mr. Short felt Ashtar's communications (through Van Tassel) should become commercial and mainstream, in order for personal notoriety, not for a truth to the public. Due to Mr. Short's difference of opinion to Van Tassel, their friendship parted on bad terms. Mr. Short soon thereafter began Ashtar Command. Mr. Short was not in contact with the original Ashtar, and George Van Tassel was never apart of Mr. Short's organization. Ashtar's personality is a distinct authority, who communicated with Van for specific messages, this was most graphically displayed in the message from Ashtar, through Van Tassel to the U.S. Government. Ashtar is not a metaphysical philosopher or rambler. George Van Tassel's organization is in no correlation with Ashtar Command and advises persons to be extremely discerning. The approach of Love is to be aware, but there is more needed to grow as a person and advance in intelligence. Giving yourself and your intelligence up to love or Light Beings, causes passive thinking and retardation of personality. Science and spirituality are one, not a divided subject. The Ashtar of Ashtar Command is a real personality, this personality is a clone of the original Ashtar. You CANNOT "channel" space intelligence. This does not mean the assistance of space intelligence is only limited in specific individuals, people who deem themselves "chosen" or the "spiritual elite". We will not define the method of communication of Ashtar through Van, as will not give a correction to the lie Ashtar Command has created."

Thelma Terrell adopted the name Tuella and organized a virtual "wing" of the Ashtar Command, on a par with Bob Short's Ashtar Command. The term *"channel"* captured the imagination of many mediums and psychics, who began identifying their skill as *"channeling."* In some instances, the information mediums received is called *"downloads."*

Tuella was a psychic channel who made no claim to be a tensor channel as van Tassel had introduced that technology. She liked the term "channel" and adopted it for her role with the Ashtar Command. Under the auspices of Tuella's psychic channeling Jesus-Sananda was incorporated into the Ashtar Command. Although their plans had been delayed, as a result of interference by "dark forces," the newly formed space command made plans for Ascension and World Evacuation under Tuella's mediumship.

Inevitable cultural iterations of familiar doctrines and theologies commingled with new slants on spirituality and science among UFO followers.

Leo Sprinkle

Leo Sprinkle's milestone research in 1964 was the first psychological study of individuals who reported UFOs. Conducted at the University of Wyoming, where he was a Professor of Counseling Services, Dr. Sprinkle used an inventory of standard tests on hundreds of experiencers. He concluded that most UFO witnesses are north in psychological functioning. He further concluded, "There is sufficient evidence to accept the hypothesis that psychic phenomena, including channeled communications, are associated with UFO encounters; further, there is emerging evidence that UFO contactees view themselves as changing from planetary persons to cosmic citizens."

In his book, *Soul Samples* Sprinkle summed up his approach to psychic experiences common for UFO experiencers. "My approach is to minimize the tendency to 'explain' (or explain away) the reality of psychic experiences, and to emphasize the willingness to 'explore' the personal meaning of these human experiences of spiritual emergence." Sprinkle's PACTS model of abductee/contactee experience, based on twenty-four years of study and published in 1988.[1]

Dr. Sprinkle reports that while growing up about 40 miles east of Pueblo, Colorado, he was taken for a ride in a UFO. The tall alien in a space suit put his arm around Sprinkle as they rode, and while watching the stars the alien told him to "learn to write." After observing a "flying saucer" (daylight disk) in 1949, Leo Sprinkle and his wife observed a silent UFO which "hovered, moved, hovered, moved, etc." over Boulder, Colorado in 1956.

"Maybe it's a fantasy, maybe it's a daydream, but whatever it is, it's affected my life to the point that I'm on a mission," he said. Part of that mission is to help others make the most of their UFO encounters, he said. He tries to help people deal with their experiences in such a way they will get something meaningful from it.

In 1980, Dr. Sprinkle founded the Rocky Mountain Conference on UFO Investigation which is still going strong. The conference has served as a focal point and beacon of hope for hundreds of abductees/contactees/experiencers hoping to come to terms with their "high strange" experiences.

Helena Blavatsky

Helena Blavatsky is especially relevant to UFO experiencers with intriguing parallels to contact development. She displayed psi abilities seen among UFO occupants and subsequently developed by UFO experiencers. A champion of the Vedic traditions, she lived and worked in India for decades. In 1976 India issued a postage stamp commemorating the 100-year anniversary of Blavatsky's first visit to the country. After living in Tibet with her master teacher, the Mahatma Morya from the Punjab region of India, Blavatsky translated into English the text of an ancient Tibetan document she reported studying, entitled *The Voice of the Silence*. Western scholars, who had never seen Eastern literature of the order Blavatsky published, scrutinized her with a critical eye. She was defamed, slandered, and accused of fraud. More than 100 years after her visit to Tibet the Fourteenth Dalai Lama affirmed *The Voice of the Silence* is authentic Tibetan literature.

Along with her voluminous publications, which included *The Secret Doctrine* and *The Veil of Isis*, letters handwritten by Blavatsky's Mahatmas (teachers) in Tibet commonly materialized in response to questions and situations of special concern. The letters, written in unique red and blue ink, are presently in the British Library. As might be suspected, Blavatsky was defamed, slandered, and accused of fraudulently writing these letters. Handwriting experts have determined that Blavatsky did not write the letters herself.

Testimony and experiments by numerous witnesses affirm the letters materialized in their presence, sometimes answering questions witnesses asked while they waited for responses. Daniel Caldwell provides hundreds of pages of testimony by Blavatsky's close associates in the book, *The Esoteric World of Madame Blavatsky: Insights Into The Life of A Modern Sphinx*.

Parallels with Helena Blavatsky's amazing faculties and UFO phenomena will be apparent as this *hidden history* unfolds. In a speech to the Theosophical Society of America in 1875 she predicted that heightened psychic sensitivity and awareness would develop among humanity in the 20th century. In an 1882 letter Blavatsky's teacher, Koot Hoomi, wrote about the intelligence of humanity as the whole host already evolved in contrast to only humanity of the earth as we see it, thus specifying the hosts of the plural solar systems representing the mother source:

"...the mystic name given by us to the hosts of... (the solar Dhyan Chohans or the host of only our solar system) taken collectively, which host represents the mother source, the aggregate amount of all the intelligences that were, are, or will be, whether on our string of man-bearing planets or on any part or portion of our solar system. And this will bring you by analogy to see that in its turn Adi-Buddhi (as its very name translated literally implies) is the aggregate intelligence of the universal intelligences including that of the Dhyan Chohans even of the highest order. That is all I dare now to tell you on this special subject, as I fear I have already transcended the limit. Therefore whenever I speak of humanity without specifying it you must understand that I mean not humanity of our fourth round as we see it on this speck of mud in space but the whole host already evolved." (Letter written by Mahatma Koot Hoomi to A. O. Hume, received July 10, 1882)

Notes

[1] After conducting his landmark study of UFO contactees and abductees, Dr. Leo Sprinkle developed the PACTS model of contact with spiritual beings, extraterrestrials and ultraterrestrials in 1988. In addition to spiritual beings, extraterrestrial or ultraterrestrial contacts that Dr. Sprinkle identified, other sources of activity have been reported since the mid-1980s.

The PACTS Model

P = PREPARATION - Family & cultural experiences

Family and/or cultural tradition of ESP and/or spiritual contacts. Childhood visitation by Spiritual Beings (SB's). Lucid dreams or precognitive dreams of possible future events. Psychic experiences (e.g., telepathy, clairvoyance, seeing auras, etc.)

A = ABDUCTION - Inducted or initiated, involuntarily, by SB's

UFO sightings and/or UFB abduction experiences or partial amnesic events. Taken aboard spacecraft by SB's or UFO entities. Unexplained body marks, scars, emotional reactions (Why me?). Feeling of being "drafted" for some unexplained purpose.

C = CONTACT - Inducted or initiated, voluntarily, by SB's

Adult visitations (by SB's or spiritual guides). Psychic experiences (telepathy, clairvoyance, PK, healing, etc.). Lucid dreams and/or precognitive dreams of possible future. Emotional reactions (Why me? Purpose of visitations?). Feelings of "volunteering" for a spiritual mission or task.

T = TRAINING - Instruction for a mission or task

Obsessive/compulsive behaviors (reading, traveling, visions, etc.) Reading various materials, including "uninteresting" materials. Change in personality; feeling of being monitored; "implanted" knowledge. Review of possible past lives.

S = SERVICE - Cooperation with SB's

Channeling verbal and/or written information from SB's. Serving as a "messenger" by conducting research, talking to others, etc. Providing instruction, healing, and/or assistance to others. Working to minimize planetary difficulties; giving assistance to Humankind. Feeling that one "knows" his/her task or purpose in life.

References

Ac Tah, translated by Ananda and James Needham. 2010. *The Night of the Last Katun: 2012 Maya.* Printed in Mexico. pp 33-34

Alexander, Eben. 2012. *Proof of Heaven: A Neurosurgeon's Journey into the Afterlife.* Simon & Schuster Paperbacks: New York, NY. pp 7-10

Barrios, Carlos, translated by Lisa Carter. 2009. *The Book of Destiny. Unlocking the Secrets of the Ancient Mayans and the Prophecy of 2012.* Harper One: New York, NY. p 211

Beaulieu, Paul-Alain. "Berossos on Late Babylonian History." *Special Issue of Oriental Studies.* 2006.

Black Elk, Wallace and William F. Lyons. 1990. *Black Elk: Sacred Ways of a Lakota.* HarperCollins Paperbacks: New York, NY. p 32, 91, 92

Blavatsky, H. P., edited by Boris de Zirkoff. 1888. *The Secret Doctrine.* Wheaton, IL: The Theosophical Publishing House. pp Vol 2, 263-276

———"Mistaken Notions on 'The Secret Doctrine'" Lucifer magazine, June 15, 1890, pages 333-35 (*H.P. Blavatsky: Collected Writings,* Volume XII, compiled by Boris de Zirkoff. 1980. Theosophical Publishing House: Wheaton, IL. pp 234-237

Bricker, Harvey M. and Victoria R. 2011. *Astronomy in the Maya Codices.* American Philosophical Society: Philadelphia, PA. pp 4-10, 53-59, 249-261

Cain, Fraser. "Comet Strikes Increase As We Pass Through the Galactic Plane."*Universe Today.* May 6, 2008. . www.universetoday.com/14082/comet-strikes-increase-as-we-pass-through-the-galactic-plane/

Caldwell, Daniel. 2000. *The Esoteric World of Madame Blavatsky.* Quest Books, Theosophical Publishing House: Wheaton, IL. pp 54-55, 57

Callaway, Ewen. "Mystery humans spiced up ancients' sex life." *Nature international weekly journal of science.* 19 November 2013. doi:10.1038/nature.2013.14196 http://www.nature.com/news/mystery-humans-spiced-up-ancients-sex-lives-1.14196

Campbell, Joseph. 1978. *Creative Mythology*. Penguin Books: New York, NY. 5-6

Cantalupo, Sebastiano, etal. "A cosmic web filament revealed a Lyman-a emission around a luminous high-redshift quasar." *Nature international weekly journal of science.* doi:10.1038/nature 12898. Published online January 19, 2014. .

Charles, R.H.1912. *The Book of Enoch*. Clarendon Press: Oxford, UK. pp 16-20, 264-272

Choi, Charles Q. "How Earthquakes in Chile Have Permanently Deformed the Earth." *Live Science.* 28 April 2013. . www.livescience.com/29091-chile-earthquakes-leave-permanent-dent.html?utm_source=feedburner&utm_medium=feed&utm_campaign=Feed%3A+C2C-InTheNews+%28Feed+-+Coast+to+Coast+-+In+the+News%29

Chopra, Deepak. "Cosmic Fire." October 21, 2012. www. deepakchopra.com/blog/view/910/cosmic_fire

Clendinen, Inga. 2003. *Ambivalent Conquests — Maya and Spanish in the Yucatan, 1519 — 1570.* Cambridge: Cambridge University Press.

Cooper, Gordon with Bruce Henderson. 2002. *Leap of Faith: An Astronaut's Journey into the Unknown.* HarperTorch: New York, NY. pp 212-214

Corso, Philip, Col. (Ret.). 1998. *The Day After Roswell.* Pocketbooks: New York, NY. pp 22-23

Cowgill, George L. "Teotihuacan and Early Classic Interaction: A Perspective from Outside the Maya Region." Braswell, Geoffrey E., editor. 2004. *The Maya and Teotihuacan.* University of Texas Press: Austin, TX. pp 10-11, 328-335

Cranston, Sylvia.1993. *HPB: The Extraordinary Life and Influence of Helena Blavatsky Founder of the Modern Theosophical Movement.* New York, NY: G. P. Putnam's Sons. p 194

Cremo, Michael. 2005. *Forbidden Archaeology: The Hidden History of the Human Race.* Los Angeles, CA: Bhaktivedanta Book Publishing, Inc. pp 796-814

Creveling, J. R., etal. "Mechanisms for oscillatory true polar wander." *Nature*, international weekly journal of science. November 8, 2012. www.nature.com/nature/journal/v491/n7423/full/nature11571.html

Cruttenden, Walter. 2006. *Lost Star of Myth and Time.* St. Lynn's Press. Pittsburgh, PA. pp 44-52

Dalley, Stephanie, translator. 2008. *Myths from Mesopotamia: Creation, The Flood, Gilgamesh, and Others.* pp 182-188, Seven Sages pp 228-277, 327-328

Duran, Krsanna. 1994. "Magnetic Change Mapped in Kennewick Crop Circle." *All Star Roundup.com: Crop Circles* www.allstarroundup.com/cc/cckennewick.html

_____2011 "Liddington Castle 2010 Crop Circle." *All Star Roundup.com: Crop Circles* www.allstarroundup.com/cc/ccliddington2010.html

_____2011. "Crop Circles Point to Breakup Region on Indo-Australian Plate." *All Star Roundup.com: Crop Circles* www.allstarroundup.com/cc/ccindonesia.html

_____2012. "Bracciano Crop Circle: Solar Wind and Earthquake Spree." *All Star Roundup.com: Crop Circles* www.allstarroundup.com/cc/ccbracciano5-20-12.html

_____2012. "America's East Coast." *All Star Roundup.com: Crop Circles.* www.allstarroundup.com/cc/ccohio9-2012.html

The Erickson Project: The Sasquatch Quest www.sasquatchthequest.com/

Fry, Daniel. 1973. *To Men of Earth.* Merlin Publishing Co: Merlin, OR. pp 82-83, 110-111

Gerson, Lloyd P. 2006. *Aristotle and Other Platonists.* Cornell University Press: Ithaca, New York. pp 113-114

Ghose, Tia. "Before Babel: Ancient Mother Tongue Reconstructed." *LifeScience.* May 6, 2013. . www.livescience.com/29342-ancient-mother-tongue-reconstructed.html

Gillessen, S., etal. "A gas cloud on its way towards the super-massive black hole in the Galactic Centre." *Nature* journal. December 14, 2011.10.1038/nature10652

Hagstrum, Jonathan T. "Antipodal hotspots and bipolar catastrophes: Were oceanic large-body impacts the cause?" *Earth and Planetary Science Letters 236* (2005) 13-27.

Handwerk, Brian. "New Underwater Finds Raise Questions About Flood Myths." *National Geographic.* May 28, 2002.

Hapgood, Charles S. 1966. *Maps of the Ancient Sea Kings.* Reprinted by Adventures Unlimited Press: Kempton, IL. pp 199-204

Howe, Linda Moulton. "Persistent Sinkholes and Unexplained Booms." *Earthfiles.com* www.earthfiles.com/news.php?ID=2087&category=Environment

Iamblichus, translated by Robin Waterfield. 1988. *The Theology of Arithmetic*. Phanes Press: Grand Rapids, MI. pp 35-40

Jung, Carl Gustav, translated by R.F.C. Hull. 1990. *The Archetypes and the Collective Unconscious*. Princeton University Press: New York, NY. pp 3-5

_____1968. *Man and His Symbols*. Anchor Books, Doubleday: New York, NY

Kannenberg, Ida M. 2013. *My Brother Is a Hairy Man: The Search for Bigfoot*. Atlantis Phoenix Books: Missoula, MT. pp 17-28, 82-84, 114-120

_____2013. *Project Earth from the Extraterrestrial Perspective: Species and Mind*. Atlantis Phoenix Books: Missoula, MT. p 163

_____2013. *Time Travelers from Atlantis*. Atlantis Phoenix Books: Missoula, MT. p 3

Kelly, Morgan. "Massive volcanoes, meteorite impacts delivered one-two punch death punch to dinosaurs." *News at Princeton* .November 17, 2011.

Ketchum, M. S., P. W. Wojtkiewicz, A. B. Watts, D. W. Spence, A. K. Holzenburg, D. G. Toler, T. M. Prychitko, F. Zhang, S. Bollinger, R. Shoulders, R. Smith. "Novel North American Hominins, Next Generation Sequencing of Three Whole Genomes and Associated Studies." *The DeNovo Special Edition*. Volume 1, Issue 1, February 13, 2013. http://sasquatchgenomeproject.org/Review posted on the *Sasquatch Genome Project* website.

Kitei, Lynne D., M.D. 2004. *The Phoenix Lights*. Hampton Roads Publishing Company: Charlottesville, VA. pp 1-11

Klingaman, William K. and Nicholas P. 2013. *The Year Without Summer:1816 and the Volcano that Darkened the World and Changed History*. St. Martin's Griffin: New York, NY. pp 121-151

Knight, Christopher and Alan Butler. 2004. *Civilization One*. Watkins Publishing: London, UK. pp 219-225

Koerner, E. F. Konrad. "The Sapir-Whorf Hypothesis: A Preliminary History and a Bibliographical Essay." *Journal of Linquistic Anthropology*. Volume 2, Issue 2. December 1992.

Kramer, Miriam. "Ancient Maya Predicted 1991 Solar Eclipse." Live Science. January 8, 2013. . http://www.livescience.com/26070-maya-predicted-1991-solar-eclipse.html

Kubler, George. 1972. "Jaguars in the Valley of Mexico." Reprinted from *The Cult of the Feline*. Dumbarton Oaks, Trustees for Harvard University: Washington D.C. p 1

La Violette, Paul. 1997. *Earth Under Fire*. Starlane Publications: Schenectady, NY. pp 70-71, 94, 150-152

_____2013 "Close Approach of Cloud G2 Around July 2013. Starburst Foundation. starburstfound. org/superwaveblog/?p=246

Lao Tzu, translated by James Legge. 1891. *The Tao-te Ching*. Internet Classics Archive. http://classics.mit.edu//Lao/taote.html

Le Plongeon, Augustus. 1877. *The Mayas, The Sources of Their History. Proceedings of the American Antiquarian Society of April 26, 2876 and April 25, 1877*. Press of Charles Hamilton: Worcester. pp 56-58

_____1881.*Vestiges of the Maya or, Facts Tending to Prove that Communications and Intimate Relations Must have Existed, in very Remote Times.* Hamburg, Germany: Tredition Classics. pp 32-33

Lewis, Martin W.; Kären E. Wigen. 1997. *The Myth of Continents: a Critique of Metageography.* University of California Press: Berkeley, Los Angeles and London. pp 31-35

Little, Drs. Gregory and Lora, and Van Auken, John. *Edgar Cayce's Atlantis.* 2008. A.R.E. Press: Virginia Beach, VA. pp 48-51

Lovett, Richard A. "Texas and Antarctica Were Attached, Rocks Hint." *National Geographic.* August 2011. .

Mack, John E. 1999. *Passport to the Cosmos: Human Transformation and Alien Encounters.* Crown Publishers: New York, NY. pp 22-49

Mails, Thomas E. 1996. *The Story of the Cherokee People from Earliest Origins to Contemporary Times.* New York, NY: Marlowe & Company.

Malmström, Vincent H. 1997. *Cycles of the Sun, Mysteries of the Moon: The Calendar in Mesoamerican Civilization.* Austin, TX: University of Texas Press. pp 102-104

Mann, Charles C ."The Birth of Religion." *National Geographic.* June 2011. www.ngm.nationalgeographic.com/2011/06/gobekli-tepe/mann-text.

Marden, Kathleen, Denise M. Stoner and Stanton Friedman. 2013. *The Alien Abduction Files: The Most Startling Cases of Human Alien Contact Ever Reported."* Career Press, New Page Books: Pompton Plains, NJ. pp 45-70

Matthias Meyer, Qiaomei Fu, Ayinuer Aximu-Petri, Isabelle Glocke, Birgit Nickel, Juan-Luis Arsuaga, Ignacio Martínez, Ana Gracia, José María Bermúdez de Castro, Eudald Carbonell, Svante Pääbo. "A mitochondrial genome sequence of a hominin from Sima de los Huesos." *Nature international weekly journal of science*, 4 December 2013; DOI: 10.1038/nature12788http://www.nature.com/nature/journal/vaop/ncurrent/full/nature12788.html

McKenna, Terence. 1995. *Timewave Zero: Terence McKenna's Software for Time Traveling*. Blue Water Publishing: Newberg, OR. pp 5-6, 50-62

Mitchell, Edgar with Dwight Williams. 2008. *The Way of the Explorer: An Apollo Astronaut's Journey Through the Material and Mystical Worlds*. The Career Press, Inc.: Franklin Lake, NJ

Mooney, James with biographical introduction by George Ellison. 1992. *History, Myths and Sacred Formulas of the Cherokees*. Bright Mountain Books, Inc.: Fairview, NC:

Mullaney, James. 2007. *Edgar Cayce and the Cosmos*. A.R.E. Press: Virginia Beach, VA. p 4, 24

Mutwa, Credo. 1996. *Isilwane, The Animal*. Struik Publishers: Cape Town, South Africa. p 24

NASA News. "Solar Storm Warning." March 10, 2006. science.nasa.gov/science-news/science-at-nasa/2006/10mar_stormwarning/

NASA News. "Solar Flare Surprise." December 15, 2008. science1.nasa.gov/science-news/science-at-nasa/2008/15dec_solarflaresurprise/

NASA News. "Are Sunspots Disappearing?" September 3, 2009. science1.nasa.gov/science-news/science-at-nasa/2009/03sep_sunspots/

NASA News. "Global Eruption Rocks the Sun." December 13, 2010. science.nasa.gov/science-news/science-at-nasa/2010/13dec_globaleruption/

NASA News. "Solar Mini-Max." June 10, 2014
http://science.nasa.gov/science-news/science-at-nasa/2014/10jun_solarminimax/

Neihardt, John. 2008. *Black Elk Speaks: Being the Life Story of a Holy Man of the Oglala Sioux*. University of Nebraska Press: Lincoln, NB. p 33

Norris, R.D. and J.V. Firth. "Mass wasting of Atlantic continental margins following the Chicxulub meteor event." *Geological Society of America Special Paper 356 — 2002*. www.oceanleadership.org/wp-conte nt/uploads/2011/10/Norris-and-Firth-2002.pdf

Oppenheimer, Clive. 2011. *Eruptions that Shook the World*. Cambridge University Press: New York, NY. pp 22-52

Pagel, Mark, etal. "Ultraconserved words point to deep language ancestry across Eurasia." *Proceedings of the National Academy of Sciences of the United States of America.* May 6, 2013.
www.pnas.org/content/early/2013/05/01/1218726110.full.pdf+html

Pasztory, Esther. 1997. *Teotihuacan: An Experiment in Living.* University of Oklahoma Press: Norman, OK. pp 6, 64-65, 83-85

_____ 1974. *The Iconography of the Teotihuacan Tlaloc.* Dumbarton Oaks: Washington, DC. p 6

Phys.org February 9, 2015. "Earth's Surprise inside: Geologists unlock mysteries of planet's inner core."
http://phys.org/news/2015-02-earth-geologists-mysteries-planet-core.html

Phys.org June 9, 2014. "Scientists May Have Identified Echoes of Ancient Earth."
http://phys.org/news/2014-06-scientists-echoes-ancient-earth.html

Plato, edited by Edith Hamilton and Huntington Cairns. 1980. "Timaeus." *Plato, the Collected Works, including the Letters.* Princeton University Press: Princeton, NJ pp 1151-1211 ("Timaeus"), pp 475-525 ("Phaedrus")

Radin, Dean. 2006. *Entangled Minds. Extrasensory Experience in a Quantum Reality.* Pocketbooks, a division of Simon and Schuster, Inc.: New York, NY. pp 1, 14-17, 209-236

Reuters. March 30, 2002."Pyramid Structure Found Off Coast Of Cuba." Cuba Headlines. January 17, 2011:

Ring, Kenneth Ph.D. 1989. "Near Death and UFO Encounters as Shamanic Initiations." *ReVision*, Vol. 11, No. 3, Winter 1989
www.near-death.com/experiences/articles011.html

Sanchez, Anthony F. 2010. *UFO Highway: The Dulce Interview * Human Origins * HAARP/Project Blue Beam.* eBook self-published. pp 51-55

Schele, Linda and David Freidel. 1990. *A Forest of Kings: The Untold Story of the Ancient Maya.* Morrow: New York, NY. pp 77-84

Schoch, Robert M. "The Mystery of Gobekli Tepe and Its Message To Us." *New Dawn Magazine.* September-October 2010.

Sejourne, Laurette. 1956. *Burning Water: Thought and Religion in Ancient Mexico.* Thames & Hudson: London. p 74

Shen, Helen. "Unusual Indian Ocean earthquakes hint at tectonic breakup." *Nature,* international weekly journal of science. September 26, 2012. www.nature.com/news/unusual-indian-ocean-earthquakes-hint-at-tectonic-breakup-1.11487

Sinnett, A.P., compiled by Alfred Trevor Barker. 1923. Letter "From K.H. to A.O.H. Received July 10th, 1882."*The Mahatma Letters to A.P. Sinnett from the Mahatmas M. and K.H.* The Theosophical Publishing House: Wheaton, IL. Letter No. XIII from A.P. Sinnett in January 1882 with responses by Morya. pp 70-78; "Letter No. XV, from Koot Hoomi to A. O. Hume, July 10, 1882 pp 88-99; Letter XXIIB, II, 1882: Koot Hoomi replies to queries pp 149-178

Sitchin, Zecharia. 2008. *The End of Days: Armageddon and Prophecies of the Return.* Harper: New York, NY. pp 245-249, 252-255

_____2007. *The Twelfth Planet.* Harper: New York, NY.

_____1985. *The Wars of Gods and Men.* Avon Books: New York, NY. p 347

Soennichsen, John. 2008. *Bretz's Flood: The Remarkable Story of a Rebel Geologist and the World's Greatest Flood.* Sasquatch Books: Seattle, WA. pp143-168

Sprinkle, R. Leo. 1999. *Soul Samples.* Granite Publishing, LLC: Columbus, NC. pp 143-154, 237-238

Stanford University Humanities Lab. "Reconfiguring the Archaeological Sensibility: Mediating Heritage at Teotihuacan, Mexico." http://humanitieslab.stanford.edu/teotihuacan/1497

Stone, Rebecca R. 2011. *The Jaguar Within: Shamanic Trance in Ancient Central and South American Art.* The University of Texas Press: Austin. p 4

Stoner, Dennis M. Special interview on Dreamland radio. June 21, 2013. www.unknowncountry.com

Than, Ker. "Ancient Lost Continent Discovered in Indian Ocean." *National Geographic News.* February 27, 2013. http://news.nationalgeographic.com/news/2013/02/130225-microcontinent-earth-mauritius-geology-science/

_____"Lost Lands Found by Scientists." National Geographic News. May 11, 2013. http://news.nationalgeographic.com/news/2013/13/130509-brazilian-atlantis-lost-continents-geography-world/

_____"Ancient Lost Continent Discovered in Indian Ocean." National Geographic News. February 27, 2013. . http://news.nationalgeographic.com/news/2013/02/130225-microcontinent-earth-mauritius-geology-science/

Thompson, J. Eric S. "Systems of Hieroglyphic Writing in Middle America and Methods of Deciphering Them." *American Antiquity*, Vol. 24, No. 4, 1959 pp 349-364

Tompkins, Peter. 1976. *Mysteries of the Mexican Pyramids*. Harper & Row: New York. pp 20-23, 171-172, 226-229, 241

Vail, Gabrielle and Christine Hernandez, editors. 2010. *Astronomers, Scribes, and Priests: Intellectual Interchange between the Northern Maya Lowlands and Highland Mexico in the Late Postclassic Period*. Dumbarton Oaks, Trustees for Harvard University: Washington D.C. pp 263-278

Van Flandern, Tom. 1993. *Dark Matter, Missing Planets and New Comets: Paradoxes Resolved, Origins Illuminated*. North Atlantic Books. Berkley, CA. pp 277-279, 332-339, 425-432

Van Helsig, Jan. 2009. *Unternehmen Aldebaran: Kontakte mit Menschen aus einem anderen Sonnensystem*. Amadeus – Verlag. Fichtenau, Germany. pp 90-93, unnumbered photos between 164 and 165

Van Tassel, George. 1958. *Religion and Science Merged*. Ministry of Universal Wisdom, Inc. Yucca Valley, CA pp 15-19

Waters, Frank. 1989. *The Mexico Mystique: The Coming Sixth World of Consciousness*. Ohio University Press Books: Swallow Press. pp 31-32, 33, 61-66, 158-159

Wethington, Nicholas. "The Milky Way's Rotation." *Universe Today*. January 26, 2009. www.universetoday.com/23870/the-milky-ways-rotation/

Williamson, George Hunt. 1973. *Other Tongues, Other Flesh*. Neville Spearman: London, UK. Book II pp 73-94, 152-191

Wittke, James H., et al. "Evidence for deposition of 10 million tonnes of impact spherules across four continents 12,800 years ago." *Proceedings of the National Academy of Sciences for the United States.* Published online before print May 20, 2013, doi: 10.1073/pnas.1301760110 , PNAS May 20, 2013

Yukteswar, Sri. 1977. *The Holy Science*. The Self Realization Fellowship: Los Angeles, CA. pp ix-xi

Zhirov, N. F. 1970. *Atlantis: Atlantology Basic Problems*. Progress Publishers: Soviet Union, Moscow. p 215

Zorich, Zach. "Popul Vuh Relief — El Mirador, Guatemala." *Archaeology Archive* .January 2010

Index

13 August anniversary, 72
13 signature number, 62
13 square root, 149
120-year lifespan, 41
2012 CE, 14, 19, 21-23, 29, 33-34, 44, 61, 63-64, 67, 92, 98, 102, 105-106, 110-111, 114, 129, 142, 145-146, 151, 155-159, 162, 169-170
3114 BCE, 27, 54, 78
Abraham, 28, 51
Ac Tah, 170
Adam and Eve, 25, 35, 39, 41, 43, 59
adept, 3, 7, 14, 42, 59, 138
Africa, 4, 7, 9, 11-13, 16, 26, 35, 39, 46-47, 55, 103, 121, 154, 156, 163, 174
Agni, 137
Aldebaran, 23, 36, 56
America, 2, 4-5, 7, 9, 11-12, 14, 16, 19, 25, 28, 35, 46, 57, 61, 70-71, 78, 80, 83, 91-93, 105, 111, 121, 128-129, 131, 145-146, 148, 157, 159, 163, 165, 180, 183, 190
ancestors, 1-3, 14, 16, 21, 32, 35-36, 61, 69, 72, 110, 113-117, 136-137, 140-141, 145
ancient astronaut, 33, 131
Ancient Earth, 4, 20, 31, 56
Angkor Wat, 54, 69-70, 95
Anu, 40, 57

Anunnaki, 37-38, 42, 44, 55, 57
Aphrodite, 28, 40
Apollo, 142
Arcadia, 27, 116
archetype, 2, 44, 140-141, 143, 177, 179
Arctic, 24-25, 36
Arcturus, 23-24, 35-36, 115-116, 119, 122
aristocracy, 39-40, 46, 56
asteroid, 31-32, 59, 141, 154
Athens, 27, 40
Atlantic Ocean, 3-4, 9, 36, 46, 148, 176
Atlantic Seaboard, 46
Atlantis, 3-5, 7-9, 11-13, 22-26, 35-36, 39-40, 47, 54, 56, 93, 111, 115, 131, 148, 154, 156, 162, 176
atmosphere, 45-47, 104, 107, 145
Atrahasis, 41, 44
August 13, 65, 72, 78, 145
Australopithecus, 37, 117, 122
authentic, 155-156, 165, 173-174, 190
Avalonia microcontinent, 3, 9, 26
awareness, 17-18, 95-96, 98, 122, 133, 137, 187, 190
axis, 4, 15, 23, 32, 72, 74, 76, 102, 148, 151, 155
Aztec, 72, 74, 77, 83, 88-92

Babel, 19, 51, 53-54, 57
Babylon, 26-28, 32-34, 39, 47, 54, 56
Baltica microcontinent, 3, 9, 12
Barrios, Carlos, 92, 148, 162
Berossos, 50, 54, 58
Bigfoot, 21, 23, 25, 34-37, 46, 56, 100, 111, 114-119, 121-126, 129, 131, 141
billion years ago, 9
bird, 6, 41, 48, 50, 54, 69, 71, 161
Blavatsky, Helena, 3-4, 7-9, 11-14, 19, 21-22, 42, 54, 137, 143, 150, 190
Bracciano crop circle, 102, 111
Brasseur de Bourbourg, Charles, 4-5, 7
Bretz's Flood, 58

Cambodia, 54, 71
canon, 74
cathedral, 72, 86, 91-92
Catholic, 86, 90, 92
cave, 78, 114, 117
Cayce, Edgar, 24-25, 36, 56, 115, 131
celestial, 27, 44, 59, 66, 71, 137, 146
Central America, 4, 46, 70-71
Chaldea, 28
channel, 44, 161, 165, 168, 172, 187-188
Chichen Itza, 6, 29, 32, 80, 89, 146-148, 151, 166
Chicxulub, 23, 36, 150-151, 154, 156
coast, 4, 13-14, 21, 23, 47, 105, 111, 148, 151, 157-159, 161
colossal head, Olmec, 72, 82

comet, 23, 33, 44, 56, 70
consciousness, 34, 82, 92-93, 99, 175-176
continent, 3-4, 9, 11-13, 19-22, 25, 36, 46, 57, 66, 74, 125, 150, 163, 174
Cooper, Gordon, 27, 71, 91, 146
cosmic fire, 137, 142
cosmic impact, 4-5, 16, 46, 66
cosmic rays, 64, 66-67, 100, 105, 109
creation garden, 35
Cremo, Michael, 7, 20
Crete, 46, 71
crop circles, 70, 100, 102, 111, 155-156, 158-159, 166-172, 174
crust (earth), 3, 9, 11, 46, 104-105
Cruttenden, Walter, 70
Cygnus, 66

divine, 13, 39, 50, 55, 95, 141, 168, 177
Divine Right to Rule, 95
DNA, 21, 25, 35, 37, 46, 58, 114-115, 118, 128-130, 141, 145, 173
dot-bar numbers, 69, 73-74, 145
dragon, 157, 166
Dresden Codex, 102, 151
dual, 61-62, 70, 146
Dulce, New Mexico, 57

Ea, 44, 50, 54
Earth, 1, 3-4, 7-9, 14, 16-17, 20-26, 28-29, 31-37, 39-41, 43-45, 47, 50-51, 53, 55-56, 59-64, 66-67, 70, 74, 78, 95-96, 98, 100, 103-105, 109-112, 115-116,

118-119, 122-126, 131, 136-138, 140-141, 145, 147-148, 150-151, 154-155, 157, 162-167, 172, 174, 177-178, 191
Earth Calendar, 33, 145
Earth glyph, 29, 32, 147-148, 150-151, 155
Earth-Human Calendar, 62, 145
earthquake, 6, 46, 100, 103, 111, 151, 156-157, 159-162
Egypt, 26-27, 54, 65, 69-71, 78, 86, 93, 121, 146, 178
electric, 83, 98-99, 104, 137, 173
electromagnetic, 98, 109, 137, 142, 145, 167
elite, 37-38, 180, 188
England, 9, 39, 154, 163, 166, 168-170, 172-174
Enki, 26, 37, 40, 42, 44, 46-47, 50-51, 54-55, 59
Enki-Ea, 44, 50, 54
Enlil, 25, 28, 36-37, 40-41, 45-47, 50-51, 54-55, 59
Enoch, 41, 45-46, 57
Enuma Elish, 31, 33, 54, 59
Epic of Creation, 31
epigenetic, 47, 58
Erickson Project, 114, 128, 130-131
Eridu, 26, 51
eruption, 5, 23, 26, 46-47, 58, 64-66, 86, 88, 102, 108, 112, 150-151, 154, 157-161
esoteric, 3, 9, 13, 22, 42, 44, 82, 190
Europe, 1, 4, 11, 25-26, 39, 46-47, 58, 74, 78, 91, 103, 113, 136, 173
exploding planet, 32-33
exploding planet hypothesis, 32

extraterrestrial, 1, 3, 7, 14, 16-17, 21, 23, 33, 35-37, 39-41, 93, 131, 183, 185-186, 191

Feathered Serpent, 6, 27-28, 54, 62, 64-65, 67, 69-71, 78, 83, 88, 137, 145-146, 166
Feathered Serpent's pyramid, 83
Fifth World, 67
firmament, 47, 176, 178
First Reich, 56
fossil, 114
Fourth Reich, 56
Fourth World, 45, 67, 78
fractal, 34, 140-141, 171
fracture, 14, 23, 29, 98, 150-151
Fry, Daniel, 14, 16, 22, 24, 29, 185-186
full collar of feathers, 6, 28, 67, 71, 83

galactic, 34, 62, 66-67, 69-70, 109-110, 112, 135, 140
Gandhi, Mahatma, 8
Garuda, 54, 69
gematria, 62
Genesis, 1, 14, 23, 33, 37, 39, 41-44, 47, 50-51, 53, 59, 115, 117, 131, 141, 176, 178
genome, 35, 37, 113-115, 128-131
giant, 13, 29, 41, 72, 109, 115, 131, 136-137, 185-186
gifts of civilization, 54
glacial lake, 53
glacial melt, 16, 46, 53, 66
glacial period, 12
glacier, 12, 46

globe, 32, 39, 43-44, 70, 102, 139-140
glyph, 29, 32, 36, 62, 72-73, 83, 89, 91, 145, 147-148, 150-151, 155, 158, 166
Gobekli Tepe, Turkey, 25-26, 46-48, 50-51, 54, 58, 66, 71, 88
gods, 1, 11, 13-14, 26, 28, 32, 34, 37, 39-41, 43-47, 51, 54-55, 57, 59-60, 82, 89, 95, 99, 137, 140-141, 148, 157, 163-166, 176-178
Gothenburg Magnetic Excursion, 25, 64-66
Gray, 38, 185
Great Britain, 9, 47, 78, 173
Great Pyramid, 25-27, 78, 86, 95, 100
Great Year, 69
Greece, 27-28, 39-40, 46, 50, 69-71, 165
Greek, 40, 50, 55, 59, 61, 89, 116, 135, 164-165, 167, 180
Gulf of Mexico, 46, 70-71, 148, 154

HAARP, 57
Harleston, Hugh, 86
heating, 64, 102
Hebrew, 51, 131, 178
Herodotus, 24
Hesiod, 39-40, 59
Himalaya, 16, 24
Hindu, 8, 25, 28, 61-62, 69, 74, 93, 95-96, 110, 137
hoax, 168-169, 171
Holy Roman Empire, 56
Homer, 55, 59, 137, 165
Homo s., 36, 118-119, 126

Homo sapiens, 37, 50, 118, 125, 129, 177
Homo sapiens sapiens, 50, 118, 125
Hopi, 45, 67, 78, 113
Human, 1-2, 5-8, 14, 16-17, 20-25, 32-33, 35-41, 44-47, 50, 53-57, 59, 61-62, 72, 82-83, 86, 90, 93, 95-98, 104, 110-111, 113-118, 122-126, 128-130, 133, 138, 141, 145, 148, 150, 155-156, 163-169, 171, 173, 175, 180, 183-184, 186-187, 189
humankind, 14, 25, 37, 44, 50, 61, 70, 86, 92, 146, 192
hybrid, 115, 129-130
hydrogen, 33, 107
Hyperborea, 24-25, 35-36, 44, 137

Ice Age, 65-66, 127, 173
Iceland, 9, 11, 58
icon, 36, 51, 147
Igigi, 41, 44
Inanna, 26, 54, 166
India, 7-8, 26, 50, 54, 69-70, 73-74, 137, 146, 150, 160, 190
Indian Ocean, 4-5, 7, 13, 20, 22-23, 32, 36, 47, 70, 148, 150, 156-158, 162
Indonesia, 73, 105, 151, 155-157, 169
Indus Valley, 7, 26-27, 51, 65
initiation, 14-15, 22, 71
Ireland, 173
Ishtar, 55
island, 11, 14, 23-25, 35-36, 40, 73, 90, 137, 148, 151, 154, 156-161, 173, 176

jaguar, 6, 20, 71-72
Java, 14, 23, 151, 155
Jewish calendar, 34, 47, 54
Jews, 39, 43
July 11, 1991 solar eclipse, 2, 29, 102, 146
Jung, Carl, 140, 143, 176-177, 180
Jupiter, 23, 32-33, 55, 59, 67, 102, 141

Kannenberg, Ida M., 24, 34, 56, 95, 110-111, 116-117, 131
Kennewick crop circle, 100, 111, 155, 158-159
Ketchum, Melba, 25, 35, 114, 117, 128-130
kingdom, 39-40, 43-44, 156, 164, 169
Koot Hoomi, 3, 19, 21, 26, 138, 143, 190-191
Kubler, George, 20
Kukulkan, 54

La Venta, 6, 71-72
La Violette, Paul, 67, 109, 112
language, 4-5, 8, 19, 25, 34, 39, 51, 53-54, 57, 74, 86, 89, 92, 110, 131, 146, 166, 175, 179-180, 183
Le Plongeon, August, 4-7, 20, 73-74, 152
Lemuria, 11-13, 16, 23, 25, 35-36, 44, 51, 115, 121-122, 125-127, 137
Liddington Castle crop circle, 70, 169-170, 174
long count, 27, 29, 34, 44, 54, 62-65, 69, 72, 78, 92-93, 110, 145-146

lord, 3, 39-41, 43, 45-46, 53, 59, 113, 146
lunar, 170
lunar eclipse, 170

Mack, John Dr., 17, 22
Madrid Codex, 4
Maez (Arcturian), 21, 98, 111, 116-118, 122, 124, 126
magnetic, 3, 25, 28-29, 47, 63-66, 83, 98, 100, 102-103, 105-106, 108-109, 111, 151, 165, 173
magnetic core, 100, 151
magnetic north, 64, 100, 102, 109
mahatma, 8-9, 11, 19, 21, 26, 42, 57, 143, 190-191
Malay, 73
Maldek, 33
Malona, 33
Manifest Destiny, 92
Marduk, 26-28, 31-32, 54-56, 59
Mars, 1, 16, 23-24, 31-33, 37, 55, 141
Masters of the Stars, 2
Maya, 2, 5, 7, 18-20, 64, 73, 90-93, 100, 110, 146-148, 151, 161, 170
Mayan calendar, 29, 73, 83, 91, 166, 171
McKenna, Terence, 34, 56
Mediterranean, 26, 35, 59, 70
megalith, 26-27, 78, 172-174
Mercury, 32
Mesopotamia, 26, 37-38, 47, 51, 53-54, 56, 58
Mesopotamia, ancient, 38, 47, 53
metaphysics, 136, 186

meteor, 36, 150, 156, 185
Mexico, 1-2, 5-7, 20, 23-24, 27-29, 46, 50, 54, 62, 67, 69-72, 80, 83, 86, 88-93, 95, 121, 137, 140, 143, 146, 148, 150, 154-156, 166, 172
Mexico City, 2, 90-91, 155
Mid-Atlantic Ridge, 11, 58, 148
Milky Way, 36, 61, 69-70, 109
million years ago, 4, 11
Millon, 76, 86
mind, 11-12, 14-15, 44, 50, 83, 95, 98, 109, 113, 117, 131, 135, 138, 141-143, 148, 156, 164-166, 175-176, 179, 183, 187
Mitchell, Edgar, 142
molten debris, 4, 46, 66
moon, 31-33, 45, 61, 71, 76, 78, 80-83, 86, 92, 97
moon pyramid, 78
Morning Star, 32, 59, 80
morphogenetic, 35
Morya, 42-44, 57, 190
mother language, 4, 25, 39, 51, 54
Mu, 4-9, 11-14, 16, 35-36, 78, 93, 150, 155, 157
myth, 15, 21, 32, 41, 56, 58-59, 70, 74, 82, 114

Nabu, 28, 55
Nabunaid, 55
NASA, 29, 61, 63-65, 98, 102, 106-108, 112
Native American Church, 80
nature preserve, 23
Neanderthal, 21, 23, 34-36, 44, 113-114, 117, 125-126
near death, 14-15, 22

Nephilim, 41, 131
Nibiru, 31-32
Nineveh, 26, 51
Nippur, 54
Noah, 41, 45, 50-51, 53
noctilucent clouds, 47
North America, 5, 9, 25, 46, 80, 128-129, 157
nuclear, 26-29, 37, 55, 96-97, 102, 109, 115, 128-129, 137, 155

Oannes, 50
Older Dryas, 25
oligarchy, 38
Olmec, 6, 27, 71-73, 82, 86, 146
ouroboros, 146

Pacific Ocean, 23, 31, 36, 46, 70, 78, 148
PACTS, 189, 191
Pasztory, Esther, 74, 77, 92
Persian Gulf, 38, 47, 51, 53
Phoenix Lights, 2, 18, 29, 185
Pillars of Hercules, 154
Planet K, 23, 32
Planet V, 32
Plato, 4-5, 13, 40, 69-70, 136, 140, 148, 166, 175-179
Pleiades, 36
pole reversal, 47
Polynesia, 73, 157
Portugal, 47, 156
Poseidon, 40, 47, 148, 156
Poseidonis, 11
Prince George, 39
psi, 96, 190
psychic, 14, 17, 95-96, 123, 138, 169, 187-192
pyramid, 6, 20, 25-28, 61, 65, 71-72, 74-78, 80, 83, 86-

89, 91-93, 95, 100, 145, 157
pyramid culture, 92
Pyramid of Quetzalcoatl, 71
Pyramid of the Moon, 76, 83, 86
Pyramid of the Sun, 6, 28, 75-77, 86, 92

quantum, 3-4, 34-35, 67, 133, 135-136, 141-142, 165, 187
Quetzalcoatl, 6, 54, 65, 69, 71, 82, 90

radiation, 24, 27, 35, 46, 55, 62, 66-67, 69, 105, 137, 186
rainbow, 47
ratio, 31, 37, 69, 146
rebel, 25, 41, 58
rebellion, 45
relativistic, 3-4
reptilian, 37, 122
resonance, 35, 83, 135, 141, 145
resonant frequency, 145
Ring of Fire, 31
Ring, Kenneth, 15
Rome, 14, 28, 39-40, 55-56, 71, 74, 88, 91, 136, 148

sages, 44, 50-51, 54-55, 58, 62, 70, 86
Sasquatch, 58, 114, 123, 128-131
satchel, 54, 71
Schliemann, Heinrich, 55
Schumann Resonance, 145
scientist, 3-4, 14, 20, 25, 31, 36-37, 40-41, 45-47, 55-56, 66, 69, 98, 102, 107-108, 110, 114, 117-118, 122, 128-129, 136, 151, 160-161

Second Reich, 56
settled, 51, 80, 88-89, 146, 173
settlement, 26-27, 51, 65, 86, 173
shaman, 154, 163
shamanic, 6, 14-15, 20, 22, 166
Sheldrake, Rupert, 35
Siculus, Diodorus, 24
Sin, 28, 45, 54-56
Sinai, 28
Sinjar Mountains, 51, 53
Sirius, 37, 70
Sitchin, Zecharia, 26, 28, 31, 47, 57, 59, 118-119, 131
Sixth World, 92-93
Soennichsen, John, 58
solar eclipse, 2, 19, 102, 146
solar flare, 64, 109, 112
solar maximum, 29, 61, 63-65, 105-108
solar minimum, 64, 102, 107-108
solar system, 28, 31-32, 61-62, 64, 67, 69-70, 86, 102, 135-136, 146, 191
solar tongue, 39
Solex-Mal, 39
sons of God, 1, 14, 37, 39, 41, 45-46
soul, 14-15, 22, 44, 125, 137, 140-141, 164, 166, 168, 175, 189
Space Age, 64
Sphinx, 9, 48, 190
spirit, 15, 41, 62, 137, 139, 141, 165, 175, 178, 181
Sprinkle, Leo Dr., 17, 22, 189-191
square root, 146
star, 1-2, 16, 24, 32, 59-61, 70, 78, 80, 96, 109-111, 115-

117, 119, 136, 146, 162-164, 166, 174, 187, 189
Stone Sages, 62, 70, 86
Stonehenge, 26-27, 154, 172-174
Strait of Gibraltar, 148, 154
Sumer, 23, 25, 28, 35-37, 40, 46, 51, 54-55, 131, 166
sun pyramid, 78
Sun Stone, 62, 72, 82-83, 86, 89, 91, 95
superwave, 66-67, 109
symbol, 15, 44, 50, 71, 74, 78, 88, 146, 154, 166, 175-177, 179-180
symbolism, 6, 54-55, 81, 110, 137, 146, 167, 176-177

Table of Nations, 39, 50-51
technology, 1, 16, 24, 36, 46, 48, 55, 106, 110-111, 131, 175-176, 183-184, 187-188
tectonic, 3, 11, 14, 23, 33, 98, 150-151, 155-157, 159, 162
telepathy, 99-100, 124, 183, 191-192
temple, 48, 74, 78, 80, 82-83, 86, 135, 155
tensor, 175-176, 187-188
Teotihuacan, 6, 28, 62, 65, 67, 71-72, 74-76, 78, 80, 82-83, 86-89, 91-93, 95, 145, 155, 157
Theosophy, 8
Third Reich, 56
Third World, 45, 67
thirteen, 62, 69, 72-74, 83, 145-146
Thompson, J. Eric, 91, 93
Thoth, 100, 146
Tiamat, 31-33, 59-60

Tibet, 7-8, 42, 54, 190
TimeStar, 23, 36, 64, 105, 108, 150, 154, 157-159, 163
timewave, 23, 34-35, 44, 56, 64
Timewave Zero, 34, 56, 64
Toltec, 74, 80, 83, 88-90
Troano Codex, 5-6, 74
Troy, 27-28, 40, 55, 59
Tula, 80, 89
Turkey, 25-27, 39, 46-48, 51, 53, 70, 88

UFO, 1-2, 7-8, 14-17, 22, 24, 28-29, 33, 36-37, 39, 54-55, 57, 96-98, 115, 131, 136-137, 140, 155, 167, 172, 175-176, 183-186, 188-191
ultraterrestrial, 191
United Kingdom, 169
Ur, 28, 54

Van Tassel, George, 14, 22, 29, 136-137, 185-186, 188
Vatican, 28, 178
Vedas, 137
Vedic, 7-8, 21, 27, 51, 65, 69, 146, 190
Venus, 1-2, 32, 67, 78, 80, 82, 102, 137, 140, 171
volcanism, 86, 150
volcano, 23, 33, 58, 65, 100, 156-157, 159-162

Wadjet, 54, 69
war, 1, 16, 24-29, 35-36, 40-41, 46, 55, 59, 65, 88-89, 93, 95-96, 172, 174, 186
warming, 24, 66, 173
weapon, 26-27, 33, 46, 92, 96, 137

web, 4, 17, 19-20, 113, 133, 135, 141, 145
Web of Life, 17, 19, 113, 133, 141, 145
Williamson, George Hunt, 33, 39, 56-57, 187
worldwide, 36, 61, 93, 102-103, 136, 154, 163, 169, 174

Yazidi, 53
yoke, 115
Yucatan, 4-5, 32, 89, 91, 93
yuga, 23, 25, 27-28, 61-62, 64-67, 69, 88, 93, 95-96, 110, 146
Yukteswar, Sri, 23, 25, 61-62, 67, 70

zero, 29, 34, 56, 63-64, 69, 72-74
Zeus, 28, 55, 59, 164-165

Krsanna Duran

A futurist and developer of the TimeStar model of planetary space-time, Krsanna Duran is a UFO experiencer and student of Trans-Himalayan adepts. She has a uniquely inspired method of forecasting planetary, solar, and galactic interactions as a cohesive whole system with synthesis of ancient and modern models of time, space, and reality. She has researched crop circles since 1993, to find correlations with planetary and human energetic conditions.

She balances an innate sense of pragmatism in contacts with time travelers and extraterrestrial sources. Krsanna and Ida Kannenberg shared mutual experiences with time travelers from Atlantis in contemporary UFO contacts.

Krsanna Duran was born and reared in Oklahoma and presently lives in Montana. A Southern Cherokee descendant of Stand Watie's Cherokee Cavaliers, she is an advocate of indigenous peoples and cultures.